LEGAL ACCENTS, LEGAL BORROWING

THE INTERNATIONAL PROBLEM-SOLVING COURT MOVEMENT

James L. Nolan Jr.

PRINCETON UNIVERSITY PRESS

PRINCETON AND OXFORD

Nolan, James L.
Legal accents, legal borrowing : the international problem-solving
court movement / James L. Nolan Jr.
p.   cm.
Includes bibliographical references and index.
ISBN 978-0-691-12952-5 (hardcover : alk. paper)
1. Criminal justice, Administration of. 2. Dispute resolution (Law)
3. Alternative convictions. 4. Restorative justice. 5. Law—American
influences. I. Title.
K5001.N65 2009
345 .05—dc22
2008037719

British Library Cataloging-in-Publication Data is available

This book has been composed in Sabon

Printed on acid-free paper. ∞

Printed in the United States of America

10   9   8   7   6   5   4   3   2

To Amy, David, Laura, and Will

CONTENTS

ACKNOWLEDGMENTS

THIS PROJECT, long in the works, has benefited from the assistance of a number of individuals and institutions. I began work on the project in England in 1999 with the assistance of a National Endowment of the Humanities grant and a Fulbright Scholarship. The Midland Centre for Criminology at Loughborough University proved an ideal location to start work on the project. Philip Bean, then-director of the Centre, was a helpful colleague and encouraging host. I also profited from two years as a Visiting Fellow at the Centre for Criminology at Oxford University between 2004 and 2006. Regular staff as well as other visitors at the Centre offered valuable input on a variety of aspects of the project. Chapter 6, for example, began as a paper presentation at All Souls College in a seminar sponsored by the Centre. Input I received in the context of the seminar, as well as in other conversations with Lucia Zedner, Federico Varese, Richard Young, Carolyn Hoyle, and Rasmus Wandall, was helpful in a number of respects.

I also benefited from feedback on work presented at two conferences focused on criminal court innovations and research—one at Columbia University Law School in 2003 and another at Tel Aviv University Law School in 2007. Among those offering helpful comments during these events were Hadar Aviram, Shai Lavi, and Malcolm Feeley. I have several to thank for reading and commenting on all or part of the book manuscript, including Philip Bean, Richard Boldt, Michael Brown, Kai Erikson, David Garland, Robert Jackall, David Nelken, Julian Roberts, Olga Shevchenko, and Glenn Took. The customary caveat is in order here; that is, only the author—and not those who so generously read and offered feedback on the work—bears responsibility for any oversights or errors that remain.

I am grateful to the many judges, magistrates, sheriffs, probation officers, treatment providers, evaluators, lawyers, clerks, and other professionals working in problem-solving courts around the world, who opened their courtrooms and offices to me and willingly and patiently responded to my many questions. It would be impracticable to name all who have helped in this way, and, of course, completion of the project would have been impossible without their cooperation. Several program directors and academics with considerable local knowledge of problem-solving courts in their respective countries took time to consult with me during my travels. Especially deserving of mention in this regard are Moira Price, Arie Freiberg, and David Indermaur.

Williams College students played an important role in the completion of this book. In the very early stages of the research, Sara Arnold worked with admirable skill organizing materials collected for the six cases represented in the comparative study. After graduating from Williams, Sara continued her quality assistance, both in transcribing interviews and in editing various chapters. Thanks goes to students on the Williams-Exeter Programme at Oxford University, including Arathi Rao, Nika Engberg, Rosie Smith, and Devin Yagel, who helped with interview transcriptions and other background research. At Williams College, Linda Saharczewski also helped transcribe interviews, and Donna Chenail, with her usual alacrity and good cheer, assisted in numerous ways during the years of work on the project. I owe much thanks to Ian Malcolm at Princeton University Press for useful input in all stages of the project and for so ably guiding the book through the editorial process.

Finally, I was once again served immeasurably by the support and patient counsel of my wife, Cathy. The research demands of the project were lightened and energized by the company and interest of our four children, to whom this book is proudly dedicated.

Chapter 2 includes revised material from "Redefining Criminal Courts: Problem-Solving and the Meaning of Justice," *American Criminal Law Review* 40, no. 1 (Fall 2003); chapter 3 contains reworked and expanded parts of "Separated by a Common Law: Drug Courts in Great Britain and America," in *Drug Courts: In Theory and in Practice* (Aldine de Gruyter, 2002); and an adapted section of chapter 7 appeared in "Ambivalent Anti-Americanism: The Ironies of Exported Culture," *Culture* 2, no. 1 (Spring 2008). Permission to use this material is respectfully acknowledged.

LEGAL ACCENTS,
LEGAL BORROWING

INTRODUCTION

ON a drizzly December morning in 1992, a fourth-grade boy at Red Hook's Public School 15 in Brooklyn, New York, got in a fistfight with another nine-year-old. Upset by the altercation, the boy walked away from school in tears. When Patrick Daly, the popular principal of P.S. 15, learned of the situation, he left the school to look for the boy—an action consistent with the character of this man, who had been teaching at the school since 1966 and had been principal since 1986. Walking through Red Hook's crime-ridden housing projects in search of the young boy, Daly eventually found himself in the crossfire of a drug-related skirmish. A stray bullet hit Daly in the chest, and he fell to the ground. Edgardo Torres, a security guard and former marine who witnessed the shooting, reached the fallen principal and attempted to administer CPR. Daly's last words to Torres: "Thank you." At 12:10 p.m. Patrick Daly—described by many as a soft-spoken, dedicated, and caring educator—was pronounced dead at the Long Island College Hospital.

Three teenagers were later arrested, tried, and convicted for the murder of the beloved school principal, but the community was left grieving at its loss and determined to do something about widespread crime in Red Hook. Just a few years before Daly's untimely death, Red Hook had been featured in *Life* magazine as a degenerating community racked by rampant criminal activity and a raging crack epidemic. The streets of the Red Hook neighborhood, as depicted in the 1988 article, were littered with empty crack vials and hypodermic needles, terrorized by near-daily shootouts between rival drug operations, and populated by residents so frightened they rarely left their apartments. Almost anticipating Daly's murder, one resident, who was interviewed for the article, said of the crack gangs, "They kill each other and anybody in the way."[1]

The death of the principal, who happened to get "in the way," served as a catalyst for action. Charles J. Hynes, Kings County district attorney, and Judge Judith Kaye, chief judge of the New York Court of Appeals, with the help of New York's Center for Court Innovation (CCI), worked together to help bring about what would become a flagship community court: the Red Hook Community Justice Center. The court, which opened its doors in 2000, is located in a renovated building that was previously the home of a local parochial school. The judge-led program, which offers court-monitored intervention for a variety of low-level "quality of life" crimes (including petty theft, drug offenses, prostitution, and illegal vending), has been presided over by Judge Alex Calabrese since its inception.

Described by Red Hook staff as "warm, friendly, and accessible," Judge Calabrese engages directly with the offenders who come before his court, and he has a variety of resources available to him at the center to assist him in addressing such underlying problems as drug addiction, housing difficulties, and lack of basic education. One participant, José Hernandez, who had struggled with a heroin addiction for eighteen years, was assigned to the Red Hook community court as a consequence of a drug-related infraction.[2] He was mandated into a court-monitored treatment program and required to return to court periodically so that Calabrese could evaluate his progress. In one court session, Calabrese asked Hernandez about his family. "I remember one time your wife and child came to court," he said. "How old is your child?" Hernandez indicated that his son was five years old. Calabrese then made reference to an essay Hernandez had written for the court (an exercise mandated by the court as one form of sanction). "What impressed me about your essay," said Calabrese, "was not only that you have to face this problem for yourself, but you have a responsibility for your five-year-old boy, as well." Hernandez agreed with the judge and added that his son is very attached to him. Calabrese continued, "Kids want to be like their dad. You have an important loved one looking up to you. There is no reason why you can't do well. You have to do it for yourself. You have to do it for your son." They talked briefly about Hernandez's work and the evening classes he had started taking. In closing, Calabrese asked Hernandez if he had a picture of his son in his wallet and suggested that it was "always a good idea to have a picture of your kids in your wallet."

Such interaction is typical of the kind of personal engagement between judge and participant to be found in the Red Hook community court. However, though the court functions in a team-oriented, problem-solving manner, the adversarial model is not dispensed with entirely. As Calabrese explains, lawyers directly engage in a more traditional adversarial manner in about one-tenth of all cases. On the same day of Hernandez's appearance, another defendant, recently arrested for a vending violation, stood before Calabrese for the first time. This defendant had been charged with selling items (including door locks and nose-hair trimmers) without a license. The district attorney (DA) offered two days of community service. The public defense lawyer objected to this offer, explaining that the defendant had only recently arrived in the United States, could speak virtually no English, had no criminal record, and did not realize that what he was doing was illegal. The DA then offered one day of community service. The defense lawyer, visibly irritated, rejected the offer and committed to fighting the case. The defendant was released and a new court date was set.

When the Red Hook Community Justice Center was launched in April 2000, then New York mayor Rudy Giuliani prophetically announced, "Today we are opening what I believe will be an exciting new model for the court system well into the century, the Red Hook Community Justice Center. People will be coming here to find out how to do it in the rest of the city and the rest of the country." In fact, visitors have come to Red Hook, not just from the United States, but from around the world. The Red Hook community court has become the prototype for the development of community courts internationally.

The first such transplantation occurred in England. After visits from such high-ranking British officials as Home Secretary David Blunkett and Lord Chief Justice Harry Woolf in 2003, Judge Calabrese was invited to England to discuss community courts with a number of British criminal justice officials. Persuaded by what they saw and heard, British officials hired David Fletcher in 2004 to be the judge of England's first community court. The Liverpool Community Justice Centre, which officially opened its doors in September 2005, looks like the Red Hook court in many respects. For example, it is located in the heart of North Liverpool, a community similarly plagued by "antisocial" behavior. Also like the Red Hook court, the Liverpool Community Justice Centre houses a range of services to help the judge address defendants' underlying problems. The court is even located in a renovated building that previously housed a local Catholic school.

Two years after the start of the Liverpool court, Australia launched its first community court, the Neighbourhood Justice Centre, in the Collingwood neighborhood of the city of Yarra (a northeastern section of Melbourne, Victoria). Here, as in Liverpool, Red Hook is credited as the model and inspiration for the new court. In laying the foundation for the court, officials from Victoria visited Red Hook and were impressed with its operations. Moreover, staff from the CCI traveled to Melbourne to meet with Victoria criminal justice officials to educate them on the concepts of community justice. When the Neighbourhood Justice Centre was launched on March 8, 2007—again in a renovated building that once served as an educational facility—Attorney General Rob Hulls recalled his trip to Red Hook. Hulls spoke of the "enormous privilege" it was to "witness the Red Hook Community Justice Center in action" and how it served as the spark that would lead to the initiation of Australia's first community court. David Fanning, the magistrate hired to preside over the Neighbourhood Justice Centre, likewise recalled Hulls's pilgrimage to Red Hook, referring to it as a "road-to-Damascus experience" during which Hulls became "a complete convert."

The conversion experience continues internationally. Plans are under way for the development of community courts in Dublin, Ireland;

Glasgow, Scotland; and Vancouver, British Columbia, Canada. In each case, officials have looked to Red Hook and other community courts in the United States to serve as the essential blueprint for the proposed initiation of community courts in their respective countries. The development of community courts, however, is just one example of a much more widespread international phenomenon. In addition to community courts, a number of other problem-solving courts—including drug courts, mental health courts, and domestic violence courts—have been developed in the United States and exported around the world. This book is the story of the international problem-solving court movement, one that is still very much in the process of unfolding.

This analysis of the movement provides the reader with not only a detailed and comprehensive description of an important international legal development, but also an interesting case study of the processes of globalization. As with other cultural products exported from the United States, this innovation is embraced abroad with a curious mix of enthusiasm and concern—a sort of ambivalence, as we will see, that characterizes international attitudes toward the United States more generally. The effects of this particular export, however, are of potentially enormous consequence to importing societies. Embedded in American problem-solving courts are cultural assumptions that significantly challenge long-held understandings of the meaning and practice of justice—assumptions that when transplanted along with problem-solving courts may significantly challenge or alter the legal cultures of importing countries.

This comparative study reveals that some countries are more conscious and protective of traditional understandings of justice than are others. Even in the cases of more deliberate resistance, however, features of American culture still manage to penetrate the local legal cultures of the receiving countries. A fuller appreciation of the law's cultural entanglements helps to make sense of the nature and extent of such infiltration. Borrowers of American problem-solving courts often speak of these judicial innovations as though they are autonomous and easily adaptable legal products. Without a deeper understanding of the ongoing dialectic between law and culture, then, importers can underestimate the degree to which these programs carry with them unwished-for—even openly denigrated—features of American culture. The infusion of such cultural qualities, whether welcomed or resented, portends to fundamentally alter understandings of justice in the receiving countries.

The book is a natural sequel to my previous work, *Reinventing Justice: The American Drug Court Movement*, in that it follows the progression of an international movement that began with the development of American drug courts. This book looks at the expansion of the drug court model to other types of problem-solving courts in the United States and to the transfer of these courts internationally. Specifically, this comparative study investigates six countries where the problem-solving court movement is most advanced: England, Scotland, Ireland, Canada, Australia, and the United States.[3] As in *Reinventing Justice*, ethnographic work features as the project's central research method. Between 1999 and 2008, I visited more than fifty different problem-solving courts around the world (some on multiple occasions) and made at least three research trips to each of the six countries represented in the study.[4] At the various courts, I typically interviewed the judge, magistrate, or sheriff presiding over the court; witnessed court programs in operation; and spoke with other staff associated with the courts, including probation officers, treatment providers, lawyers, program directors, victim support personnel, medical doctors, evaluators, and, in the case of aboriginal courts, elders and peacemakers. In addition to interviewing individuals working directly with the courts, in several instances I also interviewed government officials responsible for the initiation of specialty courts. On a number of occasions, I also observed various venues operating in conjunction with courts, including community and pre-court team meetings, as well as various treatment programs.

The fieldwork was supplemented with data from a variety of other sources, including government reports, parliamentary debates, evaluations of individual court programs, publications issued by such advocacy groups as the CCI, media accounts, public statements and articles by problem-solving court judges, and analyses of specialty courts in law reviews and other academic journals. In addition to visiting individual courts in all six countries, I also attended a number of national and international conferences on problem-solving courts (including conferences in Canada, Australia, Scotland, and the United States), where I talked with problem-solving court officials, attended relevant lectures and panel discussions, and collected materials put out by the various courts.[5]

Much of the work on problem-solving courts, especially in the United States, centers on the question of whether these courts work. Are they cost-effective? Do they reduce recidivism rates? This book is not an evaluation study. Thus, the reader will not learn about so-called best practices or find out which country is most "successful" at problem-solving courts. Rather, it is a study of the international transplantation of problem-solving courts and is particularly concerned with what the processes of legal borrowing reveal about cultural differences and changing legal cultures in a global context. From such a perspective, even the relevance of efficacy and the meaning of success are understood as culturally determined. For example, in a cultural context where a therapeutic idiom is more dominant, the notion of what constitutes success may not match up with such conventional criminal justice measurements as reduced recidivism rates.

Or, depending on the particular treatment philosophies that inform different court programs, determinations of what constitutes success will vary. Thus, such questions as those put forth by a Canadian mental health court judge and his colleagues are salient: "Who defines success? What is a therapeutic outcome? By whose standards?"[6] The answers to these questions presuppose and are determined by particular cultural assumptions. This book, therefore, endeavors to make sense of such assumptions in relationship to the law through a comparative assessment of a new and expanding international legal movement.

With this basic focus in mind, the book first traces the development of problem-solving courts in the United States and summarizes the defining characteristics of the four most prominent types of problem-solving courts: drug courts, community courts, domestic violence courts, and mental health courts. This is followed by an analysis of the international transfer of problem-solving courts against the backdrop of broader discussions about globalization, the relationship between law and culture, processes of legal transplantation, and the new legal theories (i.e., therapeutic jurisprudence and restorative justice) that are commonly associated with these courts. The middle part of the book documents and explores the comparative development of problem-solving courts in the United States and England, Canada and Australia, and Scotland and Ireland, respectively. The closing chapters consider the relevance of the international comparisons to such broader themes as American exceptionalism, contradictory anti-American attitudes, and the promise of problem-solving courts to restore public confidence in criminal justice systems around the world.

New courts in both England and Australia have directly emulated the Red Hook community court in striking ways. Yet each case represents the importation of a court innovation into a culture and legal system very different from those of the program's country of origin. The same could be said of the variety of problem-solving courts that have been transferred internationally. Countries importing problem-solving courts, therefore, must contend with these differences, either by rejecting certain parts of the American export or by adjusting the programs in such a manner as to make them more suitable to their new context. Observing the manner in which such transfers are negotiated offers insights into a range of broader social developments, including the processes of globalization, the nature of the relationship between law and culture, and the unique and contested place of the United States in the larger world community.

Chapter One

PROBLEM SOLVING AND
COURTS OF LAW

> For problem-solving judges and attorneys, a case is a problem
> to be solved, not just a matter to be adjudicated.
> —*Greg Berman and John Feinblatt*

IN HIS BOOK *The Homeless Mind*, Peter Berger identifies a "problem-solving" orientation as a defining feature of modern consciousness. "Problem-solving inventiveness," as he puts it, is a dominant sensibility in our modern technological society. According to Berger, this form of consciousness not only is found among those working directly in the productive processes of industrial capitalism, but also is carried over into other sectors of public and private life.[1] From this vantage point, it may not be altogether surprising that a legal innovation emerging at the turn of the twenty-first century would specifically refer to itself as a *problem-solving* enterprise. Consistent with the essential disposition characterized by Berger, "problem-solving courts" have surfaced as one of the most interesting and important innovations in the contemporary legal world.

Advocates may not be overstating matters when they speak of problem-solving courts as a "paradigm shift," a "dramatic wave of court innovation," as even a "revolution" in criminal justice.[2] So significant is the development in the United States that in 2000 the U.S. Conference of Chief Justices (CCJ) and the Conference of State Court Administrators (COSCA) passed a joint resolution endorsing and encouraging "the broad integration over the next decade of the principles and methods employed in problem solving courts in the administration of justice." Less than a year later, the American Bar Association (ABA) followed suit, calling for "the continued development of problem solving courts" and going so far as to encourage "law schools, state, local and territorial bar associations, and other organizations to engage in education and training about the principles and methods employed by problem solving courts." In 2004 the CCJ/COSCA passed another resolution, reaffirming its 2000 declaration, and resolving further to "encourage each state to develop and implement an individual state plan to expand the use of the principles and methods of problem-solving courts into their courts." What precisely are problem-solving courts? And what are the problems that these courts seek to solve?

Problem-solving courts have been described as "specialized tribunals established to deal with specific problems, often involving individuals who need social, mental health, or substance abuse treatment services."[3] As understood here, the problems are those of individual defendants who, because of some kind of legal infraction, find themselves before a criminal court. The court, in this case, offers to help individuals solve the problems that are commonly seen as the root cause of their criminal behavior. Among the various types of problem-solving courts developed since the late 1980s are drug courts, community courts, domestic violence courts, and mental health courts. The different courts, as the classifications suggest, are oriented toward addressing such individual problems as drug and alcohol addiction, domestic discord and violence, mental disability, and the "antisocial" behaviors that harmfully affect the quality of life in local communities.

In discussions about the purpose and focus of these courts, however, the problem sometimes appears to be not so much that of the individual offender, but that of the judicial system itself—a system viewed by many as suffering from a range of dysfunctions. Ubiquitous, for example, are complaints about overcrowded jails and prisons; the expense and burden of increasing court case loads; the "revolving door" phenomenon of repeat offenders; the impersonal and assembly-line quality of "McJustice," or expedited case management; fatigue and job dissatisfaction among lawyers and judges; the win-at-all-costs mentality of modern trial advocacy; and the adjudicative restrictions of hyper-proceduralism and mandatory minimum sentencing guidelines.[4]

Of these systemic troubles, one to receive notable attention among advocates of problem-solving courts is, curiously, job dissatisfaction among judges. In conventional courts, it is argued, stressed-out judges complain of feeling isolated, unappreciated, misunderstood, and frustrated with the endless stream of repeat offenders cycling through their courtrooms.[5] With pressure to rush through overloaded court calendars, judges protest that "there is barely time for the judge to think, let alone interact with the parties or their attorneys."[6] Judges complain further that mandatory minimum sentencing laws restrict their ability to craft sentences appropriate to the lives and situations of individual offenders. Innovators contend that problem-solving courts provide judges with an alternative judicial forum that is more personally satisfying. As they see it, in problem-solving courts, judges enjoy greater discretion, more personal interaction with defendants, and a feeling that they are actually effecting change. Two problem-solving court advocates, Peggy Hora and Deborah Chase, have actually conducted surveys comparing problem-solving court judges with regular judges. Among their findings: a higher percentage of problem-solving court judges felt their "current assignment had a positive emotional effect on them" and "made them feel happier."[7]

Not surprisingly, some have questioned whether the good feelings and personal happiness of judges should be a primary concern of the court.[8] In response, Hora and Chase argue:

> When judges are feeling productive and positive, these attitudes carry over to staff, litigants, and counsel. Likewise, if a burnt-out judge is short-tempered, the perception of the court is more likely to be negative. This suggests that . . . a judge's job satisfaction would be a predictor of litigant satisfaction and significantly affect the public's trust and confidence in the court.[9]

As intimated in this statement, judges worry that problems in the criminal justice system have resulted in declining public confidence in the American judiciary. Common is the stated belief that the American criminal justice system suffers from a deficit, if not a crisis, of legitimacy and thus struggles to justify itself vis-à-vis society.[10] David Rottman and Pamela Casey, from the National Center for State Courts, for example, report that "public opinion surveys indicate . . . low levels of trust and confidence in the judiciary."[11] Even more decidedly, Greg Berman and John Feinblatt, from the Center for Court Innovation in New York, assert that "no civic institution has experienced a greater loss of public faith in recent years" than the American criminal justice system.[12]

Judges, therefore, feel pressure to improve their standing with the public and, along with other supporters of problem-solving courts, "are united by the common belief that courts need to reassert their relevance in society."[13] As a district attorney from Portland, Oregon, put it, "I strongly believe we've got to work on public credibility, because a lot of citizens, quite frankly, they don't think judges are relevant."[14] Judge Judith Kaye, chief judge of the New York State Court of Appeals and a tireless promoter of problem-solving courts, agrees. In her 2000 State of the Judiciary address, she highlighted a key question for the next century: "How do we build public trust and confidence in our justice system?"[15] Just as Hora and Chase believe problem-solving courts will improve judicial self-esteem, Kaye firmly believes that "problem-solving courts can help counter the erosion of public trust and confidence in justice that we have experienced in recent generations."[16]

Kaye, however, does not believe the courts are the extent of the problem. As she puts it, "Courts are, after all, a mirror of society."[17] In other words, the courts' difficulties are themselves only a microcosm of deeper problems in the larger society. In this sense, then, the problems are not simply those of individual defendants or of a beleaguered court system filled with dissatisfied judges, but of society more generally. Supporters of problem-solving courts and related legal innovations argue that the need for legal change is exacerbated by the failure of other social institutions to handle a growing number of social problems. In other words, because of the failure of "traditional non-legal dispute resolution mechanisms in society," such as one's "church, community, neighborhood, friends, and family," the legal system now finds itself in a position where it must directly address various social ills.[18]

With the weakening of these nonlegal support structures, advocates of legal change believe that the courts had no choice but to attempt to fill the void. As Rottman and Casey see it, "The main push for this change came from the societal changes that placed courts in the frontline of responses to substance abuse, family breakdown, and mental illness." Because "courts cannot restrict the flow of such problems into the courtroom," they have essentially been "pulled . . . toward a problem-solving, proactive orientation."[19] Or as Timothy Casey puts it, "The failure of various agencies has led to the dumping of all social problems into the lap of the courts."[20] In light of this development, one judge mused, "It seems terribly odd that America is looking to the judicial branch to solve these problems. It seems to me that in very large measure, this is happening because of the abject failure of the other branches of government."[21] Or as another judge put it, in more colloquial terms, the courts must address these problems because there "ain't nobody else doing it." Not all are persuaded by this reasoning, and some suggest that heavy financial investment in problem-solving courts necessarily taps into public funds that might be better spent strengthening other social support structures.[22]

Regardless of where one stands on this particular question, it is clear that the problems on which problem-solving courts focus fall within three general categories. Namely, as discussed in the literature on the phenomenon, problem-solving courts address the interrelated problems (1) of individual offenders, (2) of a troubled court system seeking to regain its legitimacy, and (3) of society more broadly (due, ostensibly, to the failure of other social institutions to handle perennial social ills). The various problem-solving courts, then, as Greg Berman summarizes, "all seek to use the authority of courts to address the underlying problems of individual litigants, the structural problems of the justice system, and the social problems of the communities."[23]

While the problems of the criminal justice system and of the broader society are, at least in a tangential sense, the concern of these innovative courts, the problems to which people generally refer when speaking of problem-solving courts are those of the individual offenders. For this reason, the courts are typically classified, as noted earlier, by the particular individual problems they address. Although problem-solving courts vary considerably, they can be characterized, at least in the United States, by five common features: (1) close and ongoing judicial monitoring, (2) a multidisciplinary or team-oriented approach, (3) a therapeutic or treatment orientation, (4) the altering of traditional roles in the adjudication process, and (5) an emphasis on solving the problems of individual offenders—hence, the umbrella term that has emerged to describe this new breed of courts: *problem-solving courts.*

In the remainder of this chapter, I provide a brief overview of the variety of problem-solving courts that have emerged in the United States since the late 1980s (thus fleshing out the five defining characteristics just noted), followed by a preliminary outline of the expansion of problem-solving courts internationally. Again, what follows in this chapter is a description of courts in the United States, some features of which, as we will see, would not accurately describe problem-solving courts in the other common law regions considered in this case study.

Drug Courts

I begin where problem-solving courts began, namely, with drug courts, which—as the numbers (both nationally and internationally) readily demonstrate—are the most visible, widespread, and influential of the problem-solving courts. As Berman and Feinblatt note, "The current wave of problem-solving experimentation can be traced back to the opening of the first 'drug court' in Dade County, Florida, in 1989."[24] The Miami court became the essential model for the over twenty-one hundred drug courts established throughout the United States since that time. While drug courts vary from location to location, they share many of the same essential qualities. Drug courts offer drug offenders, as an alternative to the normal adjudication process, an intensive court-based treatment program. Participants, or "clients" (as they are typically called in drug courts), return regularly to the courtroom, where they engage directly and personally with the judge. In addition to repeated encounters with the drug court judge, clients submit to regular urinalysis tests.

Clients also participate in individual and group counseling sessions, Alcoholics Anonymous (AA) and Narcotics Anonymous (NA) twelve-step groups, and acupuncture treatment. Progress in these various treatment modalities is monitored by the drug court judge, who, during court sessions, offers praise and prizes for success and admonitions and sanctions for noncompliance. Sanctions can vary from increased participation in weekly NA meetings to community service to several days of incarceration. Clients agree to participate in drug courts with the promise that successful completion will result in dropped charges or an expunged record of arrest. The process is advertised to take one year, but it often lasts much longer.

Drug courts, in many important respects, depart from the practices and procedures of a typical criminal court. Prosecutors and defense counsel, for example, play much reduced roles and act less as adversaries than as collaborative partners on the same treatment team. In many drug courts, lawyers are not even present during regular drug court sessions. Instead, the main courtroom drama is between the judge and the client, both of whom speak openly and freely in the drug court setting. Often accompanying the client is a treatment provider, who advises the judge and reviews the client's progress in treatment. Court sessions are characterized by expressive, and sometimes tearful, testimonies about the recovery process and are punctuated with applause from those in attendance, thus leading one observer to describe the court as "something akin to a cross between a revivalist meeting and Alcoholics Anonymous."[25] Once they complete the program, clients participate in colorful graduation ceremonies, which can involve emotional speeches from graduating clients, the issuing of graduation certificates, and visits from the media and local luminaries.

The various problem-solving courts that have followed in the wake of the drug court movement are similarly team-oriented, multidisciplinary, and therapeutic in approach. They likewise have adopted a style that involves early, intensive, and regular court supervision and coordination of services aimed at addressing the defendant's underlying problems.

COMMUNITY COURTS

Included among these are community courts, which, while sharing some of the same essential features as drug courts, are also distinct in important ways. For instance, unlike drug courts (and other problem-solving courts), community courts are more directly concerned with addressing the problems of the community. Such a focus is informed, in part, by the "broken windows" theory made famous in a 1982 *Atlantic Monthly* article by James Q. Wilson and George L. Kelling. According to this theory, "street crime flourishes in areas where disorderly behavior goes unchecked."[26] That is, broken windows or, analogously, low-level offenses, if not addressed, will lead to further neighborhood decay and more serious and entrenched criminal behavior.

In keeping with this basic understanding, community courts target such "quality-of-life" offenses as prostitution, illegal vending, public drinking, disorderly conduct, graffiti, shoplifting, noise ordinance violations, fare beating, loitering, and vandalism. The extent and nature of criminal activity varies from location to location. In the San Diego community court, for example, public drinking is the "most popular charge." In Washington, DC, prostitution and cocaine possession are the most common offenses handled by the community court. The Midtown community court in New York handles a large volume of illegal vending and prostitution cases, while city ordinance violations (such as loitering and excessive noise) are among the most common offenses in the Hartford community court. Some community court buildings, such as the Red Hook Community Justice Center in Brooklyn, are intentionally situated directly within the particular "catchment area" of a local community in order to make the court and its multiple functions more visible, accessible, and relevant to local residents.

Community courts are also distinct from drug courts in that restitution plays a more central role. That is, various community service sanctions are imposed to provide "payback" and "recompense" to local communities for the various "quality-of-life" crimes to which the communities have been subjected.[27] The community service can include such assignments as painting over graffiti, picking up trash in local parks, sweeping streets, feeding the homeless, sorting recyclables, landscaping around senior centers, and removing snow from public sites. Community courts will sometimes try to match community service sentences to specific crimes. For example, a graffiti artist may be asked to clean or paint over graffiti.[28] Or someone caught shoplifting in New York's "fashion district" may be sent to the Salvation Army to distribute donated clothing.

Not all sanctions, however, come in the form of community service. As in other problem-solving courts, community courts "use the coercive power of the court" to direct participants into relevant treatment programs.[29] In the Midtown community court, for example, clients are sometimes required to attend "quality-of-life group" sessions. In Portland, Oregon, participants may be asked to write an essay or attend a "theft-deterrent" class.[30] In the Hartford community court, defendants arrested for prostitution may be ordered to participate in the "Prostitution Protocol Program."[31] Counseling sessions in this program focus on such topics as "defendants' personal experiences and feelings, their emotional needs, [and] self-esteem,"[32] themes similar to those encountered by defendants in drug court treatment programs.[33] Participants are also provided with (or required to take part in) a variety of social services, including health care, drug and alcohol treatment, general equivalency diploma (GED) classes, or job training.[34]

By imposing sanctions and requiring participation in various treatment modalities, community courts, like drug courts, provide a program that is "both therapeutic and accountable"[35]—or as an official at the Midtown community court explained, "We combine punishment and help." Significantly, therapeutic accountability can include short stints in jail, sometimes in response to noncompliance with other treatment and community service requirements. This is a defining feature of the Portland community court, where "alternative sanctions are backed up by a jail sentence if the defendant fails to comply."[36] A community court judge from Washington, DC, similarly says, "When things go wrong, we lock you up." Judge Calabrese of the Red Hook community court likewise explains,

> Sometimes this court has to use jail as a tool. Just like the treatment is used as a tool, sometimes jail is used as a tool. It's usually the last resort. . . . But it is sometimes that short jail period that gets the person to understand that if he or she continues down that road, this is exactly where it is going to get you.[37]

The first community court was established in New York City in 1993.[38] The Midtown community court remained the only community court in the United States through 1998, but by 2000 there were nearly a dozen in operation, including courts in Portland, Oregon; Austin, Texas; Red Hook, New York; and Hartford, Connecticut. Julius Lang, from the Center for Court Innovation, reports that "today there are about three dozen community courts across the country, either in planning or in operation." It is anticipated that in the near future, "most big cities in the United States and many smaller cities will have one or more community courts."[39]

DOMESTIC VIOLENCE COURTS

Domestic violence courts differ from other problem-solving courts in that the cases involve not only defendants, but also clearly identifiable victims. In domestic violence courts, therefore, both victims and offenders have problems for which the court offers therapeutic assistance. The stated goals of the Dade County domestic violence court typify this dualistic concern. Among the court's aims are "to protect the abused partner and children, to hold the perpetrator accountable for violent behavior, [and] to stop that behavior and rehabilitate the perpetrator."[40]

In spite of this unique focus, domestic violence courts still embody all five of the defining features of problem-solving courts identified earlier. The courts are characterized by the close monitoring and supervision of a specially trained judge, who works with a multidisciplinary team comprising not only lawyers, probation officers, and treatment providers (as is common in other problem-solving courts), but also representatives from victims' advocate organizations, battered women's homes, and sexual assault units. The judge is armed with "a range of creative sentencing options," as well as a variety of counseling and substance abuse programs, specifically developed to address the peculiar problems associated with domestic violence.[41] Defendants are mandated into "batterer's treatment counseling" and "anger management classes." They may also be required to participate in drug treatment programs, attend AA and NA self-help groups, and spend time in jail,[42] while victims are "linked to a variety of services and counseling."[43] Here, as in other problem-solving courts, the judge engages the defendant directly and assumes "multiple roles, including acting as authority, motivator, problem-solver, and monitor."[44]

Given the seriousness of domestic violence offenses, some courts downplay the overtly therapeutic aim of rehabilitating the offender. Judge John Levanthal of the Brooklyn domestic violence court, for example, says the purpose of his court is "to protect victims and punish the guilty." He sees his court as different, in this regard, from a drug court and does not, for instance, allow applause in the courtroom or choose to describe his court as a therapeutic enterprise. A study of the Brooklyn domestic violence court conducted by the Urban Institute confirms this quality of Levanthal's court, noting that where the drug court judge is "intent to heal the defendant" and "is cast as a supporting force within the criminal justice system, the felony domestic violence judge [i.e., Levanthal] is not."[45]

Levanthal's court, however, is more the exception than the rule.[46] Other domestic violence courts directly imitate the pattern and principles of the drug court model and are much less afraid to call attention to the court's therapeutic efforts to treat offenders. In the Dade County domestic violence court, for example, the "treatment of abusers in domestic violence cases is emphasized over punishment."[47] The court, which was established in 1992, includes among its services for offenders parenting classes, substance abuse treatment (including urinalysis and acupuncture), mental health counseling, and a twenty-six-week-long course based on the Duluth model. Significantly, the Duluth model "emphasizes the importance of using batterer intervention programs" and thus represents a "move away from victim intervention to a greater focus on perpetrator intervention and examination of perpetrator psychology."[48]

Judge Randal Fritzler, who helped launch the Vancouver, Washington, domestic violence court in 1997, is explicit about the therapeutic and problem-solving orientation of his court. His stated goal in establishing the court was to make it "an outcome-oriented, problem-solving, therapeutic court,"[49] with anticipated therapeutic benefits for victims and offenders alike. To be sure, one of the three critical phases in Fritzler's court is "an intensive treatment and monitoring phase of the offender."[50] Methods employed, in this regard, include "anger-management" exercises, "cognitive rational emotive therapy," and instructions for replacing "negative self-talk with positive self-talk." Defendants participate in various role-playing exercises and are asked to submit a two-page weekly "Feelings and Behavior Journal."[51]

Importantly, therapeutic dynamics are not realized only within the context of court-mandated treatment settings. Regular interactions between judge and victim and judge and defendant are also understood as therapeutic exchanges. As Judge Fritzler explains, "Judicial recognition of offender success in treatment . . . can give the offender a sense of self-efficacy and achievement."[52] When defendants are doing well, therefore, they are "rewarded with praise and, when appropriate, the lifting of restrictions" by the domestic violence court judge. However, when offenders are not doing well, the judge can impose a variety of sanctions, including "more frequent reviews, electronic home confinement, work crew, alternative community service . . . or actual jail time."[53] As in drug courts and community courts, then, the punitive and therapeutic aims of the domestic violence court work in a complementary fashion. These are not necessarily contradictory impulses, as many intuitively assume.[54]

Therefore, the greater emphasis on punishment in domestic violence courts does not make these courts any less therapeutic. Consider several further examples. The judge in a California domestic violence court uses a "caring attitude" and "constructive intimidation" to draw defendants closer to him, an interaction that he sees as the "most important component of the specialized court process."[55] The "a priori assumption" in this court is that "enhancing therapeutic effects for defendants has a direct relationship to enhancing victim safety."[56] A domestic violence court judge in Phoenix, Arizona, makes a similar connection between the treatment of defendants and victim safety. As she puts it, "We want these folks—mostly its men—involved in treatment, because the more and the longer they're involved in treatment, the less likely they're going to reoffend with either the old victim or a new victim." A domestic violence court judge from Washington, DC, acknowledges the therapeutic dimension to her court, where she uses civil protection orders to mandate defendants into various types of individual and group counseling, including anger management, alcohol or drug abuse, domestic violence, or sexual abuse therapy.

The Brooklyn domestic violence court was initiated in 1996. In setting up his court, Judge Levanthal visited the domestic violence court in Quincy, Massachusetts, which was established in 1987. Though it is a multidisciplinary specialty court dedicated to domestic violence cases, the Quincy court relies more heavily on probation and is not as judge-centered as the domestic violence courts (and other problem-solving courts) that were initiated in the early 1990s and beyond. Over the past decade, domestic violence courts have spread rapidly. While there were only a handful in the mid-1990s, by the end of 2000 there were more than 200 domestic violence courts in the United States, and by 2002, there were "well over 300 domestic violence courts nationwide."[57]

MENTAL HEALTH COURTS

Like domestic violence courts, the number of mental health courts has expanded in recent years. The first mental health court was established in Broward County, Florida, in 1997. By September 2005, there were 111 mental health courts in the United States.[58] Defendants in mental health courts have typically committed minor offenses, such as trespassing, shoplifting, disorderly conduct, petty theft, urinating in public, drug abuse, or "spitting at people in the street."[59] The criminal infractions, therefore, are not unlike those committed by some defendants in drug courts and community courts. The important difference, however, is that mental health courts only accept "persons with a demonstrable mental illness" that is determined to have "contributed" to their offense.[60] A diagnosed mental illness, therefore, is usually required for participation in the program. This is the case in Broward County, where potentially eligible candidates must be "diagnosed with an Axis I mental illness [e.g., schizophrenia, mood or anxiety disorders, certain impulse-control disorders, bipolar disorder, or major depression], have an organic brain injury or head trauma, or be developmentally disabled."[61] In order to treat underlying disorders, mental health court programs offer defendants a judge-led multidisciplinary team comprising representatives from both legal and treatment communities.[62]

Judges are sometimes specially trained in mental health issues in preparation for this unusual judicial role. Consider the following description of the mental health court judge put forth by Arizona judges Michael Jones and Louraine Arkfeld:

> A mental health court judge must understand mental health issues, problems, and a new mental health vocabulary. . . . It is important for a mental health court judge to understand the various diagnoses and prognoses of the parties who appear before him or her in the mental health court. A mental health court judge must understand the limitations of certain illnesses and disabilities, as well as their potentials.[63]

Though retrained according to this new "vocabulary," judges still rely throughout court processes on the input of community mental health providers in a number of respects. For example, judges look to mental health professionals in their efforts to ensure the appropriate use of prescribed medications, an important and unique feature of mental health courts.[64] As one mental health court judge explained, "Medication compliance" is "usually the first goal that I set for these folks." In court, she finds herself encouraging participants to take and stay on their medications, including such drugs as Zoloft, Paxil, and Wellbutrin. She acknowledges the importance of having a doctor present in court, whom she regularly turns to for information about particular disorders and the effects of certain drugs. She readily confesses her own ignorance in this regard: "I'm perfectly willing to admit that I don't have all the information or all the educational background in these cases on the medications and even the illnesses. I'm certainly willing to learn about them."

Apart from monitoring the use of prescribed medications, mental health courts function much like drug courts in many other respects. Like drug courts, mental health courts can be both pre-plea (or pre-adjudicative), where participation is offered as a kind of diversion from the normal adjudication process, and post-plea, where participation is either a condition of probation or part of a deferred sentence. Moreover, the court sessions and the overall program are judge-led. Judges, as such, are at the very "center of the treatment and supervision process."[65] In this capacity, judges often behave in the proactive, therapeutic manner characteristic of drug court judges. Indeed, several mental health court judges (including judges in San Bernardino, California, and Maricopa County, Arizona) previously served as drug court judges and thus brought to mental health court the new therapeutic paradigm with which they had become familiar.

As in drug courts, mental health court participants regularly return to the courtroom, where they engage directly and personally with the judge. In the Anchorage, Alaska, mental health court, for example, the judge "discusses the participant's progress in treatment with him or her directly, identifies any problems, and encourages continued participation." During court sessions, participants "who have passed important milestones or have good reviews may receive praise from the judge and even applause from other participants seated in the courtroom."[66] A Minnesota judge, while not allowing applause in his courtroom, believes reviews "are essential in mental health court." He says, "It really makes a difference for two reasons . . . defendants are much more likely to comply if they know they have to answer to a judge at some point. And at the same time, they're really anxious to come back and see me." This judge thoroughly enjoys the more personal interactions with defendants in the mental health court setting and was happy to move away from a more traditional judicial disposition.

> I was one of those people who found being a judge very isolating and remote and not really part of the events. They just kind of happened in front of you and you reacted rather than tried to be proactive. So for me, this was really like a duck to water. I really enjoy this.

Though judges are personal and interactive in mental health courts, when participants fail to meet the treatment conditions set by the court, judges can also be quite tough and impose a variety of sanctions, including jail.[67] As an observer of the Broward County mental health court notes, "Patients who fail to follow their prescribed treatment plan can be ordered to jail, much like a defendant who breaks parole."[68] In the San Bernardino mental health court, participants who have not complied with court requirements can receive a range of sanctions, including "stern lectures and reprimands" from the judge, "sitting in the jury box during the court proceedings," assignment to "a more restrictive and structured treatment setting," and "jail."[69] Ann Remington, an assistant public defender in Minnesota, describes the oversight role of Judge Richard Hopper, a Minneapolis mental health court judge, as follows: "Judge Hopper in mental health court can review these cases as frequently as he wants." Of one client he may say, "I want to see him back in 90 days and make sure he is doing what he needs to do." If a client "falls or strays from that line, the accountability is immediate. Judge Hopper can bring him back into court, put him back into jail, get those resources back in line very, very quickly."[70]

As in other problem-solving courts, then, the mental health court judge has a variety of options—both punitive and therapeutic in quality—that can be imposed on the defendant. A detailed overview of four mental health courts in the United States offers the following summary discussion of the role of the mental health court judge:

> The judge plays a hands-on, therapeutically oriented and directive role at the center of the treatment process. The judge deals and interacts with the participant directly, and assigns rewards and sanctions as may be appropriate, including selective use of jail.[71]

Interestingly, the use of jail in mental health courts is regarded as "appropriate in a therapeutic not a punitive sense."[72] Similar euphemistic reclassifications have likewise been used to justify incarceration and other sanctions in drug courts and other problem-solving courts.[73]

Mental health courts, however, are unique in that, perhaps more than any other type of problem-solving court, they exist in response to the failure or abdication of other social institutions. Arguably, the growing presence of mentally ill defendants in the criminal justice system is attributable, in part, to the "deinstitutionalization movement in mental health during the 1960s and 1970s."[74] With the subsequent failure of community-based treatment services to fill the void, the criminal justice system was forced to handle an increasing volume of mentally disturbed offenders. The sometimes tragic consequences of the failure of nonlegal social support structures for the mentally ill are cited as a justification for the court's increased involvement in this regard. In Seattle, for example, retired fire department captain Stanley Stevenson, while returning to his car following a Mariners baseball game, was randomly and brutally stabbed to death by a mentally ill defendant in 1997. The assailant, a misdemeanor offender with a history of mental health issues, had been found incompetent by the court and had only recently been released back into the community prior to the murderous assault. Just as Patrick Daly's death spurred the initiation of the Red Hook community court, so Stevenson's murder served as a catalyst for the launching of Seattle's mental health court.[75]

The fact that criminal courts have moved to fill the void of addressing the problems of the mentally ill invites the criticism noted earlier: that problem-solving courts absorb funds that could (and should) more appropriately be invested in other social institutions. Indeed, it has been suggested that "effective community intervention could prevent the need to find and treat mentally ill citizens in the criminal justice system."[76] In spite of this criticism, significant resources have been (and are being) invested in the mental health courts and other problem-solving courts, which are increasingly viewed as a viable and welcome forum in which to address social problems previously handled by other social institutions. Resources devoted to problem solving in courts of law, however, are not limited to the four new specialty courts discussed thus far.

OTHER PROBLEM-SOLVING COURTS AND "GOING TO SCALE"

In addition to drug courts, community courts, domestic violence courts, and mental health courts, more recent versions of problem-solving courts include reentry courts, which provide recently released prisoners intensive court oversight as they return to life in the community; homeless courts, which are designed to provide judicial oversight, drug treatment, and other services for homeless repeat offenders; DUI (driving under the influence) courts, for drunk-driving offenders; teen courts, for youths who have committed minor offenses, where fellow teenagers serve as a jury of peers; tobacco courts; gambling courts; truancy courts; and prostitution courts.[77] Beyond specialty courts that focus on specific problems, a number of hybrid models have emerged, including combined domestic violence/ mental health courts, combined community/mental health courts, and combined DUI/drug courts. Some community courts, moreover, have a youth court component. Other variations of problem-solving courts include further specialties within specialty courts. There are now, for example, at least four different varieties of drug courts, including adult drug courts, juvenile drug courts, family drug courts, and even a campus drug court at Colorado State University. In all, there are more than three thousand problem-solving courts in operation in the United States, with hundreds more in the planning and implementation stages.

While the primary manifestation of judicial problem solving is represented in these so-called specialty courts, advocates have begun to promote the inculcation of a problem-solving orientation into the American criminal justice system more broadly. Personnel at the Center for Court Innovation in New York, among others, speak forcefully and enthusiastically about taking the problem-solving orientation "to scale." By this they mean applying the methods and principles of problem solving within the criminal justice system on a comprehensive scale. In some instances, problem-solving approaches have even been introduced in court settings that handle at least some civil matters, such as in unified family courts and integrated domestic violence courts.[78] As Francis Hartman, at Harvard's Kennedy School, puts it, "Going to scale is importing some of the values and operations from problem-solving courts into the court system as a whole."[79]

A sort of judicial cross-fertilization is one manner in which "going to scale" is beginning to take place. This happens in a couple of different ways. First, problem-solving court judges may influence colleagues who work in the conventional courts of their own courthouses. Atlanta community court judge Clinton Deveaux, for example, tells how a colleague used to view his judicial problem-solving efforts critically, as a "social worker on the bench." Over time, however, this colleague not only began to refer cases to Deveaux's court, but also started to make judgments himself based on what was "really needed to solve the problem" and came to realize that "this is the only way to deal with this stuff if you're going to actually stop the recidivism and actually solve some of the problems that are bringing these people to the court." Deveaux goes so far as to observe that "increasingly now, everybody is trying to find ways to solve whatever the problem is that got the case in front of the court, rather than just processing it."

Another instance of judicial cross-fertilization occurs when judges return to a conventional court after completing their problem-solving court assignment, and bring with them the ideas and methods learned in a specialty court context. A study commissioned by the California court system, for example, included interviews with several dozen problem-solving court judges. These judges, upon returning to their conventional court, felt that it was "not only possible but desirable" to transfer problem-solving principles and practices to their new court assignment. Among the qualities they viewed as transferable were "the value of a problem-solving mindset, direct interaction with defendants, monitoring offenders' performance in treatment, and reaching out to social service providers."[80]

In describing (and endorsing) this process of judicial transference, David Wexler and Bruce Winick anticipate the "creation" of a fundamentally altered criminal justice system:

The new problem-solving courts have served to raise the consciousness of many judges concerning their therapeutic role, and many former problem-solving court judges, upon being transferred back to courts of general jurisdiction, have taken with them the tools and sensitivities they have acquired in those newer courts. Indeed, the proliferation of different problem-solving courts, and the development of various "hybrid" models, suggests to us that the problem-solving court movement may actually be a transitional stage in the creation of an overall judicial system attuned to problem solving, to therapeutic jurisprudence, and to judging with an ethic of care.[81]

Other problem-solving innovators are equally ambitious in their wish to push for a fuller application of the problem-solving mentality within the broader criminal justice system. Berman and Feinblatt, for example, strategize: "We must figure out how to 'go to scale' with problem-solving justice, altering the DNA of state court systems so that problem solving becomes part of the practice of every courtroom."[82] Similarly, Robert Boruchowitz, director of the Defender Association in Seattle, anticipates that "if we can show people the benefits of treating each defendant as a whole person with a history and a future like we do in problem-solving courts, then we could alter the whole criminal justice system."[83]

These are, of course, rather bold (or at least boldly stated) aspirations—and boldness is a quality, as we shall see, that is distinct to the American version of the problem-solving court movement. That is, international comparisons reveal the extent to which boldness, as such, is not as common a feature of innovative courts in countries outside of the United States.

INTERNATIONAL TRANSFERENCE

Not only has the problem-solving court model been applied to an expanding range of populations in the American criminal justice system, but these courts have also been exported internationally. Some version of the American drug court, for example, has been transplanted to Australia, Canada, England, Scotland, and Ireland. Domestic violence courts have been developed in England, Australia, Scotland, and Canada. Australia and Canada have both introduced a type of mental health court. As noted in the introduction, Liverpool, England, launched the United Kingdom's first community court, based directly on the community courts in New York (i.e., the Midtown and Red Hook community courts). England has since initiated a second community court in Salford, and in early 2007, Australia started its first community court in Melbourne, Victoria. Plans are under way for the launch of community courts in Vancouver, Dublin, and Glasgow, as well. Versions of other problem-solving courts have also been initiated in these five other countries, including aboriginal courts in Canada and Australia; youth courts in Hamilton and Airdrie, Scotland; and DUI, homeless, prostitution, and therapeutic diversion courts in Australia.

Problem-solving courts have taken on very different forms in the other regions. Understanding these differences within a broader cultural context is, of course, a primary focus of this book. Chapters 3 through 5 explore in greater detail the processes of legal borrowing and the comparative differences among problem-solving courts in the six different countries. Before moving to a more detailed analysis of the comparative cases, however, it is necessary to reflect more generally on the relationship between law and culture, and on the legal theories that have been drawn upon to undergird problem-solving courts in differing cultural contexts. The cultural sources of both problem-solving courts and related legal theories are rarely discussed in the literature, an oversight the present comparative study aims to avoid. Indeed, a comparative perspective, based (as this one is) on the analytical assumption that law and culture are integrally related, promises to shed light on defining legal and cultural differences. A theoretical understanding of the relationship between law and culture from a comparative perspective, therefore, sets the stage for making sense of the international borrowing of this important legal innovation, and will be the focus of the next chapter.

Chapter Two

LAW AND CULTURE IN COMPARATIVE
PERSPECTIVE

> We should not lose sight of the cultural ties of the laws
> and closely observe what happens to them when laws are
> decoupled from their national roots.
> —*Gunther Teubner*

A USEFUL starting point for making sense of the international transplantation of problem-solving courts is found in the expansive literature on globalization. An important question explored within this literature is the extent to which the process of globalization is best characterized as one of *homogenization*. That is, one "popular intellectual view," as Roland Robertson puts it, holds that "the entire world is being swamped by Western—more specifically, American—culture."[1] Homogenization, as such, is viewed as the process by which American-styled capitalism, mass culture, and consumerist habits are imperialistically advanced in a world that is progressively more interconnected through electronic communications, the Internet, television, and transnational corporations. Local practices and habits give way to an increasingly homogenous and convergent global culture. Accepting the essential merits of this viewpoint (at least as a starting point), Peter Berger similarly observes: "What everyone assumes is not always wrong. There is indeed an emerging global culture, and it is indeed heavily American."[2] Both Robertson and Berger, however, also recognize that the process (or processes) of globalization are not nearly as monolithic, uniform, or unidirectional as this basic view conveys.

Another part of the equation—occurring sometimes in direct response to homogenization—is the local rejection of the dominant global culture and the reassertion of indigenous practices and commitments to local identities. *Heterogenization,* or *localization,* is thus sometimes put forth as the counterpart to homogenization. Hsin-Huang Hsiao highlights this feature of globalization in his description of localizing processes in contemporary Taiwan: "Globalization also involves the promotion or facilitation of local difference and diversity—the rise of local heterogenization."[3] In Benjamin Barber's terms, this is "Jihad" rejecting "McWorld." One is reminded, in this regard, of the European unwillingness to import or grow genetically modified foods, or of the recent renaissance of indigenous languages in the Celtic regions of Wales and Scotland. As characterized here, then, when the global and local intersect, at least two very different responses are possible: homogenization or heterogenization, acceptance or rejection, globalization or localization, universalism or particularism.

The reality, of course, is more complex and more interesting than a simple dichotomy such as this would suggest. Benjamin Barber, for one, warns against viewing the emerging global world as one characterized by "Jihad versus McWorld."[4] Rather, as he sees it, "McWorld and Jihad do not really force a choice between such polarized scenarios. Together, they are likely to produce some stifling amalgam of the two."[5] Or as Roland Robertson puts it: "The concept of globalization has involved the simultaneity and the interpenetration of what are conventionally called the global and the local."[6] The fusions, or "cases in-between acceptance and rejection," are not only "more intriguing," as Peter Berger puts it,[7] but arguably more numerous, as well, and have been given a variety of names in the literature. Berger, for example, speaks of "hybridization" and Roland Robertson of "glocalization"—that is, the synthesis of the global and the local, or "difference-within-sameness."[8] George Ritzer even speaks of heuristic gradations in types of hybrids, with some conceptualizations tending toward heterogenization and others toward homogenization.[9]

Though the international transplantation of local court programs is rarely considered in discussions about globalization, the analytical categories offered in this literature are certainly relevant. For example, one could ask whether the international borrowing of an American-made legal product such as problem-solving courts represents the triumph of American legal culture over the local legal cultures of the receiving regions, leading to the further homogenization of law and culture on a global scale. Or one might wonder whether the programs, when transplanted from one location to another, are so fully transformed, indigenized, and diluted of their defining American qualities as to represent a fuller diversification or heterogenization of legal programs throughout the world.

Interestingly, the legal actors in the five non-U.S. regions considered here most often see themselves as producing a hybrid. In other words, they say they are importing an American product but are adapting it to fit their local situation. Consider the following example offered by an Irish judge in 2000, who was at the time helping to start a drug court in Dublin. He acknowledged the U.S. origins of the program but was very clear that it had to be adjusted to fit the particularities of the Irish situation.

> You can take the huge enthusiasm of the Americans. You can take their generos-
> ity in sharing their ideas with people and giving their time and knowledge. . . .
> But in the natural order of things, you tailor the program to what suits you best.
> Not because you think there's anything wrong with the American system—but
> all you're saying is, we're three thousand miles away from you, we have a differ-
> ent culture, etc. And we've just got to tailor that, put up the cuffs, and make
> the suit fit us.

As the example makes clear, the judge identifies the process as one of
adaptation. An American-made suit is shipped across the Atlantic. Without proper alteration, it is likely to fit awkwardly or not at all. The sleeves
may be too long, the style out of place, or the fabric not suitable for
the climate. Though the essential pattern may represent a useful starting
point, the suit needs to be re-tailored or remanufactured to "fit" the
new owner.

Most practitioners think (or at least talk) in terms of synthesis or adaptation and recognize that if a proper adjustment is not made, the transplantation may prove unsuccessful. That is, conscious of cultural differences, they recognize the very real possibility of rejection. Consider, in this
regard, an alternative, more mechanical metaphor offered by a treatment
provider in Glasgow, who was, at the time, endorsing the importation of
drug courts to the United Kingdom.

> In terms of the drug courts in Britain, I'll share with you a salutary experience
> I had last year. When in the U.S., I saw this light that I really liked in a shop
> and I bought it. I thought, all I have to do is change the plug over when I [get]
> back to Britain. And I took my light home, showed it off, and was very proud
> of it. I changed the plug and nothing happened. I think it blew a fuse or some-
> thing. And what I discovered was that the electrical system that the light
> worked from was different, the plug was different, the bulb was different. I
> think that this is a useful metaphor, and one which we in the UK need to take
> on board in terms of looking at the transplantation of drug courts.

The Scottish treatment provider warned his fellow Brits that the legal
program could not be transferred wholesale. UK lights use different bulbs,
have different plugs, and run on different electrical currents. Without necessary adjustments, the American-made product simply will not work.
However, with the appropriate transformer unit, electrical adaptor, and/
or plug converter, the light can be made to function in its new context.

As these two examples suggest, the in-between cases can vary in terms
of the degree of adjustment that is required. Shortening the cuffs of a
sleeve is less of an adjustment than remanufacturing a jacket with a different type of fabric. Using an electrical currency transformer is a more
significant (and more expensive) adaptation than attaching a small three-

pronged British plug to an American version of the same. Therefore, in terms of conceptualizing synthesis, it makes more sense to think in terms of a continuum, with some adaptations requiring more preparatory efforts than others in order to ensure acceptance and avoid rejection.

LEGAL TRANSPLANTS

Given the variations in degree and type of adaptation, it may not be surprising that a number of metaphors have been used to describe legal transplantations. These include mechanical, economic, discursive, and organic metaphors. As with the example of the American light fixture, mechanical images refer to the relocation of manufactured parts from one system or machine to another. For example, a car part in one automobile is removed and reused in another. In the language of economic transactions, others speak in terms of transferring, importing, exporting, or borrowing legal products. Still others employ discursive images and speak of the variation of meanings embedded in language and of translating legal codes from one context to another.

Perhaps the most common images used to describe legal transfers are organic metaphors. Indeed, the very notion of transplantation calls to mind the process by which an organ is extracted from one human body and placed into another. Organic metaphors also come in the botanical variety. A branch is cut and grafted, or a seed is grown in one location, uprooted, and then replanted in another. While each type of metaphor enables one to envision adjustment—e.g., the use of an electrical converter, the tailoring of a suit, or the translation of a foreign language—organic images may most helpfully illustrate the extent to which the receiving entity must be prepared for the transplanted part, whether through the cultivation, fertilization, and watering of soil or the use of powerful drugs (e.g., cyclosporine) to prevent the human body from rejecting a foreign organ.

Why does it matter which metaphors are used? Most significantly, metaphors serve important heuristic purposes, enabling us to conceptualize more or less precisely the nature of particular social processes. As it specifically concerns legal transfers, metaphors provide different understandings of how law and society relate to one another.[10] Organic metaphors, for example, convey a closer relationship between law and society than do mechanical metaphors, because, as just noted, organic images better illustrate the necessity—and sometimes difficulty—of adaptation. As Otto Kahn-Freund observes, "It makes sense to ask whether the kidney can be 'adjusted' to the new body or whether the new body will 'reject' it—to ask these questions of the carburetor is ridiculous."[11] Thus, a good choice of metaphor allows us to more clearly understand and describe what actually happens when a legal transplant is attempted. However, as David Nelken explains, "Any one metaphor is unlikely to enable us to capture all that is important about legal transfers." Rather, we should view the variety of metaphors as "more or less useful" in helping "us to think in new and imaginative ways," recognizing that "any one metaphor is bound to be misleading."[12]

Scholars and practitioners alike employ metaphors (more or less successfully) to communicate certain understandings of legal transfers, of the relationship between law and society, and, correspondingly, of the need for some kind of adaptation. Consider the suit and lamp metaphors cited at the start of this chapter. Not only do both practitioners speak of the need for adaptation, but both also depict an understanding of law as something closely connected to society. We have a "different culture," says the Irish judge. Our institutions run on a different "electrical system," says the Scottish treatment provider. Adaptation, as such, is required because law is deeply ensconced in a particular cultural context.

In the literature on legal transplants, not all scholars hold to this understanding of the culturally embedded nature of law. Alan Watson is perhaps the most well-known critic of the so-called "mirror theory of law,"—that is, the view that law directly reflects and is significantly shaped by social forces outside of the law.[13] According to Watson, because law is essentially insular and autonomous, legal rules easily move from one society to another. Indeed, for Watson, legal change occurs not because of social change within a given society, but from the borrowing of laws from one society to another. Curiously, Watson himself favors the "transplant" metaphor and thus obscures his own proposed understanding of the process.

As Nelken points out, "Watson's own chosen metaphor of legal transplants suggests that transplanting laws should be arduous; certainly medical transplants are not everyday affairs or something one undergoes lightly!"[14] Cultural anthropologist Donald Joralemon highlights the difficulty of transplantation when he discusses the indispensable role of drugs in persuading a human body to accept a foreign organ. He notes, for example, that "the body never [actually] accommodates the presence of foreign tissue." It is only coaxed into doing so by being put in a "pharmacologically induced stupor."[15] A complicated mix of drugs is often required to prevent a body from rejecting a transplanted organ. If the drugs are discontinued, the body will begin to attack the foreign part. Given the difficulty and complexity of this process, one quite rightly questions the conceptual accuracy of the transplant metaphor for describing, as does Watson, the "ease and inevitability of legal transfers."[16]

Even Watson, however, in his selective use of historical cases, admits the significance of extralegal factors in shaping the nature of legal change. Following a lengthy discussion of the development of Scottish law, for example, Watson acknowledges that the important influence of European civil law in Scotland is attributable, in part, to Scotland's checkered historical relationship with England. Scottish attitudes toward England continue to shape Scotland's legal and political practices, a reality that is evident in the contemporary devolution process. Watson concedes that Scotland's openness to the influences of civil law "shows how much legal relationships may owe to non-legal historico-political factors."[17] Moreover, Watson admits that law undergoes change when transplanted from one culture to another. As he puts it, "A voluntary reception or transplant almost always . . . involves a change in the law, which can be due to any number of factors, such as climate, economic conditions, religious outlook."[18] He even acknowledges that the manner in which a law is altered may be the most telling indicator of cultural difference. "Speaking broadly though, if one were trying to discover 'the Spirit of the People' from its law one should look not to the overall system but to the details where it diverges from other systems."[19] This is a suggestion the present study endeavors to follow.

Given these concessions, it is understandable that others have called into question Watson's basic argument: that the source of legal change is the borrowing or imposition of foreign laws, and that such a process is indicative of the essential autonomy of law. Lawrence Friedman states rather bluntly that Watson's basic "premises are ludicrous."[20] Friedman argues instead that law is "never totally autonomous. Legal systems do not float in some cultural void, free of space and time and social context; necessarily they reflect what is happening in their own societies."[21] Like Watson, however, Friedman views the transferability of law as easy, inevitable, and increasingly common. He is "as optimistic as Watson concerning the extent to which legal transfers take place successfully," but for very different reasons.[22]

Approximating the views of those globalization theorists who emphasize homogenization, Friedman argues that the increasing mobility and harmonization of laws around the world is made possible because societies are becoming more alike. The ease of legal transferability is attributable not to legal autonomy, as Watson would argue, but to law's cultural embeddedness in an increasingly homogenous and convergent global culture. "There is a tremendous amount of globalization in business and the economy," says Friedman, "and the law follows along."[23] Therefore, Watson explains the ease of legal transplantation by emphasizing legal autonomy and cultural difference, whereas Friedman explains the same by emphasizing law's social embeddedness and social sameness.

LAW AND CULTURE

While some globalization theorists (e.g., Roland Robertson) would question Friedman's observation that the world is increasingly homogenous, Friedman shares with notable company his views regarding the close relationship between law and culture. Indeed, his essential position has a distinguished legacy in comparative law scholarship. As far back as the middle of the eighteenth century, Montesquieu, "the first of all comparative lawyers,"[24] advanced a socially embedded understanding of law in his famous work, *The Spirit of Law*. So profoundly is law an expression of a certain people, according to Montesquieu, that only in the case of *un grand hazard*—a great coincidence—is a law that is framed in one nation suitable for another. The difficulty of legal borrowing, as such, has everything to do with the socially determined quality of law, bound as the law is, according to Montesquieu, to such cultural factors as the religion of the people, their inclinations, manners, and customs.[25]

The German comparativist Bernhard Grossfield goes so far as to argue that "the idea that the law of a culture stems from the material and spiritual life of the people is as old as law itself: phrases such as 'common sense' (from sensus communis), 'vox populi, vox die,' and 'Volksgeist' are there to show it." Providing a rather full expression of this position, Grossfield adds that

> every legal system is a "unique product of a particular complex of determining factors": "Every culture has its particular law, and every law its particular cultural life." Every legal system has a unique individuality. This is entailed in the saying that "law varies directly with culture."

In short, according to Grossfield, "law is culture and culture is law."[26] Such a full explication of the mirror image of law, of course, requires qualification. For example, it is difficult today to speak of a uniform national culture, both because of the porous quality of national boundaries and because of the variety of (sometimes conflicting) cultures within a given society. Moreover, as Teubner argues, different types of laws within an individual society are more or less tightly bound to varying cultural currents.

Accepting these qualifications, the basic view that law is significantly related to culture has much support among contemporary comparative law scholars, sociologists of law, and legal anthropologists. Pierre Legrand, for example, says that "law is the symbolic apparatus through which entire communities try to understand themselves better."[27] Likewise, Mary Ann Glendon, Michael W. Gordon, and Christopher Osakwe observe that "law is a concentrated expression of the history, culture, social values and the general consciousness and perception of a given people."[28] In a similar way, cultural anthropologist Clifford Geertz sees the law "as a distinctive manner of imagining the real."[29] That is, the law tells the story about a particular culture, a particular people. The distinctives of the law, as such, provide a glimpse into the peculiar social realities of a given society. "Law," moreover, according to Geertz, is local knowledge: "local not just to place, time, class, and variety of issue, but as to accent."[30] The notion of accent is especially helpful as it concerns a comparison among six English-speaking countries. Just as the distinctive accents of a shared language often indicate very profound cultural and regional differences, so the varying accents of legal initiatives—such as problem-solving courts—within a shared common law tradition reflect significant political, cultural, and historical differences.

One of the more comprehensive and persuasive recent articulations of this position is offered in the work of David Garland. Following a careful review and critique of Marxian, Durkheimian, and Foucauldian theories of law and punishment, Garland makes a convincing case for the central import of culture in determining a society's criminal law and punitive practices. In this regard, Garland argues that the law "is necessarily grounded in wider patterns of knowing, feeling, and acting, and it depends upon these social roots and supports for its continuing legitimacy and operation."[31] Moreover, he speaks of the extent to which a penal culture "will always have its roots in the broader context of prevailing (or recently prevailing) social attitudes and traditions."[32]

Thus, like the advocates of problem-solving courts cited in chapter 1, Garland acknowledges that culture serves a legitimating or justificatory role vis-à-vis the law. Recall that recent legal innovations are often justified by advocates on the grounds that problem-solving courts promise to renew confidence in the criminal justice system. In observing the justificatory rhetoric and strategies employed by supporters of problem-solving courts, one simply cannot ignore the multiple references to two new legal theories of justice. That is, it is rare to read about problem-solving courts or to talk to someone associated with the movement—especially in the United States—and not hear some reference to *therapeutic jurisprudence* (TJ) and/or *restorative justice* (RJ). Practitioners regularly discuss both theories, sometimes interchangeably and with varying levels of familiarity, to justify their problem-solving efforts. Therefore, in order to make sense of the important relationship between law and culture as it concerns problem-solving courts, one must necessarily account for the essential place of developing legal theories in the larger equation.

THERAPEUTIC JURISPRUDENCE AND RESTORATIVE JUSTICE

One interesting analysis that links all three (law, culture, and emerging legal theories) can be found in the work of Susan Daicoff. In her discussion of what she calls the "comprehensive law movement," Daicoff identifies various intersecting "vectors" that, in response to the legal system's perceived ailments, endeavor to make the system "more humane, therapeutic, beneficial, humanistic, healing, restorative, curative, collaborative, and comprehensive."[33]

Among these so-called vectors are problem-solving courts, therapeutic jurisprudence, and restorative justice. While it is clear that these are related phenomena, for conceptual purposes it is important to distinguish problem-solving courts (a practical legal innovation) from therapeutic jurisprudence and restorative justice (ideas about justice theorized within the academic world). In other words, it makes more sense to characterize problem-solving courts as a legal innovation, the philosophical justifications for which are drawn from the principles articulated within therapeutic jurisprudence and restorative justice, rather than to characterize both as vectors on the same conceptual plane. The undeniable link between the theories and the practice invites a fuller understanding of the defining components of the former.

While there are important similarities between therapeutic jurisprudence and restorative justice, there are also significant differences. With respect to what they hold in common, both theories have a normative dimension to them. That is, they are not merely analytical frameworks, but propose to alter legal practices in accordance with new ways of thinking about justice. For therapeutic jurisprudence—which understands the law "to function as a kind of therapist or therapeutic agent"— this means identifying and enhancing legal processes determined to be therapeutic and altering or reducing legal processes determined to be antitherapeutic.[34] While the scope of restorative justice is broader and more varied, normative considerations generally refer to the aim of promoting legal processes that "attempt to repair the harm caused by criminal behavior."[35] The reparative focus can include such efforts as "restoring" the victim, "reintegrating" the offender into society, healing the conflict between victim and offender, and/or repairing "the breach in the community's sense of trust."[36]

A second similarity between TJ and RJ is that both theories are therapeutic, in the sense that they place an emphasis on emotions, empathy, healing, and the psychological well-being of individuals encountering the legal system. John Braithwaite, an Australian criminologist and leading RJ theorist, highlights this area of common concern. "The biggest methodological similarity between Therapeutic Jurisprudence and Restorative Justice is empathy for human survivors of legal conflicts; this demands a holistic grasp of the human consequences—in loss, pain, emotion and relationships—of the legal encounter."[37] This shared holistic perspective leads both theoretical perspectives to support a problem-solving orientation. Indeed, as Braithwaite argues further, "Perhaps the most solid common ground between Therapeutic Jurisprudence and Restorative Justice is that they are both part of a return to problem-oriented adjudication," where "narrow framings like 'what is the right punishment?' are eschewed in favor of 'what is the right solution to the problem?'"[38]

In a final area of common ground, both theories rhetorically defer to elements of more traditional theories of justice, even while they advocate fairly radical changes in the legal system. For example, restorative justice includes among its "priority list of values" the following: "honoring legally specific upper limits on sanctions" and respecting "fundamental human rights."[39] Regarding the former, it should be noted that though upper limits on sanctions are typically understood within the limiting principle of "just deserts" theory, Braithwaite (along with Philip Pettit, in an earlier discussion on the topic) does not attempt to defend it on these grounds.[40] Indeed, as Andrew von Hirsch and Andrew Ashworth point out, "no persuasive reason is offered" in their analysis for "why those limits should exist."[41]

This disagreement is emblematic of the varied and often conflicting schools of thought one finds within the vast literature on restorative justice. Some RJ scholars, including Braithwaite and Pettit, have (at least initially) portrayed restorative justice as fundamentally distinct from a retributive or "just deserts" theory of justice, a characterization with which retributivists like Ashworth and von Hirsch have readily agreed. Other scholars, including Russ Immarigeon, Kathleen Daly, Richard Young, and Carolyn Hoyle, hold that retributive and restorative principles can actually find much common ground.[42] Still others argue that the two perspectives "are not merely overlapping concepts but are integrally interlinked."[43] Antony Duff, for example, claims not only that the two theories are "compatible," but that "restoration . . . requires retribution."[44]

Even those RJ scholars who try to distance themselves from retributivist principles nevertheless also wish to maintain features of just deserts theory, even if they do not explicitly define them in retributivist terms. John Braithwaite, for example, follows the retributivist emphasis on proportionality, as noted earlier, when he maintains that upper limits of punishment should somehow be sustained. He even allows that he is "happy to retain various due process protections and other fundamental justice values."[45] Such a concession is consistent, as Braithwaite acknowledges, with qualifications offered by TJ scholars, who likewise say that they wish to avoid "subordinating due process and other justice values" in their promotion of therapeutic consequences.[46]

Indeed, Bruce Winick and David Wexler, the two most prominent therapeutic jurisprudence scholars, regularly assert that therapeutic values should not "trump" certain traditional values of justice. As Bruce Winick puts it, "Therapeutic jurisprudence has always suggested that therapeutic goals should be achieved only within the limits of considerations of justice . . . law should be applied fairly, evenhandedly, and non-discriminatorily. Legal actors should seek to apply the law therapeutically but only when consistent with these values."[47] Therefore, like restorative justice, therapeutic jurisprudence defers, at least rhetorically, to "just deserts" principles.

Along with these similarities, therapeutic jurisprudence and restorative justice also differ in important respects. For one, therapeutic jurisprudence scholars are a little uncomfortable with the emphasis on "reintegrative shaming," a concept John Braithwaite has made central to his understanding of restorative justice.[48] In an April 2000 panel discussion at Western Michigan University, David Wexler was asked specifically about restorative justice and reintegrative shaming. He acknowledged some compatibilities between TJ and RJ but thought the term "reintegrative shaming" was "unfortunate." In particular, he thought "the word shame . . . throws a lot of people off track." He also feared that the restorative justice emphasis on reintegration may not give enough attention to rehabilitation and suggested that "more needs to be introduced into the restorative justice paradigm regarding efforts at rehabilitation."

A second difference between the two theories is the broader scope of restorative justice. As noted earlier, both theories include a normative dimension. Again, for therapeutic jurisprudence, this specifically means that "therapeutic consequences are good, antitherapeutic consequences are bad."[49] Restorative justice, in contrast, "is concerned with a much wider net of consequences."[50] While the wider and more diverse scope of RJ has invited a variety of critiques (including concerns about the absence of "dispositional criteria"), the more restricted, if somewhat vague and ambiguous, analytical focus of therapeutic jurisprudence has left others wondering whether TJ practices ultimately supplant the preservation of traditional justice principles.[51] In other words, with the focus centered on promoting therapeutic outcomes and discouraging antitherapeutic outcomes, are other justice values ignored or disregarded, in spite of the stated wishes by TJ theorists to retain these values?

As I have argued elsewhere, the preoccupation with identifying and promoting therapeutic consequences in legal processes can result, if only unwittingly, in the eventual disregard of just deserts principles.[52] Therapeutic jurisprudence scholars may not be openly hostile to retributivist principles, but concerns about due process, proportionality, procedural fairness, and the like can fade into the background in the context of a legal culture fixated on promoting therapeutic processes. The wider scope of RJ considerations and the growing number of scholars sympathetic to a composite view of restorative and retributivist principles suggest that a disregard for traditional justice principles in RJ-inspired legal programs may be less likely.

This will depend, of course, on particular understandings among practitioners of RJ and TJ, which, as noted earlier, vary considerably. Awareness of and commitment to restorative justice and therapeutic jurisprudence also appear to vary with respect to region. For example, therapeutic jurisprudence, in contrast to restorative justice, is more clearly an American phenomenon. TJ grew up in the United States at approximately the same time as did the early problem-solving courts. It has more recently received a sympathetic reception in Canada and Australia, but its influence is less often evident, if not openly resisted, in Ireland, England, and Scotland.

The origins of restorative justice are more diverse. "Victim-offender reconciliation" programs in North America, such as the one developed in Kitchener, Ontario, in 1974, are often cited as one place where modern restorative justice practices first emerged.[53] In the 1980s, the peacemaking processes among First Nations people in Canada and family group conferencing in New Zealand are additional practices celebrated by restorative justice theorists.[54] John Braithwaite picked up on and developed the "powerful ideas" of family group conferencing, which began taking root in Australia and Canada in the early 1990s (and to a lesser extent in England and the United States).[55] References to RJ principles are evident in each of the cases considered in this comparative study but are clearly more pronounced (particularly in academic communities) in Australia, Canada, and England than in the United States, Scotland, and Ireland.[56] Just as there are regional differences regarding the relative concentration of RJ and TJ in different countries, the relevance of these theories also seems to vary from one type of problem-solving court to another. For example, therapeutic jurisprudence has been more closely aligned with drug courts than any other type of problem-solving court, while community courts (with their emphasis on reparation and community service) are more aligned with restorative justice principles in important respects.[57] In spite of these differences, practitioners invoke therapeutic jurisprudence and restorative justice in varying ways, and often demonstrate only nominal understandings of the central tenets of both.

Without denying the important influence of these theories, some argue that the problem-solving court movement is actually, at its core, fundamentally pragmatic. That is, the movement is not so much about adjusting court processes to fit therapeutic and/or restorative principles as it is about achieving a system that is more efficient and effective. Greg Berman, for example, says that what most appeals to him about the movement is that it is "deeply pragmatic." As he puts it, the movement has not so much been "born out of theory" as advanced by "practitioners on the ground, struggling to do something better than what they were doing." He does not deny the influential role of TJ and RJ in the movement but is careful not to align himself with any one school. Rather, he sees the movement as informed by a "bricolage" of theories. Even scholars closely aligned with therapeutic jurisprudence acknowledge that, at least initially, "the problem solving court revolution" was "largely atheoretical."[58] The deep pragmatism Berman sees in the movement, however, does not necessarily equate with the absence of theory. Pragmatism itself is a singular perspective, the application of which significantly influences legal processes. Richard Posner, today's leading legal pragmatist, himself admits that "legal pragmatism . . . is a theory."[59] It is, in fact, a theoretical perspective that has experienced something of a renaissance in recent years.[60] Even more than RJ, legal pragmatism encompasses a varied and eclectic range of perspectives.[61] Among the common themes emphasized by legal pragmatists are a result-oriented preoccupation with "what works," an experimentalist approach, a skepticism toward foundationalist claims, and a forward-looking instrumentalism.[62] Though perhaps unaware of academic theorizing by legal and philosophical pragmatists, U.S. problem-solving court practitioners often act in a manner commensurate with these themes, even if they do not invoke legal pragmatism nearly as often as they do TJ and RJ.[63] It should be noted that pragmatic considerations are not necessarily antithetical to therapeutic jurisprudence. A therapeutic orientation and pragmatism (or therapeutic pragmatism) can actually work in a complementary manner. The perspectives are often offered in tandem, at least in the United States, to justify problem-solving courts.

Regardless of claims about the absence of theory in the early stages of the movement, problem-solving courts are rarely discussed today (especially in the United States) without some reference to therapeutic jurisprudence and/or restorative justice. Recall, once again, the notion of vectors introduced by Susan Daicoff. Problem-solving courts, TJ, and RJ all arrived on the legal scene at approximately the same time, though they were concentrated in different locations and within different types of specialty courts. What explains the simultaneous development of these related phenomena? Daicoff takes a step toward answering this question when she suggests that behind the emergence of all three were "certain philosophical shifts . . . in the late twentieth century." Without elaborating on the substance of these philosophical shifts, she identifies the growing "appreciation of psychological dynamics" and awareness of individuals' "emotional well-being."[64] These societal qualities that Daicoff highlights are, in fact, consistent with the defining tenets of what a number of sociologists and cultural critics have referred to as a conspicuously therapeutic cultural ethos emergent in American society—what Philip Reiff famously called "the triumph of the therapeutic."[65]

In other words, the significant influence of another vector (or variable)—namely, a therapeutic culture—may help to explain, at least in part, why features of both the theories and the practices emerged when and where they did.[66] Legal historian William Nelson makes this essential point in a discussion about problem-solving courts. Highlighting qualities of the therapeutic culture and its institutional concomitants, Nelson acknowledges the societal decline in influence of family and community structures and notes the emergence of "professional psychiatrists, social workers, and the like," who now help judges "engage in improving behavior." Importantly, however, Nelson adds that this change is not so much a "comment on the judiciary, but a comment on the changing structure of American society."[67] Thus, societal changes have directly affected the judiciary, just as they have the plausibly of emergent legal theories. When considering the important interplay between problem-solving courts and culture from a comparativist perspective, therefore, it makes sense to consider the role of theory; the theories, like the courts themselves, are reflections of their cultural context. If certain courts are justified by a kind of therapeutic pragmatism, as they arguably are in the United States, what happens when these courts are transplanted? Do the culturally embedded theories transfer as well? If so, what effect will the imported legal program have on a receiving culture that is not defined by such qualities?

LEGAL IRRITANTS

This question points to a second part of the ongoing dynamic between law and culture, namely, the important influence of law on culture. Those sensitive to the influential role of culture on law recognize that law shapes, just as it is shaped by, culture. As David Garland puts it: "It is a two-way process—an interactive relationship—and if one is to think in terms of cause and effect or vectors of determination, then the arrows must run in both directions simultaneously."[68]

Thus, law not only reflects cultural sensibilities, but also helps to shape them. Law serves a pedagogical role, as Mary Ann Glendon observes, "by influencing the way people interpret the world around them as well as by communicating that certain values have a privileged place in society."[69] Law may serve this role even if the values expressed in the law cannot be directly enforced at a particular historical moment. As political scientist Gary Jacobsohn demonstrates in his insightful comparison of constitutional law in Ireland, India, Israel, and the United States, law can sometimes have an intentionally "aspirational dimension" to it. That is, accepting the constraints of the political and cultural realities of a given historical moment, a country's laws, though perhaps "immediately unenforceable," can advance ideals with which society may one day more fully comply.[70]

So, what happens when a new legal program (with certain culturally embedded values) is transferred from one country to another? The dialectical nature of the relationship between law and society invites the comparativist to consider the effects of legal transplantation on social change. This case study does not simply compare societal responses to a certain type of crime—say, grand theft—and analyze different adjudicative and punitive practices with respect to this crime. The international development of problem-solving courts is something more fluid and evolving—it involves the transfer of related legal programs from one society to another and the process of adapting these programs to fit varying legal cultures. Given the close relationship between law and culture, we realize that the introduction of a new legal program hardly represents the end of the story. Therefore, we wish not only to make sense of the manner in which law is adapted to fit its new context, but also to understand (if only in a preliminary manner) how the imported legal program might influence the new social context.

Regarding this second analytical focus, one encounters certain conceptual limitations in the most popular metaphors of legal transplantation. As noted earlier, the acceptance or rejection of an imported legal program is not the conclusion of the story, as the transplant metaphor might lead one to conclude. Gunther Teubner makes just this point. He argues that the transplant metaphor is, in fact, "misleading" and "creates the wrong impression that after a difficult surgical operation the transferred material will remain identical with itself, playing its old role in the new organism. Accordingly, it comes down to the narrow alternative: repulsion or integration,"[71] a false dichotomy very similar to that challenged by globalization theorists.

Moreover, acceptance itself is a rather relative term. As discussed earlier, the successful reception of a transplanted organ is contingent upon the continuing use of powerful immunosuppressant drugs. Precisely because the body's immune system has been suppressed or weakened, the drugs, rather than the transplanted organ, can produce significant side effects—including anxiety, depression, diabetes, and/or high cholesterol. Envisioning the metaphorical relevance of immunosuppression in the context of legal transplantation is not easy. The distinct processes of transplanting an organ and prescribing a variety of drugs do not clearly approximate what happens when a legal rule or program is transferred from one society to another. Certainly there are side effects to legal transplantation (which, to be sure, represent a useful feature of the transplant metaphor), but are these caused by something akin to an immunosuppressant drug? If so, what is the social or cultural equivalent of a pharmacological suppressant?

In light of difficulties such as these, Teubner questions the usefulness of the transplant metaphor altogether and offers instead what he calls the notion of a "legal irritant." As he explains, "When a foreign rule is imposed on a domestic culture, I submit, something else is happening. It is not transplanted into another organism, rather it works as a fundamental irritation which triggers a whole series of unexpected events."[72] Such a view is sensitive not only to law's relationship to other social institutions but also to the potential social consequences of a given imported law when it becomes part of the law-culture dynamic in a new society. Reflecting on this dynamic, Teubner adds:

> Legal irritants cannot be domesticated, they are not transformed from something alien into something familiar, not adapted to a new cultural context, rather they will unleash an evolutionary dynamic in which the external rule's meaning will be reconstructed and the internal context will undergo fundamental change.[73]

According to Teubner, then, the irritant metaphor is helpful in two important ways. First, it better captures the complexity of a legal transfer and thus moves beyond the more limited analytical choice of either rejection or acceptance. Again, this is a corrective that corresponds directly with the views of those globalization theorists who emphasize processes of synthesis or hybridization. Second, the legal irritant metaphor aids us in thinking about what unexpected consequences may be triggered as a result of introducing an imported legal program into a new legal culture. Though he does not take up the notion of legal irritation, Jack Hiller does much the same thing as Teubner in his discussion of the transferability of Western law to developing countries. With a more explicitly cultural focus, Hiller argues that laws transferred from one country to another "carry with them so much imperceptible and incommensurable cultural 'baggage' that the receiving country will inevitably experience far more internal cultural change than it either realized, intended or would have intended."[74] Hiller holds that each culture has "its own integrity and internal consistency"[75] and that law, like language and sport, "is a product of culture."[76] Because law is a product and thus a carrier of culture, when it moves from one place to another, it not only functions differently in the importing country (i.e., adapts), but it "will 'skew' the receiving culture in profound ways."[77] In terms very similar to those used by Teubner, Hiller argues that the importation of foreign laws "generates unknown and un-perceived 'ripple' effects upon the culture."[78] Ignoring these conse-quences, according to Hiller, will inevitably result in an increasingly ho-mogenous "mass world culture."[79]

PROBLEM SOLVING IN A GLOBAL CONTEXT

To review, an examination of the international expansion of problem-solving courts promises to yield insights with respect to both cultural dif-ferences and concomitant social change. Regarding the former, because law is a product of culture, adaptations signify defining cultural distinc-tions. Thus, a legal program such as a community court in the United Kingdom, though directly borrowed from the United States, looks very different in Liverpool than it does in New York City. The nature and extent of the differences provide insights into the particular cultural con-texts within which the programs are situated. As both Hiller and Teubner maintain, however, the adjustments made to the legal programs are not the end of the story. The programs themselves also effect change in the legal culture to which they have been transferred. The alteration may be quite subtle and not easily detectable, but it is change to which the com-parativist should pay attention.

To illustrate the latter point, consider an example from the globaliza-tion literature. Berger observes that when "Mexicans eat *hamburguesas*," they are not simply consuming an imported type of food under the guise of new nomenclature. In the process, "Mexicans are consuming whole chunks of American values 'in, with, and under' the American hamburg-ers."[80] Such values might include cultural understandings of what it means to share a meal with others; the significance of where food is grown and how it is prepared; and what is regarded as the appropriate time one should take to consume a meal. This example raises an important ques-tion: with the importation of an American product, legal or otherwise, is more of American culture brought on board than the receiving country realizes, in spite of deliberate efforts to domesticate the product?

In his discussions of McDonaldization, George Ritzer argues that, in fact, the processes by which McDonald's restaurants have been indi-genized really represent more homogenization than heterogenization. For example, McDonald's restaurants in Russia may produce "pirozhok" to suit local tastes and may have spawned the development of such localized chains as Russkoye Bistro, but at the end of the day, the fundamental values embodied in McDonald's are still advanced by these develop-ments—and to the detriment of local customs and habits. As evidence,

Ritzer cites obsequious comments from the Russkoye Bistro's deputy director: "We need to create fast food here that fits our lifestyle and traditions. . . . We see McDonald's like an older brother. . . . We have a lot to learn from them."[81] Ritzer suggests that the prima facie perception of adaptation is only skin-deep. Even the ostensibly indigenous developments represent more acquiescence to the global culture than they do the advancement of something that is locally distinctive.

Applying a related analysis to criminal law, Arie Freiberg comes to a similar conclusion in his discussion of foreign (particularly American) influences on Australian sentencing laws and practices. Like Hiller, Freiberg taps into themes developed in the globalization literature. He notes, for example, the significant impact of American "television, film, books, the Internet, newspapers, and academic journals" on Australian society and observes how these influences "tend to permeate and possibly eclipse local cultures, including legal and sentencing regimes and practices."[82] While he highlights the ways in which Australia has partially resisted certain influences and successfully sustained practices distinctive to its own culture and traditions, he worries that the homogenizing effects of globalization will diminish national distinctives. According to Freiberg, the Australian criminal justice system is "becoming internationalized, globalized or, perhaps, colonized, but not necessarily without resistance."[83]

Like Teubner, then, Freiberg understands that legal borrowing results in something other than full acceptance or rejection. He recognizes that Australian culture and law are being deeply influenced by an American-inspired global culture. But he also accepts that these influences sometimes come from sources other than the United States (e.g., the United Kingdom), and that Australia has, at least in the short term, been successful in resisting certain features of American criminal justice practices. The British criminologist Philip Bean comes to a similar conclusion with respect to the American influence on drug control policy in the United Kingdom. As Bean observes, "What one can see is that American policies have been changed to fit British experience and made to fit British culture . . . there is a willingness in Britain to accept some American ideas and a reluctance to accept them all. Some are worth taking on board, some not."[84]

The question remains, however, whether the legal actors importing these programs are really successful at adapting the programs in such a way that the American features incompatible with the importing culture are truly jettisoned. If a legal product, such as a problem-solving court, is developed in a uniquely American context, is it not intrinsically American to the core? Is it possible to fully extricate the culturally determined qualities of American problem-solving courts—such as their distinctively therapeutic tendencies—when the programs are transported to other countries?

We can only begin to answer questions such as these by turning to the empirical cases, which will be the focus of the next three chapters. Common themes synthesized from discussions of law and culture, globalization, and legal transplantation will provide the backdrop for an analysis of these cases of legal borrowing. To summarize, several questions inform the investigation. Is the view that problem-solving courts can be successfully domesticated, common among practitioners, an accurate interpretation of the process? Or is more of American culture being imported than the borrowing countries realize? Are some countries more successful than others at resisting the influence of American sensibilities and legal habits, and if so, why? How does this comparative study inform the larger debates about the processes of globalization? Does the importation of American legal products result in greater harmonization, or does it serve as an irritant affecting local cultures in unexpected ways? If the latter, in what ways might problem-solving courts irritate, and thus change, the legal cultures of receiving countries?

Chapter Three

ANGLO-AMERICAN ALTERNATIVES:
ENGLAND AND THE UNITED STATES

> These courts are examples of a new kind of court that is
> now an established feature of the American system, known
> as "problem-solving courts." . . . As a direct consequence,
> pilot schemes have been set up in this country to follow
> the American example.
> —*Lord Phillips, Lord Chief Justice*
> *of England and Wales*

OUTSIDE of the United States, England is among the countries furthest along in transplanting variations of these American judicial innovations.[1] Since 1998, England has initiated three types of problem-solving courts: drug courts, domestic violence courts, and community courts. In each instance, the courts were inspired by their U.S. counterparts but have taken on different forms as influenced by the particularities of local circumstances. In keeping with statements reviewed in chapter 2, English practitioners see themselves as adapting the American model to suit their own local needs. Particularly in the early years, English versions of problem-solving courts assumed qualities noticeably distinct from those of the American variety. While these distinctions have faded somewhat in recent years, they are still observable and have been determined by both structural and cultural factors.

Structural factors refer to those features of Britain's legal and political system that constrain or place limitations on the particular form that problem-solving courts assume in England. Included among these would be Britain's unique and widespread use of lay magistrates; the more prestigious, centralized, and better-funded British probation service; and the top-down quality of the British political system. These traits clearly distinguish the British from the American political and legal systems and play an important role in determining the unique features of problem-solving courts in England.

In addition to the structural factors, important cultural forces also shape the form and manner of problem-solving courts in England. That

no p-solve in England

is, even when the system might legally permit certain courtroom behaviors and practices, such conduct is nevertheless resisted because of local cultural sensibilities. For example, U.S. problem-solving courts are often characterized by a high level of theater—applause when someone has done well in treatment, tearful testimonies by defendants who have made successful improvements in their life circumstances, and even hugging between judge and defendant at court-sponsored graduation ceremonies. One California judge who strongly endorses hugging also allows clients to visit with her in her judicial chambers. In order to be seen as more approachable and caring to clients, a Kentucky judge does not wear his black robe and has even appeared in court with acupuncture needles in his ears as an advertisement for a form of treatment common in American drug courts. A North Carolina judge literally does cartwheels when clients successfully attend "ninety meetings in ninety days." British judges and magistrates are less inclined to behave in this manner and have been generally disapproving of American practices of this sort—sometimes quite forcefully and explicitly.

Over time, however, the strength of this resistance seems to have weakened. That is, in the more recent manifestations of English problem-solving courts, as will be explored in this chapter, some of the very qualities of the American courts that British legal actors once expressly deplored—even judicial hugging—are now detectable. In the earliest versions of English problem-solving courts, in contrast, Anglo-American differences were more pronounced, even while the U.S. inspiration for the courts was acknowledged, albeit sometimes only reluctantly. To consider the nature and extent of Anglo-American differences (and growing similarities), this chapter compares and contrasts English and American varieties of problem-solving courts, beginning with drug courts—the first type of problem-solving court to find its way across the Atlantic.

Drug Courts, DTTOs, and DRRs

There have, in fact, been several incarnations of drug courts in England. The first so-called English drug courts were initiated in Wakefield and Pontefract, two West Yorkshire cities located approximately two hundred miles north of London. The West Yorkshire drug courts—also referred to as STEP (Substance misuse Treatment and Enforcement Program)—came into being following a 1995 visit to the Miami drug court by Keith Hellawell, then chief constable of the West Yorkshire police (and later the UK anti-drugs coordinator, or "drugs czar"). Hellawell was inspired by what he saw in the United States, and he subsequently invited the first U.S. drug court judge, Stanley Goldstein, to speak at a British police conference the following year. Val Barker, the assistant director of public health of the Wakefield Health Authority, attended the conference. She describes what happened next.

> I first heard about drug courts when I went to an Association of Chief Police Officers conference in 1996, and I saw Judge Goldstein speak with such passion and emotion about how his drug court worked. And those people who know me know that I am a very determined woman. And I was pretty determined to go see what happened in Dade County. So, in February of 1997, I went to the [Miami] drug court with a police officer, probation officer, and my medical colleagues from Public Health in Wakefield, and we went to the court and to the treatment centers. . . . And I came back a convert, and a real enthusiast for what was happening there.

Upon returning to England, Barker applied for funds from the West Yorkshire Police Authority and, with the support of Keith Hellawell (who was still chief constable of the West Yorkshire police at the time), was awarded £200,000 to start two pilot drug court programs. Barker and her colleagues were also successful in obtaining funds from private sources, including from Marks and Spencer, a British department store chain. With this funding in place, the Wakefield "drugs court" was launched on May 5, 1998, and the Pontefract program on July 6, 1998.[2]

The two West Yorkshire courts were only briefly referred to as drug courts, because of a second related development in the United Kingdom: the initiation of Drug Treatment and Testing Orders (DTTOs), probation-based court orders that borrow some features of the American drug court model. As with the West Yorkshire courts, DTTOs were directly inspired by U.S. drug courts.[3] In 1995, Justin Russell, an important player in UK drug policy, went to the United States to observe drug courts. Upon his return he met up with others, including Paul Hayes, chief probation officer of the Southeast London Probation Service, and came up with DTTOs. According to Hayes, without the American drug court model, "we wouldn't have gotten DTTOs."[4]

In April 1998, encouraged by the positive accounts of U.S. drug courts offered by British visitors in the mid-1990s, the New Labour government issued a report: "Tackling Drugs: To Build a Better Britain." The report recommended the development of DTTOs, which were then legislatively mandated in the 1998 Crime and Disorder Act. As directed by this legislation, three pilot programs—in Gloucestershire, Liverpool, and Croydon (South London)—were initiated in October 1998. Based on the ostensible early success of these programs, the government then spent £60 million to roll out DTTOs in all forty-two of Britain's probation services in the summer of 2000. Included in this national scheme was funding for the West Yorkshire courts. Therefore, the Wakefield and Pontefract courts were folded into the larger national DTTO program, and the term "drug court" was, at least for the time being, dropped from the lexicon of contemporary British criminal justice.

With the passage of the Criminal Justice Act of 2003, DTTOs were phased out in name, though not in essential practice. The act incorporated DTTO processes into a larger Community Order scheme, one feature of which is a Drug Rehabilitation Requirement (DRR). Functioning in a fashion similar to that of DTTOs, DRRs can be tougher and more tailored to the specific circumstances of individual clients. Moreover, additional requirements, such as a curfew, residential restrictions, and mental health treatment, can be "bolted on" to the DRR. Even the specific DRR itself gives the judge or magistrates greater flexibility in imposing requirements at varying levels of intensity. One judge I interviewed, who had worked with both DTTOs and DRRs, described DRRs as a "much better vehicle"—this because they are tougher and allow him to "do all sorts of mixing and matching." The new Community Order scheme, and the specific DRRs within it, went into effect on April 4, 2005.

Interestingly, just eight months later, England once again initiated courts specifically referred to as drug courts—one in West London and a second in Leeds.[5] As with previous manifestations of drug courts in England, these courts were directly inspired by the American model. Judge Justin Philips, the first drug court judge in the West London court, explains how he "started reading about the American model." He notes specifically his "online research of the American courts" and his discovery of the "donut court in Florida," presumably referring to the Fort Lauderdale drug court, where successful clients are rewarded in court with fresh donuts. Holding up the American innovation as the model, he laments that "the UK is ten-plus years behind the U.S.A." The Lord Chief Justice of England and Wales, Nicholas Phillips (no relation), who attended the December 2005 opening of the West London Drugs Court, complimented the "inspiring leadership" of Judge Justin Philips and also noted the manner in which the judge and the court are "following the American model."

Undeniably, the West London court looks more like the American variety than any previous iteration of drug courts in England. While the U.S. model has been the acknowledged source of inspiration throughout the nearly decade-long experimentation with drug courts in England, it is only in recent years that some of the conspicuously American qualities have become more apparent. In spite of the gradual evolution toward the American model, important structural restraints still limit the scope and style of these experimental courts—limitations, again, that were even more evident in the earliest versions of English drug courts.

Lay Magistrates

Perhaps the most important structural restraint shaping British drug courts is the widespread use of lay magistrates in England. Most low-level offenses in England are handled by lay magistrates' courts, which differ markedly from America's single-judge criminal courts. British lay magistrates' courts, the origins of which can be traced back to the fourteenth century, handle the "great bulk of minor criminal charges."[6] Indeed, magistrates' courts handle approximately 95 percent of all criminal cases in England. England and Wales have approximately 30,400 lay magistrates, all of whom are appointed by the Lord Chancellor (who now also takes the title Secretary of State for Justice).[7] Lay magistrates typically sit as a panel of three, with one, selected by the panel, serving as chair. Lay magistrates have no formal training in the law, though each panel of three is assisted by a court clerk, who does have formal legal training and who advises on substantive and procedural points of law.

In larger cities, some magistrates' courts are presided over by a district judge, previously referred to as a "stipendiary magistrate," who, more like the American judge, has formal legal training and sits alone on the bench.[8] However, only about 100 full-time district judges and 150 part-time deputies sit singly as such. Thus, lay magistrates handle the vast majority—approximately 91 percent—of all criminal cases dealt with in magistrates' courts.[9] The lay magistracy is an important and central feature of the British criminal justice system, and one of which the British are quite proud. Lord Chancellor Falconer typified this attitude when, in a February 2004 speech in London, he stated unequivocally that "the lay magistracy is right at the heart of our justice system, particularly the criminal justice system. . . . The government remains totally committed to the role of the lay magistracy in our justice system."[10]

Dealing with the more serious criminal cases are the British Crown Courts, which are famous for their "colorful ceremonial trappings of court dress."[11] Crown Court judges can impose longer sentences and stricter sanctions. The majority of offenders who find themselves under a DTTO or DRR come before a panel of three lay magistrates, though in some circumstances Crown Court judges will handle these orders (usually with defendants with more serious criminal backgrounds). Again, lay magistrates handle the vast majority of these cases.

This feature of the British criminal justice system has shaped the development of drug courts in important ways. For example, English magistrates can only sentence a defendant to a maximum of six months for a single conviction and to no more than twelve months for multiple charges. Moreover, magistrates do not have the power to impose intermediate sanctions, a defining feature of American drug courts.[12] Lay magistrates, for example, cannot sanction clients to short, one-day to two-week jail terms, as are commonly imposed in the American drug courts. Their only real power is to revoke the probation order—an action that, if employed, effectively ends the client's involvement in the program. A Liverpool probation officer viewed this as one of the major differences between British and American courts.

> The magistrates—their power, if you like—is still restricted on the DTTO, because we have to breach [the defendant's order] before they can send them to prison. Whereas in America the judge can say if someone is not complying, "I'll bring them back and I'll sentence them to prison for two weeks." They are not on a [probation] order.

Contrastingly, when participants come before the British magistrates for their monthly reviews, they come before a panel that has very little actual authority.

Another difference determined by the lay magistrate system is the degree to which the English courts can provide continuity in their management and oversight of drug clients. Because lay magistrates serve in panels of three on a rotating basis, DTTOs and DRRs often lack the kind of continuity and close personal interaction between judge and client that is at the very heart of the American drug court model. In the United States, each time a drug court client returns to the court, he or she faces the same judge. Because of this format, the judge knows the client, the client knows the judge, and a relationship between the two develops. This relationship is regarded as a critical feature of the American model.

English DTTOs and DRRs do have "review hearings," where the client regularly returns to court. These review hearings may well be the feature of the American model that has been most consistently applied in all varieties of the English drug courts. In England, as in the United States, defendants must regularly—usually once per month—appear before a British judge or panel of three lay magistrates, who review their progress in the program. As in U.S. drug courts, solicitors are not typically present during the review sessions. Instead, the courtroom drama assumes a more inquisitorial than adversarial model, with the judge or magistrates engaging the client directly in conversation.

However, because of the rotating schedule of lay magistrates, clients in the English court programs often face a different panel of magistrates each time they return to court. Lay magistrates are required to sit a minimum of twenty-six half days a year, or an average of half a day in court every two weeks.[13] Local DTTO and DRR programs typically have four or five panels of magistrates trained to handle review sessions. Thus, it is difficult for the courts to achieve the kind of continuity typical of an American drug court program, where a single judge presides.

Some probation officers have tried to arrange schedules so that clients come before the same panel of magistrates for each review session, thus making more likely a growing relationship between the magistrates and defendants over time. One probation officer who had worked with DTTOs and DRRs in both Nottinghamshire and Oxfordshire attempted such a strategy. When she began working at the Oxford magistrates' court, it did not have "set magistrates" working the review sessions. When clients came up for review, then, "it could be any magistrates, who were just put on for that particular session."[14] Viewing this arrangement as a liability, she tried to implement a system in Oxford that followed the format in place in Nottinghamshire, where individual clients were assigned "fixed magistrates" for the review sessions. In Nottinghamshire, because "the same magistrates would see the same clients every time they came back . . . there was a rapport built up between the magistrates and the client."

Such an arrangement more closely approximates the processes of an American drug court. Even closer to the American model are some of the practices in Judge Philips's West London drug court. Here, too, the issue of judicial continuity has been a central concern guiding the innovation. In fact, Judge Philips himself served as a DTTO judge before launching the West London drug court. He found the DTTOs less than fully satisfying. "I had no training, and for a year or so the heavily addicted and I talked with little enthusiasm on either side." His lukewarm attitude toward DTTOs stands in stark contrast to his unfettered zeal for drug court. One feature of the new drug court about which he is so enthusiastic is this issue of continuity. "Whoever sentences, reviews," he says—thus "you get continuity, which in my view is the most important thing, because you build a relationship." Susan Williams, another district judge in West London who has served as both a domestic violence and a drug court judge, agrees that the format allows the judge to establish "rapport" with the clients. Lord Chief Justice Phillips, himself a strong supporter of problem-solving courts, likewise highlights this important difference between DTTOs and drug courts. In drug courts, unlike in DTTOs, offenders "immediately start a relationship with the judge of that court," in which "you get a much more ready focus on the problem."

Regarding lay magistrates, then, adjusting drug courts to a British context has necessarily involved suiting the program to fit a system in which the lay magistracy is a central and defining feature. The translation process has resulted in the development of a program with less consistency as it concerns the relationship between judge (or magistrate) and client. Recognizing this difference, some practitioners have attempted to adapt the program in order to achieve greater continuity. Even with the more recent adjustments, however, judges and magistrates still do not have the kind of power that judges in the United States have. Moreover, it is telling that, at least in the case of DTTOs and DRRs, the adjustments that have been made were initiated and orchestrated by probation officers, which speaks to the singular place of probation in the British criminal justice system.

The Strength of Probation

If British magistrates have less power than American judges, British probation officers have more authority than their American counterparts. In the United Kingdom, probation has more status, is more centrally organized, and has more funding. In all three drug court varieties in England, probation officers have played a very prominent role. In the United States, contrastingly, individual drug courts and the drug court movement are judge-led. Probation officers may play a role, but they certainly do not play a leading role in the program or the movement. As summarized in a 1992 *Federal Probation* article written by American and British coauthors, "Probation in Britain is better funded, more highly trained, and more favorably regarded by justice officials."[15] This defining orientation has significantly affected the shape that drug courts have assumed in England.

The DTTO and DRR programs are clearly led not by judges or magistrates but by probation officers. As one judge explained, "Up until now, and certainly under DTTO, they [probation] were everything; they ran the orders." To represent their country at major international drug court conferences, England, unlike other countries, has sent probation officers rather than judges. When starting a DTTO or drug court, probation officers typically provide training for the magistrates. So central is probation to running these orders that some have described DTTOs as "little more than a special type of probation order."[16] Because of this, British criminologist Philip Bean anticipates that probation will be the agency most opposed to the development of full-fledged, American-styled drug courts in England. "Most of this formal opposition would come from the probation service, which after all has the most to lose." Drug courts, says Bean, "would replace the DTTO in importance and thereby relegate the probation service and probation officer to a more lowly position."[17]

Observation of DTTO and DRR review hearings quickly reveals the central place of the probation officer, who speaks on behalf of individual clients, advises the magistrates, and oversees the treatment component of the order. One probation officer, who worked with both DTTO and DRR programs, discussed the manner in which lay magistrates are very willing to follow her lead. "They are lay magistrates. They are not legally trained.

They're willing to learn about drugs, and they're very willing to take advice." She recounted a DTTO review session in which a magistrate had instructed an offender to "just concentrate" and "make sure *all* your drug tests are clean for next time." The probation officer found these instructions objectionable and explained to the magistrate in court that "with all respect, this is not an achievable objective for her." Instead, the probation officer felt that the client should be encouraged to "try reducing what she is going to use." The magistrate accepted probation's advice in this instance. As the probation officer explained, "Magistrates are willing to take that from us." Highlighting the differences between magistrates' courts and Crown Courts, she added, "Now, I wouldn't do that in a Crown Court."

As noted earlier, the West London drug court, led by Judge Philips, more closely approximates the judge-led version of the American drug court model. Even in his drug court, though, Judge Philips must contend with a probation service that is accustomed to being in charge. He is quite candid about his frustration with the probation service. For example, during the time Philips was running his court's DTTO reviews, a client on the program was charged in a widely covered murder case. In Philips's view, a major reason for the unfortunate outcome was the fact that the case "was not being properly processed by probation." Specifically, he was critical of probation's "breach mechanism," the timing of urinalysis testing, even the kind of technology that probation used to test drug use. If Philips had his preference, he would "cut probation out of drug work" and put treatment organizations in charge instead. He rightly notes that "this is the American way" of running a drug court.

Though his drug court is clearly more judge-led than the DTTO program in which he formerly worked, even Philips has had conflicts with probation. In one court session, for example, he openly chastised the probation service for failing to produce a report for a client who had already been in custody for some time. He reflected further on this incident in a later interview.

> It is very much a judge-run court, and that's how it must be, because if you don't keep your foot on the accelerator, probation will ask too much. They asked for two weeks to get a probation report for a guy in custody. And I said, "No, one week, and that is the end of the matter." And if it doesn't happen, the senior probation officer will report to me.

Though Judge Philips would like to reduce the role of probation in drug court, he realizes that this is unlikely to happen and understands that he is forced to contend with an institution that has, especially when compared to its American counterpart, considerable power and responsibility.

Directionality of Innovation

Another structural difference between the American and British legal systems is the directionality of innovation. That is, in the United States, the drug court movement has largely been a grassroots kind of movement. Louisville drug court judge Henry Weber asserts that apart from receiving some federal dollars, the drug court movement is "a grassroots kind of movement. It's not something where the bureaucrats in Washington tell you what to do. Each community has developed its own program for its own particular needs, and they all deal with it on a local level. . . . It's totally a grassroots kind of thing." Tim Murray, former director of the Drug Courts Program Office in the Department of Justice, notes the same. It's a "movement," says Murray, "in the judicial system that has bubbled up from the grassroots to the federal government."[18]

Having bubbled up to the federal level, the government did become involved in helping to fund drug courts. Candace McCoy, in fact, argues that "the rapid growth of the movement as a whole was catalyzed by a considerable infusion of resources from the federal government."[19] Laurie Robinson, former U.S. assistant attorney general, however, qualifies that though there has been significant federal support, the movement has been "from the outset a grassroots, 'bottom up' movement." She goes so far as to argue that "one would be hard pressed today to find a dozen members of Congress—or even many state legislators—who would know what a problem-solving court is."[20] The important point here is not that the U.S. drug court movement is only a grassroots phenomenon, but that the starting point—and the ongoing initiative and energy behind the movement—is at the local level. "Elected officials are not the champions or central players in the arena."[21]

In England, contrastingly, legal innovations such as drug courts are more commonly initiated from the top, rather than at the local level. Jonathan Freedland emphasizes this point in his celebrated comparison between American and British political processes. As he puts it, where "bottom-up power" is a defining feature of American society, "in Britain power flows in the reverse direction, from the top down."[22] When I asked a probation officer from the Croydon program why she and her colleagues decided to implement a DTTO, her response lacked the missionary, entrepreneurial zeal typical of American drug court advocates. Instead she simply shrugged and explained that they had been told by the government to do so. In her words: "We've been basically told to get on with it. Here's the legislation. Here are the Home Office guidelines. Work with it." When I asked a medical doctor from the same program whether she anticipated that drug courts would spread in the United Kingdom, she likewise deferred to the wishes of the British government. "It will be for the government to decide. Largely, we will have to move the way the government wants. . . . One of the things that is true about the British system is that we are totally dependent on government funding. . . . We are going to have to do what the government says."

The most recent English drug courts represent something of a departure from this model. Jocelyn Green of the Ministry of Justice (previously called the Department of Constitutional Affairs), for example, says that it was local officials at the Leeds drug court who "started this model by themselves," though she also acknowledges that "legislation and drug treatment orders" enabled them to do so. Thus, she views it as a kind of "coming together" of support and direction "from the top" and "local initiative." Likewise, Judge Philips played a major role in starting the West London drug court, and he tells the story about the court's origin in the personal, enthusiastic, entrepreneurial, even "messianic" (his word) style common among some American judges. He speaks, for example, of how a cousin's struggle with cocaine addiction and his own serious illnesses (i.e., his "two appointments with the grim reaper") motivated his interest in drug courts. The experiences led him to conclude that it was for drug court work that he "had been spared." In terms of ownership of the program, he says that "the initiation came from us," and that the Lord Chancellor and Lord Chief Justice attended the court's opening because he invited them.

That said, he also acknowledges that at the same time his interest in drug courts was growing, the Home Office was looking to start drug court pilot programs, and "the powers that be have put me in charge." He even realizes that his court and the Leeds court must prove the success of their programs in order to convince the Ministry of Justice to roll out drug courts nationally—the government, according to Judge Philips, is "talking about rolling out another twenty-five courts." In fact, a year before Judge Philips started his court, the Ministry of Justice issued a report stating the government's intention of setting up "the first full drugs court in 2005" and extending "these to all areas where there is a need by 2008."[23] So, even though Judge Philips has taken more personal initiative, there is still a sense in which his program, the Leeds drug court, and future drug courts have always been (and will remain) very much dependent upon the direction and support of the British government.

Cultural Differences

In addition to the determinative features of Britain's legal and political structures, important cultural differences have also caused English drug courts to look very different from their American counterparts. A feature of American culture that has received considerable attention over the past several decades is an increasing societal preoccupation with feelings. This defining quality of the American therapeutic culture has been the subject of much commentary since Philip Rieff's seminal work, *The Triumph of the Therapeutic*, was published in 1966. Robert Bellah, Edwin Schur, Richard Sennett, and Jean Bethke Elshtain are among those scholars who have given attention to the ethic of emotivism in American culture.[24] Alasdair MacIntyre perhaps sums it up best: "Emotivism has become embodied in our culture . . . we live in a specifically emotivist culture."[25]

Reflecting this basic cultural orientation, one finds in American drug courts and in the treatment programs associated with them a great deal of expressivism. It is not atypical for clients at the various graduation ceremonies, for example, to cry and thank the judge and others for their help. And it is not just the defendants or clients who express emotions in this way. When a dozen drug court judges were asked to list the "six most important characteristics of an effective drug court judge," the most often-reported response was "the ability to be empathetic or to show genuine concern."[26] Such empathy is sometimes communicated through physical contact. Even hugging, particularly at graduation ceremonies, is not uncommon. Sally Satel observed physical contact between judge and client in fourteen of the fifteen American drug courts that she studied.[27]

Such public expressions of emotion do not go over so well in British courts. Consider comments from several West Yorkshire magistrates on the issue of hugging. One said, "We won't hug." Another added, "That is where we draw the line." Still another: "I'm not in favor of that." He went on to add that "these are really criminals at the end of the day. The decency of the court must be upheld." Another noted: "*I* haven't gotten that close." British courts are more formal than American courts. Solicitors bow when entering or exiting the courtroom and refer to magistrates as "Your Worship." Crown Courts, accoutered as they are with wigs and black robes, are even more formal. Many find it difficult to imagine the kind of expressivism that characterizes American drug courts on display in a British court. As a British member of Parliament put it after witnessing the emotionally laden processes in two American drug courts, "This was impressive—indeed moving—even if, at the same time, it proved difficult to envisage such emotional events taking place in the courts in this country."[28]

I found British judges and magistrates generally indisposed toward this type of behavior. In the West Yorkshire courts, probation officers provided a two-day training session for the magistrates who would be involved in the drug court program. The training included watching videos of U.S. drug courts in action. According to a West Yorkshire probation officer, the magistrates saw the practice of hugging clients and were "ap-

palled at that concept and they still remain appalled at that concept."
A medical doctor at the Croydon DTTO program likewise said of the
kind of emotionalism that characterizes the American drug courts, "Well,
the British magistrates just will not do it. . . . British judges are part of
the British establishment. They are the British establishment. They are the
last group of people who would respond to a rather more emotional . . .
sort of program." According to this doctor, not only judges but everyone
in the system, including clients, would be uncomfortable with such a style.
"British drug users don't like it at all. They wouldn't like the emotional
intensity of it."

Just as there are signs that structural restraints have weakened over
time, so it appears that some of the cultural checks on American-styled
expressivism are also beginning to give way. On one level, the theatrical
qualities of the American drug court have been, at least to a degree, appealing to the Brits from the time they first began importing problem-
solving courts. Recall how Val Barker was so taken in 1996 by Judge
Goldstein's "passion and emotion." Even British "drug czar" Keith Hellawell was impressed with the intense and personal nature of Judge
Goldstein's court when he visited it in 1995. Hellawell offered the following description of the Miami drug court:

> It is very much as if he [Goldstein] was talking to his son or his daughter. He
> chastises them openly. He will reward them openly by kissing them, or putting
> his arm around them. He'll say, "Come up here. Come and let me see you."
> And he will get hold of their hands or he'll point his finger at them and say,
> "I'm not going to have this. You know, you are making a mess of this. You
> are not going to do it." And then when they get through the program there
> is a ceremony and they cry and everybody cheers and they give them the
> certificate. And Stanley is there and he's holding them and hugging them. . . .
> It is the end of something great. . . . It really is something you have to experience
> to understand.

Similarly, Paul Hayes, who helped put the DTTO program together in
the late 1990s, spoke almost enviously of the American ability to emote
publicly. During a 1999 interview he said that "the whole context of the
English courtroom is more formal than the context of the U.S. court."
Thus, he saw the conspicuous expressivism in American drug courts as
"alien to our culture." At the same time, however, Hayes also believed that

> we are getting more like you, while we watch all of these terrible [U.S. daytime
> talk show] programs where people confess that they slept with everyone under
> the sun and all this. . . . So, we are getting more used to baring our souls, I
> think. But we still are not as good at it as you are.

The newest versions of drug courts in England give Hayes's observations a sort of prophetic quality. Though the British may still not be "as good at it" as Americans, the British are, it seems, getting more used to baring their souls.

In recent DRR reviews, clients and magistrates speak more personally and emotionally. A probation officer from the Oxford magistrates' court, for example, spoke of the benefits of solicitors being absent from the review hearings. This is advantageous, in her view, because "you don't have the legal-speak of solicitors." Instead the clients speak for themselves. When this happens, "you get far more of a sense of reality, and you get real, raw emotion and feelings, and I think that is really important." In the Oxford court, magistrates also hand out certificates when clients succeed on the program. Clients get a bronze certificate for their first drug-free urinalysis test, a silver for five drug-free tests, and a gold for ten drug-free tests. When a client reaches one of these milestones, the chair magistrate will, during a review session, walk off the bench, present the certificate, and shake the client's hand.

In one court session, a client was presented with a gold certificate in this manner. Upon receiving the certificate, he simply shook the magistrate's hand and said, "Thank you very much." There was no applause, no tearful testimony. In fact, the presentation was notably subdued and understated compared to American graduation ceremonies, but it was still out of place for a British courtroom. In this particular instance, the client, prior to receiving his certificate, was slightly reprimanded for leaving a group meeting early. When asked why he left early, he explained that the meeting in question involved acting and role playing, and that he was uncomfortable standing in front of people—a response, arguably, that one might expect of someone with stereotypical British reserve. Interestingly, instead of accepting this explanation, one of the magistrates encouraged the client at some length to give it a go next time. "If you try it just once," he said, "the next time it won't be so bad." A second magistrate reminded the client that "this is a court order." Unresponsive and hunched in his seat, the client appeared unconvinced as to the merits of court-mandated role playing.

Judge Philips, of the West London drug court, has moved his court even closer to—or, some might say, beyond—the kind of expressivism typical of American drug courts. For review hearings, he will literally change clothes to look more informal. He makes clients sit near him, on his level. That is, clients stand not before an elevated bench, but side by side just a few feet from the judge. Philips speaks in familiar terms, often calling clients by their first names, and is not afraid to make physical contact. Consider his own description of his behavior in the courtroom:

I do my reviews in a completely and utterly informal way. I pick a shirt or T-shirt or football shirt or whatever it is, and the most revolting socks. . . . And it breaks down the ice. And I call them by their first names, and if they come in and call me Justin, I actually say, "As long as you give me negative [urinalysis] tests, I don't mind." . . . And the language I use—well . . . I'm correctly quoted as saying to one guy, "If you give me another positive [urinalysis test], I'll kick you out on the ass." And this is my way of doing things.[29]

Recall the comments of magistrates involved in the early DTTO programs, who were explicitly disapproving of the American proclivity for physical contact with clients. Judge Philips has no such misgivings. In fact, he regularly shakes hands with and/or hugs drug court participants. As Philips puts it, "I've got no problem, if someone's done well, whether it's a woman or a man, in giving them a hug and a kiss. Because I think it is absolutely essential that we show them (1) we're human, (2) we care, and (3) if they've done well, they've got to be told."

As Judge Philips's court makes clear, some of the cultural restraints that once limited the style and scope of British drug courts have, at least in some instances, been relaxed. Even in the West London drug court, though, certain limits are still in place. For example, though British drug court judges may come across as more personal and familiar, they have not yet achieved the theatrical behaviors so central to American drug courts. As I discussed at length in a previous work, American judges explicitly use the "court-as-theater" metaphor to describe their proceedings and will intentionally arrange the court calendar and format in such a way as to achieve particular theatrical effects.[30] This involves, among other things, having all participants remain in the courtroom "audience" as individual clients are called before the judge.

In England, contrastingly, DTTO, DRR, and drug court clients appear before the judge or magistrates individually. Without other clients present, there is no large audience before which the judge can perform. Judge Philips, in fact, identifies this as an important difference between British and American courts. "I don't believe in group review," he says. "I won't allow anybody in when I'm reviewing a case, unless they're invited by me." One reason he opposes "group reviews" is that he feels clients will be less inclined to open up with him if others are present. He and other British judges realize that there is a cultural resistance to emotionalism among the British more generally, not just as displayed in public criminal court proceedings.

Therefore, both with respect to what takes place in the courtroom and in concomitant court-mandated treatment settings, emotionally laden confessional accounts of one's life are much less often on display. West

London drug court judge Susan Williams sees a major difference between Americans and Brits in this regard. "We are different," she explains. "It's a completely different attitude."

> You have a different culture in the States—the culture of being in therapy, going to counseling. . . . There isn't that culture or ethos here. If you've got a problem, if you're able to talk, you go and talk to your friends, if you can. If you don't, the idea of sitting around in group therapy is actually very difficult for some individuals.

Judge Williams adds that with Brits, "there is an in-built resistance" to this kind of therapeutic discourse. Judge Philips agrees, "Brits are like that. We're very buttoned-up" (and this from a judge who tells drug clients in court that the "nasty" short-sleeve yellow shirt he is wearing "is the color of urine when it's got cocaine in it").

Though acknowledging some loosening-up among the British, Judge Williams maintains that in Britain there is "a completely different attitude" where "there is still a lot of reserve." She accepts that this reserve may not be "in the prewar or the postwar sense of being terribly stiff upper-lipped or buttoned-up." But it is still the case that "Brits won't talk to each other in the free and easy, relaxed, and very open way that Americans will talk to each other." She says this is particularly the case among British men, for whom this kind of discourse "doesn't come naturally," but rather is viewed as "a sign of weakness." According to Williams, the only way British men can speak in such an open manner is "when they get very drunk," a method unlikely to find much support in a criminal justice program aimed at reducing substance misuse.

As it concerns treatment methods, while group work, especially of the self-help AA and NA variety, is less common in the United Kingdom, methadone maintenance is often a main staple of the treatment program. Some American drug courts use methadone maintenance, but this is actually much more rare in the United States. In fact, 20 percent of American drug court programs specifically prohibit the use of any pharmacological interventions.[31] Relatedly, Britain's emphasis on "harm reduction" also sets it apart from the treatment orientation in the United States. That is, reduced use rather than no use is acceptable in the United Kingdom, whereas in the United States, total abstinence is the more common goal and requirement of drug courts. In the British versions of the program, harm reduction or reduced use is commonly viewed as success. This orientation is attributable in no small measure to Britain's particular history of drug control, in which doctors have always played a more central role and providing maintenance drugs for the "stable addict" has been a more common practice.[32]

The central role of the medical doctor is still observable today. In the British drug court sites I visited, there was typically a medical doctor who played a significant role in the treatment. Treatment, as such, has a more medical/clinical than therapeutic/counseling orientation in England. I cannot recall an instance at any of the treatment sites I visited in the United States in which a treatment provider was a medical doctor. Joel Best says that the backgrounds and credentials of treatment providers in the United States today vary wildly, in general, and that many of "these therapists are 'professional ex-s,' individuals with little formal training who . . . have now begun careers helping others into recovery."[33] This is certainly true of the treatment providers in the U.S. drug courts, where there is great variation in levels of training, and where many treatment providers are themselves recovered (or recovering) addicts. In the United Kingdom, where the professional medical community has treated addicts for decades, levels of medical expertise are much higher, and one does not typically find "professional ex-s" in their ranks.

Concerning British drug courts, then, we find important differences that, though somewhat diminished in recent years, still affect the style and shape of this transplanted legal program. Turning to the second type of problem-solving court imported by Great Britain, we find similar differences—even more pronounced in some instances—determined by related structural and cultural factors.

DOMESTIC VIOLENCE COURTS

On June 5, 1999, approximately one year after the initiation of the Wakefield and Pontefract drug courts, England launched its first domestic violence court in Leeds, another West Yorkshire town. By 2003, four additional pilot schemes had started: in Cardiff, Derby, West London, and Wolverhampton—two more, in Croydon and Caerphilly, were added in 2004. Based on the "success" of these programs, an additional twenty-five programs were rolled out in 2006. By April 2007, there were a total of sixty-four domestic violence courts in England and Wales.

As in the case of drug courts, American innovations directly influenced the development of domestic violence courts in the United Kingdom. One of the first academic discussions of problem-solving courts in England, for example, notes the manner in which the Leeds court adopted the "judge-centered, treatment-oriented, multi-agency approach from the United States."[34] In some cases, officials traveled to the United States to observe American domestic violence courts in operation. Representatives from Croydon, for example, made two trips to the United States to examine courts in New York and Florida and even contracted with the New York–

based Center for Court Innovation to assist with the development of the Croydon domestic violence court.[35] While clearly inspired by the U.S. innovations, English domestic violence courts vary from the American model. In keeping with the adaptation view held by British practitioners, Dee Cook, who coauthored a comprehensive evaluation of the first five domestic violence courts in England and Wales, observes that though all the courts were inspired by the United States, they were "always modified according to local conditions."

The process of adaptation is, of course, influenced by the particularities of the local situation. As with English drug courts, the majority of cases in the British domestic violence courts are handled by lay magistrates. In the case of domestic violence courts, magistrates have even less direct interaction with offenders. This is due mainly to the absence of review hearings in nearly all British domestic violence courts. As Catherine Elkington, the point person for the development of domestic violence courts at the Ministry of Justice, explains, "The court makes the order, and then the person passes into the hands of the probation service. Whereas with the drug court, you've got that continuing review, and at the moment the [domestic violence] court doesn't have the power to bring defendants back for review." With the absence of review hearings, even the opportunity for greater interaction between defendants and magistrates, as has been realized in British drug courts, has simply not been part of court proceedings.

UK domestic violence courts, like their American counterparts, are multiagency. That is, representatives from probation, victim and witness support services, the police, prosecution, defense, and the magistracy work together in a court-based program to help address the problem of domestic violence. However, in England, services and extra resources made available through the court are directed primarily to the victims, not the offenders. As Victoria Hill of the West London court explains, "Our whole ethos is about keeping the survivors at the heart of what we do." An underlying principle for the West London domestic violence court, according to Hill, is "holding the perpetrator accountable for his behavior and supporting the woman through the process." A police officer who worked with the court at the time it was launched agreed that the court's "focus on the victim rather than the defendant" was important. "For once," he said, "victims are at the forefront of everyone's mind."[36]

In keeping with this position, British domestic violence court programs emphasize a fast-track system oriented toward quick adjudication, higher conviction rates, and the protection and support of witnesses and victims. The West London domestic violence court, for example, goes to great lengths to help the victim avoid contact with the accused, even allowing videoconferencing so the victim will not have to face the perpetrator in court. One trial I witnessed in West London was delayed for over half an hour so that court personnel could set up two large portable barriers between the witness stand, where the victim sat, and the dock, where the accused stood. Court personnel even tested various arrangements to ensure no possibility of eye contact between the victim and the accused.

With the absence of regular review sessions, an English domestic violence court does not look much different from a regular criminal court, which, as some British officials believe, is as it should be. Gly Plant, of the Leeds domestic violence court, for example, explains, "We're a criminal court dealing with criminals, and that is how the court is set up. . . . It's treated as a normal criminal court." Such an emphasis is not limited to the Leeds courts. The domestic violence courts rolled out in 2006 and 2007 focused even more clearly on prosecutorial outcomes, highlighting the courts' central aims of adjudicating quickly and providing protection and support for victims. Courts will now even pursue cases without the support of victims. Often a victim in a domestic violence case will retract or withdraw her case, either due to reconciliation with the offender or out of fear of reprisals for having taken legal action. British domestic violence courts have taken steps to reduce victim attrition of this sort and to pursue convictions even without the continuing cooperation of a victim.[37]

Among the British, then, there does not seem to be much inclination to extend an overtly therapeutic orientation toward the offender. Consider, for example, an introductory discussion of U.S. courts in the evaluation of the first five domestic violence courts in England and Wales. The report discusses several varieties of domestic violence courts in the United States, including the Clark County court, discussed in chapter 1 (which includes treatment for offenders). The authors note, in a manner suggesting not only a degree of unfamiliarity but also a trace of disapproval, that the court "was designed with a judicial paradigm in mind, incorporating what the founders describe as [a] 'therapeutic' approach."[38] Thus, they see the therapeutic nature of the court as somewhat gratuitous, unique to the United States, and not really transferable to England and Wales.

> Court specialization in the U.S. has not always been just about improving the court processes for victims of domestic violence, it has sometimes been grounded in promoting particular approaches to domestic violence; "problem-solving" or "therapeutic intervention." It is therefore important to scrutinize the different models of domestic violence courts in [the] U.S. to identify the benefits and limitations of the various approaches.[39]

The whole of the report makes clear that "therapeutic intervention" is not to be understood as one of the so-called benefits and has not found its way into the British variety of domestic violence courts. Mary Burton, a coauthor of the report, confirmed this when she said that in England and Wales, "more emphasis is placed on victim safety than on therapeutic intervention." Charlotte Walsh agrees with this assessment in her specific discussion of the Leeds domestic violence courts. She acknowledges the important influence of U.S. courts on the development of domestic violence courts in England but warns that the U.S. model should be adopted with "extreme caution." In particular, she recommends very limited application of rehabilitative processes.[40]

In spite of this initial resistance, more recent developments reveal some signs of greater openness to the American emphasis on treating offenders of domestic violence. As just noted, Mandy Burton recognizes the relative lack of interest in court-monitored treatment of domestic violence offenders. Based on her analysis of domestic violence courts in the United States, however, she has more recently argued, albeit somewhat cautiously, in favor of ongoing judicial involvement with defendants. Referring to the American model, she writes:

> Some specialist courts in other jurisdictions, particularly some of those developed in the United States of America, are strongly premised on "problem-solving" approaches. In "problem-solving" courts there is often an enhanced role for the judge in working towards ongoing compliance with programmes for treating or reforming the defendant.[41]

She rightly notes that in the United States, "the treatment and monitoring of offenders is regarded as an important aspect of the goals of the courts." In light of this emphasis, Burton endorses a new practice in the Croydon domestic violence courts in which "the defendant's compliance with community rehabilitation orders is reviewed at three months." All those interviewed in her coauthored study of the Croydon domestic violence court "agreed that the introduction of 'compliance hearings' in the style of the USA's problem-solving courts was a beneficial feature of the court."[42]

There is some evidence that British officials might be open to this kind of practice more broadly. A 2005 Home Office "guidance" report on domestic violence courts, for example, identifies the new "compliance hearings" in Croydon and, in a section on "judicial monitoring and offender accountability," recommends that probation submit "regular reports to the court" or that the court conduct "regular review hearings."[43] While the latter would represent a movement toward the American model on one level, it should be noted that the preferred form of treatment in England is a probation-led "perpetrator programme." Recall Catherine Elkington's observation that in British domestic violence courts, after the court makes an order, "the person passes into the hands of the probation service." Here, as in drug courts, then, we see the central place of probation in the British criminal justice system. Additionally, the purpose of the review session is not so much for magistrates to engage in some kind of therapeutic interchange with defendants as it is to make sure that the accused is attending the probation-run program.

Moreover, the actual treatment overseen by probation in these programs is less focused on such therapeutic notions as victimization, low self-esteem, anger management, and the open expression of one's emotions. Instead, the emphasis in British "perpetrator programmes" is on a "cognitive-behavioral approach combined with gender analysis." That is, the perspective views violent behavior as "learned behavior that can be unlearned (rather than as a consequence of individual pathology, stress, alcohol abuse or a dysfunctional relationship)." The program's "gender analysis" dimension "tackles the belief system that convinces male perpetrators that they have the right to control women in intimate relationships."[44] Thus, as with drug courts, even the nature of treatment is different in the United Kingdom, and its orientation is clearly less therapeutic.

Finally, regarding hoped-for changes in Britain's domestic violence courts, those associated with these courts agree that changes will not be possible without some enabling legislation. In other words, according to those working in these courts, the directives must come from the legislature. Consider, for example, concluding remarks from a review of the Leeds domestic violence court. In this case, a steering group viewed the practices of the Leeds court as only a good first step. That is, the Leeds court *clusters* domestic violence cases on a single court calendar and provides some extra resources for victims, but it is not really a *specialty* court, nor is it therapeutic in orientation. The steering group, however, expressed the hope for legislation that would allow British domestic violence courts to become more like courts in the United States. Consider the following:

> The Steering Group recognizes that the next critical step would be a move from a Domestic Violence Cluster Court to a Domestic Violence Specialist Court . . . it is recognized that legislative changes would be required to move to a Specialist Court process. The United States provides models for such innovative developments.[45]

Thus, the steering group accepts that realizing the U.S.-based model, which places greater emphasis on a "rehabilitative, treatment-based approach," could only be achieved "through a new legislative framework."[46] Unlike judges in American problem-solving courts, British officials do not think the court could or should pursue these additional features without some sort of legislative approval. Thus, evident in both

British drug courts and British domestic violence courts is the kind of top-down orientation Freedland identifies as characteristic of Britain's legal and political structures. Initiation from the top, as such, is perhaps most evident in the final type of imported problem-solving court to be considered in this Anglo-American comparison.

COMMUNITY COURTS

Community courts are the most recent type of problem-solving court to find its way across the Atlantic. Community courts are also, as noted in the introduction, the most publicly profiled case of legal transference considered thus far. Beginning in 2003, a number of high-ranking British government officials visited community courts in New York and then championed the importation of such courts to England. This process began when British Home Secretary David Blunkett and then Lord Chief Justice Harry Woolf visited the Red Hook community court in New York in early 2003. Both Blunkett and Woolf were impressed with what they saw and became convinced that community courts could work in the United Kingdom. "What I saw in Red Hook," said Blunkett, "was about engaging the community in finding a way of resolving problems, dealing with the consequences, engaging the individual in changing their chaotic lifestyle."[47] Lord Chief Justice Woolf likewise said,

> I learnt many things from the day I spent at Red Hook. One of the most important was that we might be making a mistake in [Britain] by not appreciating that courts . . . should primarily be focused on solving the problems of the community in which the crime took place.[48]

Only a few months after returning to England, Blunkett announced, "I am bringing the pioneering U.S. community court model over here."[49] A month after this announcement, British government officials convened a national conference "with more than 300 of the UK's major players in the delivery of criminal justice" to unveil plans for the development of pilot community courts in England.[50] Employing a strategy previously used in the promotion of drug courts (recall Judge Stanley Goldstein's 1996 trip to the United Kingdom to speak on drug courts), officials invited Red Hook's Judge Alex Calabrese to address this conference, held at the Queen Elizabeth II Centre in Westminster London in July 2003. Both Home Secretary Blunkett and Lord Chief Justice Woolf also spoke at the conference, and they announced the government's commitment of £3 million for initial funding of community court pilot schemes in England.

With the adoption of community courts in the United Kingdom gaining considerable momentum, officials made another high-profile visit to the

United States later in the same year. On December 15, 2003, amid much ceremony and media attention, Lord Falconer visited the Midtown community court in New York on its tenth anniversary of operation. He was "utterly delighted" with what he witnessed and declared that he would be "taking a little more back to Britain from New York than some Christmas souvenirs."[51] In fact, he announced that England would introduce a new community court in Liverpool by the end of 2004. New York officials in attendance, including Chief Judge Judith Kaye and New York City mayor Michael Bloomberg, were clearly pleased with the international interest in New York's community courts. Mayor Bloomberg said, "Lord Falconer, you're welcome to take all of our ideas and copy them."[52]

Lord Falconer wasted little time in acting upon Bloomberg's permission to borrow, as he immediately began promoting community courts back in the United Kingdom, with the stated intention of building "upon the innovative work done in New York City's Midtown Community Court . . . and the Red Hook Community Justice Centre."[53] In a speech before a group of chair magistrates in February 2004, he said,

> Just before Christmas, I was in the USA, looking at a range of criminal justice practices there. I was in a place called the Midtown Community Court in New York, which has helped to turn Times Square (which is at the heart of Manhattan) from a magnet for low-level criminal activity—most of it drug-related—to a new hub of the city, a magnet now for the consumers who swarm in and out of its stores. . . . Its focus on local justice for the local community is remarkable and one of the principal reasons for its success.[54]

As with drug courts and domestic violence courts, then, we see not only that American innovations directly inspired the development of community courts in England, but also that the program was initiated at the highest levels of government; it was not a grassroots sort of effort. The British experiment with community courts is overseen by the Community Justice National Programme, an oversight team sponsored jointly by the Home Office, the Ministry of Justice, and the Attorney General's Office. Beginning in 2004, the Community Justice Programme implemented two very different types of community courts in England, one in Liverpool and a second in Salford.

Of all the problem-solving courts operating in England, the Liverpool community court looks the most like its American counterpart, in particular, the Red Hook community court. After Liverpool was identified as an ideal location for a community court, David Fletcher was appointed the first judge of the Liverpool Community Justice Centre in October 2004. Following his appointment, the forty-seven-year-old Fletcher held a series of meetings around the Liverpool area to solicit input from local residents. The court began temporarily in the Liverpool magistrates' court in November 2004, and then in September 2005, like the Red Hook community court, moved into a renovated parochial school building as its permanent home. The renovated building in Liverpool, as in Red Hook, houses all the agencies and services that work directly with the court, including police, probation, prosecution, victim support services, drug and alcohol counseling, a mentoring program, housing support services, and debt advice. As Judge Fletcher explains, "All the relevant agencies are right here." The services, as at Red Hook, are available not only for those brought before the court because of some kind of criminal infraction, but also as "a resource for the whole community."[55]

As just noted, a second pilot community court was initiated in Salford, a town within the larger Manchester metropolitan area approximately thirty miles directly east of Liverpool. The Salford community court, launched in November 2005, is less resource-intensive than the Liverpool court. That is, instead of being established as a stand-alone justice center with all necessary agencies in-house, the Salford community court was developed within an existing magistrates' court. Those working with the court were tasked to network with local stakeholders and draw upon resources already in place in the community. In a certain sense, Salford represents the kind of "going to scale" process promoted by the Center for Court Innovation that was discussed in chapter 1. British officials intended the Liverpool and Salford programs to serve as models for the development of additional community courts in England. As Lord Chief Justice Phillips (Lord Woolf's successor) explained during an important speech at Oxford University in May 2006, he did not foresee a national rollout of community justice centers based on the Liverpool model, principally because of the expense, but he did see the application of a "new ethos" of community justice as informed by the Liverpool and Salford alternatives. In keeping with this essential position, Britain's Community Justice Programme issued a document in August 2006 in support of "the development of new projects" built on "the lessons learnt in Liverpool and Salford."[56]

Then, in November 2006, after asserting that "Liverpool and Salford are showing that community justice works," Lord Falconer announced the initiation of ten new community courts—in "Birmingham, Bradford, Devon and Cornwall, Hull, Leicestershire, Merthyr Tydfill, Middlesbrough, Nottingham, and two projects in London."[57] Once again, Falconer acknowledged the United States as the source of inspiration for these courts. "Community courts, this approach to community justice, were pioneered in the USA," he explained. "Many of us in this room have trodden the well-beaten path to New York: to Red Hook, to the Midtown court in Manhattan. We've seen how they work. We've seen their impact." He added that Britain's effort in Liverpool "was a clear attempt to emulate that success."[58]

That the Liverpool Community Justice Centre is a deliberate attempt to emulate the New York community courts is evident in several respects. Most importantly, the court is unambiguously judge-led. As we have seen, the majority of cases in British drug courts and domestic violence courts are handled by lay magistrates, who have limited power. Moreover, these court innovations are typically probation-led, rather than judge-led. The Liverpool community court, in contrast, is decidedly judge-led in ways more characteristic of American problem-solving courts. That is, the judge plays a more prominent and central role both inside and outside the courtroom. Even before starting the community court, Judge Fletcher set up meetings in several locations around Liverpool, including the Anfield, Everton, and Kirkdale wards, to meet and talk with local residents. At these meetings, Liverpool residents were "encouraged to have their say in plans for the North Liverpool Community Justice Centre." In a manner slightly self-congratulatory, residents were told how unusual it was for someone like Judge Fletcher to meet with them in person and solicit their views.

At these meetings, the more central role of the judge in the courtroom was also highlighted. For example, a handout distributed to residents at a December 2004 meeting in Anfield stated that the new Community Justice Centre would "contain a courtroom, run by a single judge, who will work closely with the community to provide consistency for offenders and check that they carry out sentences they have been given." During the meeting, Judge Fletcher elaborated on this point, explaining further, "I'm the only judge, and I will remember them, and they will remember me." He noted that he would be able to hold defendants accountable by bringing them back to court for regular review hearings.

Interestingly, Fletcher also noted that because of his capacity as a circuit court judge, he could function in the new community court as either a district or Crown Court judge—a kind of flexibility highly unusual in a British criminal court. In the Liverpool community court, Judge Fletcher normally functions as a district judge. However, if required by the circumstances of a given case, he can transform the court into a Crown Court. At the Anfield meeting, he highlighted this feature of the court in order to underscore the nature and extent of the kind of judicial power he would have in the new community court, evidently to reassure those in attendance that the community court would not be a "soft-option" court.

It is a kind of power that has, in fact, been realized. Consider a court session in March of 2006. During the day's proceedings, Judge Fletcher literally went back into his chambers to "don a wig and gown." Barristers were brought in, and all the necessary components of a Crown Court were put in place. The case driving the transformation was that of a man who had hit a young woman in the face and broken her jaw in six places. The man pled guilty to the charge. The conviction, however, required a more lengthy sentence than could be imposed in a magistrates' court—thus the need to switch to a Crown Court setting. In his capacity as a Crown Court judge, Judge Fletcher sentenced the man to two years and four months in prison. An official at the Liverpool court offered the following description of the process: "It's like Superman. He suddenly changes into a different sort of, you know, sort of god . . . and he can impose a sanction, which is quite remarkable . . . a total change of direction, which is good; it gives him that flexibility. . . . In the magistrates' court . . . we haven't got the appropriate powers to deal with it." Eventually, the Liverpool court instituted the practice whereby the court would regularly function as a Crown Court on one Monday per month.

Like Judge Philips in the West London drug court, Judge Fletcher behaves more like an American judge, particularly as it concerns his activist orientation and his public visibility in the community. He clearly exhibits the kind of energy, drive, and charisma typical of some American problem-solving court judges, and he is not averse to making the sort of effusive promotional claims for which some American judges are famous. "The Centre," says Judge Fletcher, "represents the most radical change to occur in the justice system for decades."[59] He is also willing to engage with clients in a more direct and personal manner. One representative from the Liverpool court described Judge Fletcher's style: "He always talks to the offender on a Christian-name basis. He'll address them in that way, and he'll use some of the local vernacular, and he'll try [to] get down to their level. . . . He will be friendly with them." Another staff member said much the same: "He's very much on a level with everybody he deals with and I think that has a big impact. He's willing to get down on a level with people and communicate."[60] Fletcher even allows applause in the courtroom to reward successful clients. Also consistent with practices in American community courts, Judge Fletcher will impose sanctions directly related to particular criminal infractions. For example, a local canal had been harmed by vandalism, rubbish dumping, and the illegal operation of motorbikes. Community penalties for these infractions have included orders to dredge the canal, to improve the canal-side park, and to develop a children's nature trail. Similarly, those arrested for vandalism have been ordered to clean up their own graffiti.[61]

Though they run the program in a regular magistrates' court, officials at the Salford community court pursue many of the same goals as officials at the Liverpool court. Recognizing the importance of judicial continuity, for example, they aspire to have review hearings in which clients come before the same panel of lay magistrates. According to Brenden Beckett, project manager of the Salford community court, the hope is to "have at least one [magistrate]—the person who chaired the sentencing bench—chair the review." Beckett says that magistrates like the "monitoring aspect" and want the kind of continuity afforded by set reviews because "from a job-satisfaction point of view," it allows them "to encourage and congratulate on progress" and to "wag the finger if progress isn't good." It gives magistrates the "opportunity to see things through." However, according to Beckett, "because of listing issues" and some of the same obstacles faced by those working in British drug courts and domestic violence courts, as of the summer of 2006, "set reviews," as such, had not yet been realized.

Though given more discretion, flexibility, and authority, community court judges and magistrates in England act within, and are conscious of, certain limits. Consider several examples. During the Anfield meeting, mentioned earlier, a resident told Judge Fletcher that "what we need is discipline" and even suggested the implementation of American-styled boot camps for young offenders. The judge responded by clearly stating the limits of his judicial authority. "I can't deal in any way with how the government deals with its prisoners." In deference to the dictates of the political/legal system within which he works, he added, "I can only use the tools that the government is giving me." He stated specifically that "every judge is hidebound by maximum sentences." In an interview some nine months later, Judge Fletcher, while acknowledging the variety of in-house resources he could utilize for both offenders and victims, also noted that, unlike some American problem-solving court judges, he does not have the power to impose "intermediate sanctions." His court, like British-styled drug courts, must work with the existing Community Order scheme, though he acknowledged being "a little bit inventive" with Community Orders. Still, within Community Orders, the judge cannot impose a several-day jail sentence as part of the order. His only real power as it concerns incarceration is to revoke the order. Therefore, as another Liverpool official put it, "Judge Fletcher is very limited [as to] what he can actually impose." Unlike in American community courts, moreover, Judge Fletcher does not participate in the court's daily pre-court meetings in order to "ensure independence in court."[62]

British community courts also differ from American courts in another important respect: no reference is ever made to therapeutic jurisprudence. It is never discussed by court officials, nor is it mentioned in court or government documents on community courts. When I asked representatives from both Liverpool and Salford whether and to what extent therapeutic jurisprudence informed the operations and philosophy of their courts, I was told that they had not even heard of the concept. On the other hand, the notion of "problem solving" is very central to British

community courts. One of the eight "key principles" informing community courts, according to the Community Justice Programme, is that they
are "problem solving in approach and outcome."[63] The Liverpool court
even has a "problem-solving team," to which the judge will refer clients
in order to determine the most appropriate type of community order for
individual cases.

Restorative justice has also taken on institutional form in UK community courts. Since April 2006, a part-time "Restorative Justice Co-ordina-
tor" has helped to facilitate various "restorative justice interventions" at
the Liverpool community court. Such interventions have been used in a
small number of cases "where the offender accepts responsibility for caus-
ing harm to a victim and is willing to cooperate in repairing this harm,"
and where the victim, of course, is also "willing to participate."[64] Some
interventions involve a "restorative justice conference," in which the offender meets directly with the victim. Others involve use of a "restorative
justice facilitator," who mediates dialogue between the offender and the
victim, while disallowing any direct contact between the parties.[65] In these
cases, offenders sometimes write letters of apology to victims. One of the
original stated goals of the Salford community court was to "implement
strong restorative justice principles." Due to fewer resources, the Salford
court's ability to deliver in this area has been more limited. Nevertheless,
reparation or "pay back" to the community—one dimension of restorative justice—has been achieved through "unpaid worker schemes."[66]

A final similarity between British and American community courts is
the manner in which advocates defend these courts on the grounds
that they serve as an antidote to a perceived problem of declining confidence in the criminal justice system. Recall the discussion in chapter 1 of
the way in which officials in the United States highlight declining "public
faith" in the judiciary and endorse problem-solving courts by asserting
that these court innovations will restore confidence in the criminal justice
system. British officials have fully embraced this rhetoric in their advocacy
of problem-solving courts, as well, repeatedly promoting problem-solving
courts on the grounds that the new programs will increase public confidence in the criminal justice system. This, of course, presupposes a
general perception that the British criminal justice system suffers from a
lack of confidence, which apparently is what British officials believe to be
the case.

Lord Falconer, for example, makes frequent references to a lack of confidence in the criminal justice system. In a 2004 speech, he said, "Confidence in the criminal justice system has been falling because the system is
insufficiently effective." Thus, "we need to increase confidence in the justice system."[67] When he announced the initiation of ten additional community courts two years later, Lord Falconer again asserted that "people

often feel that the courts do not understand their problems. . . . If there is no confidence, if there is no connection, there is no justice." According to Falconer, "Community justice and community courts are an attempt to right these wrongs."[68] The notion of building confidence can even be found on the sign in front of the Liverpool Community Justice Centre, which reads, "Community Justice Centre, North Liverpool, Reducing crime, building confidence."

One finds similar justifications offered for domestic violence courts and drug courts. A 2005 Home Office report on domestic violence courts, for example, anticipated that the national rollout of these courts would "improve the level of public confidence in the Criminal Justice System."[69] And a government strategy document introduced by Lord Falconer in 2004 identifies drug courts as one of the "strands" for "improving public confidence in the performance of the courts, and the criminal justice system as a whole."[70] Thus, we find that the British have not only transplanted problem-solving courts from the United States, but have imported the same themes used to justify the introduction and development of these programs, as well—a feature of the borrowing process we will consider more fully in chapter 8.

PROBLEM-SOLVING COURTS IN BRITISH CULTURE

While the transplantation process has differed slightly for drug courts, domestic violence courts, and community courts, the three cases are revealing in the important common themes they share. First, it is clear in each case that the inspiration for the courts came from the United States. Court officials read about and studied American courts, visited the United States, and invited American "experts" to speak in the United Kingdom. It is notable that the transplantation process has not taken the form of a one-time event. Rather, court officials continue to look to the United States as they make adjustments. Both local courts and government officials have maintained "ongoing communication" with the Center for Court Innovation in New York to assist them with the continuing development of British problem-solving courts.[71]

Second, in each case, the courts have, in the main, been initiated from the top, which stands in contrast to the more grassroots orientation of the development of U.S. problem-solving courts. There is in England a detectable movement toward emphasizing local initiative, but even there the stress on the local is, perhaps ironically, dictated from the top. The Community Justice Programme, for example, encourages local areas to be as "creative and innovative as possible" in designing community courts "which fit with local needs and circumstances."[72] But this is a directive from the central government. Thus, there may be a growing emphasis on local initiative, but it is not in lieu of government supervision and support. Jonathan Monk, head of Courts Innovation at the Ministry of Justice, sums it up best: "In the UK there is a drive from the top to establish such initiatives, but then things are developed locally."

Perhaps the most important common element revealed in the transference of the three types of problem-solving courts from the United States to England and Wales is the role of the judge. In all instances, one finds that British judges and magistrates work within particular structural and cultural limits. This condition prevents a wholesale adoption of the more conspicuously American qualities of problem-solving courts. The structural issues that limit a fuller Americanization of these courts include the centrality of the lay magistracy, the more prominent role of probation, and the deference of those within the judiciary to the directives of the legislature. Even in instances where court actors would like the discretion and power of American judges, they are reluctant to introduce changes without legislative direction and approval. As a consequence, several defining features of American problem-solving courts have not been realized. First, judges and magistrates are not able to impose short stints of incarceration as a type of intermediate sanction, as is common in American courts. Second, British courts have struggled to achieve continuity in the ongoing judicial monitoring of clients that is so central to American problem-solving courts. Third, at least until recently, judges have been reluctant to engage clients in the overtly therapeutic and theatrical manner more typical of American judges.

Concerning this last point, one finds among those involved with British problem-solving courts a consistent hesitancy to embrace therapeutic jurisprudence. Recall that Brits either knew little to nothing about TJ or were openly resistant to overtly therapeutic practices in the courtroom. One of the very few multinational comparative studies commissioned by the British government on problem-solving courts highlights the degree to which the "completely new role for the judge" envisaged by "therapeutic jurisprudence" is one that stands in "stark contrast with judicial tradition in the UK."[73] The study observes further that "problem-solving courts represent a major departure from the current operational structures of the judicial system in England and Wales. The challenge their creation presents to court culture cannot be overestimated."[74]

Indeed not. The fact that TJ-oriented problem-solving courts represent such a formidable challenge helps to explain why change has come slowly, and why TJ has largely been resisted. It is telling that the study speaks of a "court culture" challenged by the development of problem-solving courts. As we have seen, even when greater judicial engagement is structurally permissible (e.g., in review hearings), judges have been generally hesitant to push the envelope too far. In the early courts, particularly among the magistrates, there was notable resistance to behavior that was too much like that of the Americans. This has changed some in recent years, especially in Judge Philips's West London drug court and, in slightly different ways, in Judge Fletcher's Liverpool community court. Both courts are unusual in the British context. In his courtroom, Judge Philips is more personal and demonstrative—even, one could say, more therapeutic. He has, in fact, described himself as being "like a psychiatrist with authority."[75]

Judge Fletcher, because of the unique structure of his court, is able to achieve the kind of ongoing judicial monitoring that has eluded other problem-solving courts in England. Though he clearly maintains a higher level of judicial formality than Judge Philips, Judge Fletcher is very much an activist judge. He regularly meets with and seeks input from people in the community. In court, he engages clients in a personal and direct manner.[76] He even allows applause in his courtroom to recognize compliance with court orders. Evidence of this evolution toward American ways is not limited to what one finds in these two courts. Even magistrates in some recent DRR programs now hand out certificates and encourage more open expressions of emotion, though they do this in a manner decidedly understated when compared to practices in American problem-solving courts. Still, these more recent developments raise an important question: Is the general reluctance to embrace the therapeutic qualities of problem-solving courts giving way? If so, is British culture changing in a manner that would make this kind of courtroom behavior more culturally acceptable?

Not a few social scientists and cultural critics believe that British society has, in fact, begun to exhibit change more commensurate with the therapeutic qualities of American culture. The highly emotional aftermath of Princess Diana's death is often cited as a critical turning point in this regard. As the British sociologist Frank Furedi put it, "After the unprecedented display of pubic emotionalism over the death of Princess Diana in 1997, it is difficult to sustain the myth that Britain is the land of the stiff upper lip. Since this event, the powerful influence of therapeutic culture on British society has been widely acknowledged."[77] Among those acknowledging this development is novelist A. L. Kennedy, who "hailed the response to Diana's death as evidence of Britain's newfound 'emotional maturity.'" Though Jonathan Freedland thinks viewing the reaction to Diana's death as "an overnight conversion by the British to the gushy confessionalism of the U.S. . . . . might be an exaggeration," he also concedes that the "British people *are* becoming more expressive."[78] Richard Davenport-Hines concurs with this basic assessment and places the credit (or blame) on "American cultural infiltration," and on American television in particular.[79]

Recall Paul Hayes's similar assessment: that through exposure to American daytime talk shows, Brits are getting more used to baring their souls. Interestingly, when, in 2006, I asked several British government officials about the transferability of American-styled emotionalism to British problem-solving courts, they did not outright object to these practices or to the essential assessment put forth by Furedi and others. Jonathan Monk, at the Ministry of Justice, for example, said, "British culture, I think, is probably less buttoned up than it was thirty, forty years ago. . . . You can say that there are more displays of sentimentalism, shall we say, in British public life now. . . . The Princess Diana funeral, that sort of stuff, would never have happened in the past. So maybe it leads that way." That is, culture "leads the way" for similar developments in the courts. Even Lord Chief Justice Phillips, while careful to acknowledge that hugging and the like are "entirely at odds with the British ethos, which is that you shake hands with your son before he goes off to the war," also said that it was "not impossible to imagine quite emotional interchanges in the court." An aide who was present during the same interview quickly qualified this comment, though, by stressing the importance of "the dignity of the court proceedings" and maintaining a "balance between that— the necessary emotions—and dignity, which would maybe prevent the theatrics, or the theatrical elements" found in the American courts.

Taken together, these comments echo those of Judge Susan Williams (cited earlier) who believes that, though Brits aren't as "buttoned-up" as they used to be, "there is still a lot of reserve." Even Judge Philips, the most demonstrative of Britain's problem-solving judges, still says of his compatriots: "We're very buttoned-up." Therefore, to the extent that it reflects broader social tendencies, the ambivalence evident in the emerging British problem-solving courts suggests a culture in flux—one in which stoicism and reserve may be giving way to more open and emotional forms of public communication. In the main, however, it seems that judges and magistrates are still, with a few exceptions, reluctant to engage with clients in a fashion that approximates the levels of intimacy and expressivism displayed in some American problem-solving courts. The manager of the Gloucestershire DTTO pilot program summed it up: "The Home Office, when they saw the American judges, they loved that, and they loved the judges giving badges and giving donuts and stuff like that." As for the transferability of these practices to Britain, he added, "I've heard this wonderful comment since then that American culture doesn't cross the pond easily."

It may not do so easily, but it clearly has arrived. Just how far its influence will extend remains to be seen. Again, the advancement of problem-solving courts in Britain is still very much a work in progress. That said, there are signs that the kinds of warnings offered by Teubner, Hiller, and the like are proving prescient. Though practitioners speak of adaptation, of adjusting American-made legal products to fit local conditions, one finds over time more evidence of conspicuous Americanism. There are also signs that British culture is changing in such a manner as to make these practices less alarming. In the rare cases when Brits were even aware of TJ, they largely resisted it, advising "extreme caution" against what portends an inestimable "challenge to" and "major departure from" the judicial tradition in England. However, as discussed in chapter 2, both problem-solving courts and TJ stem from the same cultural impulses. They are vectors, to use Susan Daicoff's term, with similar cultural roots. By embracing problem-solving courts, are not Brits, perhaps only unwittingly, bringing on board the very same therapeutic tendencies they find unappealing in the legal theory? If so, what will be the consequences of this adoption in the long term? Will it, in Teubner's terms, irritate, or will it be domesticated? In hopes of shedding light on these and related questions, we turn in the next chapter to an analysis of the borrowing of problem-solving courts by two additional common law countries.

Chapter Four

COMMONWEALTH CONTRASTS:
CANADA AND AUSTRALIA

> The collaborative, team-based, therapeutic approach of
> United States problem-solving courts inspired the establish-
> ment of similar courts in Australia. . . . We may well be in
> the process of a paradigm shift.[1]
> —*Michael S. King*

TWO other major importers of problem-solving courts are the commonwealth countries of Canada and Australia. Though the United States is often credited as the primary source of inspiration, officials from Canada and Australia also cite the influence of other countries, particularly the United Kingdom, in discussing the importation and growth of problem-solving courts in their respective countries. Furthermore, Canadians and Australians make reference to the role of each on the other, which is understandable given the similarities in the scope and timing of emerging problem-solving courts in both places. Officials in both countries see many similarities between Canada and Australia more generally, in terms of size, political structure (e.g., commonwealth status vis-à-vis the United Kingdom), and culture. With respect to the structure and style of these programs, problem-solving courts in Canada and Australia represent something of a hybrid of British and American courts, exhibiting some features of the American variety, some of the English, and some that are unique to Canada and Australia.

One example of an apparent synthesis is found in the manner in which the courts were developed. Recall the difference between American and British problem-solving courts as it concerns the directionality of innovation: what has been a largely grassroots movement in the United States is more top-down in the United Kingdom. In both Canada and Australia, one finds something in between. There are cases of local innovation, to be sure, but in both commonwealth countries, the level of initiative, guidance, and funding from both state (or provincial) and national governments has been significant. Moreover, especially in Australia, there is a greater sense of judicial deference to the directives of the legislature, even in the cases where the innovation started at the local level.

Recall also that therapeutic jurisprudence is one feature of the American variety of problem-solving courts that has been mostly resisted in England. Contrastingly, in the process of importing problem-solving courts, Canada and Australia have more fully embraced TJ. Arguably, it is therapeutic jurisprudence rather than problem-solving courts, as such, that has been the dominant "vector" driving changes in both countries. However, while they embrace therapeutic jurisprudence, judicial officials in Australia and Canada, as in England, show greater restraint than is generally demonstrated in American problem-solving courts. Relatedly, both countries show more concern for the protection of offenders' due process rights (or "natural justice," as the Australians call it) and the preservation of the dignity of the court. Particularly in Australia, there is considerable evidence of critical reflection about the potential hazards or harmful consequences of these court programs.

Further evidence of an American/British hybrid is found in the role of the judge in Australian and Canadian problem-solving courts. In Australia, as in England, for example, most of the problem-solving courts are run in magistrates' courts, which handle most low-level offenses. Australian magistrates, however, are professionals (not lay judges) and sit singly on the bench; they are more like district judges, or what used to be called stipendiary magistrates in England and Wales, and also more like the single judges of the American variety. In both Canada and Australia, then, professional judges play a more central role, and they are able to impose some of the intermediate sanctions, such as short terms in jail, that British judges cannot. Even with this increased discretion, however, judges evince more reticence than do many American problem-solving court judges.

Though problem-solving courts in Canada and Australia are typically judge-led (as in the United States), probation generally still plays a critical role in overseeing treatment and managing the court-based programs in Canada and Australia (though not as central a role as in the United Kingdom). A New South Wales probation officer was surprised to learn that "only 22 percent of drug courts in the U.S. actually have a probation component." She could not conceive of a drug court without a probation service and noted that the "probation component in the New South Wales drug court is seen as intrinsic to the whole process." Also more like in England, treatment programs are typically, though not exclusively, defined by a harm reduction or harm minimization philosophy. Finally, because of the national health care systems in both countries, the availability, accessibility, and nature of treatment are generally more similar to that found in the United Kingdom than in the United States.

Finally, there is a unique type of problem-solving court found in both Canada and Australia whose presence distinguishes these commonwealth countries from their British and American counterparts: new aboriginal courts. Given that aboriginal courts represent, in part, a recovery of traditional indigenous practices, there is some debate about the degree to which these courts should be classified as TJ-based problem-solving courts. However, the "modern kind" of aboriginal courts emerged at the same time as did the other problem-solving courts considered here. In part, the development of aboriginal courts was afforded by the spirit of innovation engendered by the problem-solving court movement. Moreover, there is, at the very least, an elective affinity between new aboriginal courts and the other problem-solving courts in terms of some of their common therapeutic qualities. Thus, it is probably safe to conclude, along with Australian criminologist Arie Freiberg, that aboriginal courts are "a specialist court with some problem-solving and therapeutic overtones."[2]

Before considering more fully the significance of the common themes and distinguishing qualities of problem-solving courts in Canada and Australia, I will first provide a brief overview of the various types of problem-solving courts that have emerged in the last decade in these two countries, highlighting in both cases some of the sources of inspiration for the development of these courts and the processes of international transplantation.

CANADIAN PROBLEM-SOLVING COURTS

One of the first problem-solving courts to find its way across the U.S./Canadian border was the Toronto drug court, launched as a four-year pilot program in December 1998. The Toronto drug court was, in fact, the first drug court initiated outside of the United States. In 2001, Canada started a second drug court in Vancouver; then, in 2005, the Canadian government announced a commitment of $13.3 million to fund four additional drug courts in Edmonton, Regina, Winnipeg, and Ottawa. At the beginning of 2007, Canada had a total of seven drug courts, including a drug court launched at the end of 2006 in Oshawa, a town just east of Toronto. Not surprisingly, the United States has been the primary influence in the development of drug courts in Canada. The Toronto drug court "grew out of the inspiration of your courts in the United States," Paul Bentley, the first Canadian drug court judge, told a mostly American audience just six months after the start of the Toronto drug court.[3] In keeping with the adaptation view common among importers of American problem-solving courts, Bentley understood that the U.S. model had to be adapted to suit the Canadian context. Several months prior to the launch of the Toronto drug court, Bentley said, "We want to use what you've done well, ignore what you haven't done so well, and adapt the model [to] our own local use. . . . I think we can use the ideas that you have and create our own drug courts to suit our own local communities."

Judge Bentley, however, has not always been keen to highlight this source of inspiration, because, as he explains, "though Canadians love Americans, they also dislike Americans because of cultural imperialism." Conscious of Canada's "particular love-hate relationship with the U.S.," he has been careful of the manner in which he sells drug courts to his fellow Canadians. For example, he has sometimes argued in support of Canadian drug courts by saying, "Look what a mess the Americans made in their criminal justice system all these years," an allusion to some of the "tough on crime" measures introduced in the 1980s and beyond. Only after making such a "terrible mess" he explains, did the Americans finally "come up with an idea." Thus, though he acknowledges the importation of a clearly American product, he pitches the innovation in a way more palatable to an audience with misgivings about the relentless impact of American culture on its society. In other words, to be persuasive, he has sometimes had to sell drug courts in almost anti-American terms. Moreover, Bentley, like other importers of American problem-solving courts, emphasizes the manner in which the courts have been adapted to fit the Canadian context. "We basically went into this exercise," Bentley explains, "with the purpose of developing a model that fit the Anglo-Canadian criminal justice system." Taking more serious offenders, employing a harm reduction treatment model, and prescribing methadone are among those features of the Canadian court, according to Bentley, that represent adjustments to the American model to suit the Canadian context.

Mental health courts are a second type of problem-solving court to find its way into the Canadian criminal justice system. The Toronto mental health court was launched in May 1998. As in the Toronto drug court, those eligible for the Toronto mental health court are assigned a range of conditions for participation in the court-based program. Importantly, participants in this program are ordered to "re-attend court on a regular basis" so that the judge can "monitor and encourage compliance" with program requirements. "Thus, judicial supervision and intervention is present in the Court process throughout."[4] In the spring of 2001, three years after the start of the Toronto mental health court, the Alberta Health Innovation Fund awarded a grant for the establishment of a similar program in Calgary. Unlike the Toronto mental health court, the Calgary court is not a stand-alone specialty court, as such, but a diversion program. That is, if the police and/or Crown (prosecutor) determine that someone who has been arrested for a low-level offense suffers from mental illness, the individual will be recommended for a diversion program involving a court-approved treatment plan. Unlike in Toronto, then, ongoing judicial monitoring is not a feature of the program. As Judge Bill

Pepler, who helped to start the program, explains, the judges in these cases "see very little." Nevertheless, it is a problem-solving enterprise in the sense that it is nonadversarial, multiagency, and oriented toward addressing the difficulties faced by individuals with mental health issues. A number of satellite courts in Ontario have established programs based on the Toronto model; in 2007, several other towns in Alberta, including Lethbridge, St. Paul, and Edmonton, began mental health court programs based on the Calgary model; and in 2000, a pilot project that developed into a mental health court was started in St. John, New Brunswick.[5]

Calgary, Alberta, is also the location of one of Canada's growing number of domestic violence courts. The Calgary domestic violence court, started in June of 2000, reflects qualities of both the British and American varieties. Recall that British domestic violence courts lack the review session venues more common in U.S. courts, where clients regularly return to the court for ongoing judicial monitoring. In the Calgary domestic violence court, according to Judge Sherry Van de Veen, "It is not uncommon . . . to include mandatory court-ordered reviews of the offender's progress."[6] However, not all the judges who rotate through the Calgary domestic violence court regularly use the review process. As Judge Pepler explains of his own experience, "With somebody on probation, sometimes I will say, 'I want to see you in three months, or six months, or two weeks, or whatever.' But that's not an integral part of this court, as it is with drug courts." Thus, the approach falls somewhere between U.S. and UK practices: review sessions are available at the discretion of the judge but are not necessarily regarded as a standard feature of the court.

More in keeping with the American model, however, the treatment of offenders is central to the program. The aim of the Calgary domestic violence court "is to effect changes to offender behavior at the earliest exposure to the justice system, through treatment and support, so as to restore family harmony."[7] According to Judge Pepler, treatment of the offender is "key to it." One of the stated goals of the program is not only to "hold the offender accountable for his/her behavior through the imposition of legal sanctions," but also to provide "opportunities for treatment and rehabilitation."[8] The nature of the treatment, however, seems to be something of a mix between British and American tendencies. In Calgary, a nonprofit organization called HomeFront works alongside the court and coordinates the various treatment options for offenders. According to Kevin McNickle, a representative from HomeFront, the Calgary domestic violence court works with treatment agencies that use "a combination of group and individual therapy" and "address issues of anger, emotions, communication, positive relationships, what is abuse, all of those things." McNickle acknowledges, moreover, that the content of the treatment was modeled on programs developed in the United States and Canada, and that staff from HomeFront had traveled to the United States to look at various programs. Treatment facilities associated with the Calgary court also reflect some of the "gender analysis" themes emphasized in British domestic violence courts. That is, the content of treatment focuses not only on such therapeutic themes as emotions and self-concept, but also on matters of "power and control" between males and females.[9]

Canada has a variety of domestic violence courts. Some, such as the Calgary court, have a central treatment component, and others are more focused on "vigorous prosecution for serious repeat offenders."[10] Of the various domestic violence courts in Canada, the Calgary court is most often referenced in association with problem-solving courts and therapeutic jurisprudence,[11] but a range of other Canadian domestic violence courts have been established, including courts in Winnipeg, Whitehorse (Yukon), and Edmonton.[12] In 1997, Ontario started two domestic violence courts, including the "K Court" in Toronto. By 2003, Ontario had established a total of twenty-two such courts, and by the end of 2006, some type of domestic violence court program had been established in all fifty-five Ontario jurisdictions.[13]

With respect to treatment, Ontario officials prefer the terms "education" and "intervention" over "treatment," and they are not inclined to view the court-ordered intervention as a therapeutic enterprise. According to Barbara Kane, who works in the Victim Services Division of the Ontario Ministry of the Attorney General, "We see domestic violence as learned behavior that can be unlearned; attitudes and behaviors can be changed with interventions." She does not like to call the intervention "therapy, which kind of pathologizes it" and believes domestic violence is not "a kind of illness that needs some kind of therapy." Some judges still assign offenders to participate in anger management programs, she notes, but the basic philosophy of the Ontario domestic violence programs opposes this form of intervention. Instead, offenders are assigned to a sixteen-week partner assault (PAR) program, which is loosely based on the Duluth model and emphasizes such themes as power and control, accepting responsibility, and changing attitudes and values.[14] Thus, compared to the Calgary court, the Ontario courts more closely resemble the British domestic violence court model.

The establishment of a community court in Vancouver was first recommended by the Street Crime Working Group, a task force set up by the attorney general of British Columbia in 2004. The Working Group, comprising over a dozen individuals from a range of government agencies, received input from Julius Lang of the Center for Court Innovation. It formally recommended the establishment of a Vancouver community court in its final report, which was released in March 2005.[15] A year later, when Vancouver mayor Sam Sullivan announced his support for the court, he specifically mentioned his visit to the Red Hook community court, where "offenders go immediately from sentencing and into services to address their underlying problems."[16] Judge Thomas Gove, who will preside over the Vancouver community court (scheduled to open on the summer of 2008), also visited community courts and other problem-solving courts in New York to prepare for his new role.

Aboriginal courts make up a final type of problem-solving court found in Canada. Just east of Calgary is the 108-square-mile reserve of the Tsuu T'ina Nation. In October 2000, a provincial court was established on the reserve to handle less serious offenses committed by Tsuu T'ina people. The court represents a fascinating synthesis of traditional Western common law processes and the "peacemaking" practices indigenous to the eighteen hundred Tsuu T'ina people living on the reserve. The courtroom, built in the shape of a circle, is presided over by a judge of aboriginal descent. The court opens with a traditional "smudge ceremony" involving the burning of sage, the smoke from which both the judge and the "Peacemaker Coordinator" allow to pass over them. Depending on the particular case, a defendant may be given the option of a peacemaking process, a type of diversion program overseen by one of the Tsuu T'ina peacemakers. In this alternative adjudicative process, members of an assembled peacemaking circle discuss the offense and determine what sort of restorative and/or punitive measures are warranted. When these requirements are completed, the circle has a ceremony, which, interestingly, has been likened to a drug court graduation.[17] Once the defendant completes the peacemaking process, the case is returned to court and, depending on the seriousness of the offense and the extent of the offender's compliance with imposed requirements, the charges may be dropped. Judge Van de Veen sees close parallels between the processes of the Tsuu T'ina court and the therapeutic jurisprudence central to other problem-solving courts.

> The [Tsuu T'ina] Court exemplifies the underlying principles of Therapeutic Jurisprudence and Restorative Healing in that it is intent upon dealing with the root causes of the criminal activity, offering treatment and counseling where needed in the case of both victims and accused persons. The peacemaking circles themselves are therapeutic to all parties coming before the court.[18]

One year after the start of the Tsuu T'ina court, a second Canadian aboriginal court was launched in Toronto. The court was created largely in response to a 1996 legislative amendment to the Criminal Code of Canada that reads, "all available sanctions other than imprisonment that are reasonable in the circumstances should be considered for all offenders, with particular attention to the circumstances of aboriginal offenders."[19] In a 1999 interpretation of this language, the Supreme Court of Canada stated that the "drastic over-representation of Aboriginal peoples within both the Canadian prison population and the criminal justice system reveals a sad and pressing social problem."[20] The Supreme Court interpreted the legislature as directing criminal courts to "inquire into the causes of the problem and to endeavor to remedy it, to the extent that a remedy is possible through the sentencing process."[21] In compliance with these directives, the Gladue court (named after the Supreme Court case, *R. v. Gladue*) opened in October 2001 in Toronto's Old City Hall. The Gladue court emphasizes noncustodial sentences and provides a variety of resources oriented toward the particular needs of aboriginal peoples. The Gladue court is distinct from the Tsuu T'ina court in that it deals with a variety of indigenous peoples in a large urban context rather than with a smaller, single group on a rural and more isolated reserve. In addition to the Old City Hall court, two additional Gladue courts are now running in the larger Toronto area.

AUSTRALIAN PROBLEM-SOLVING COURTS

Problem-solving courts in Australia and in Canada have a number of similarities, including the timing of their emergence in both countries. In 1999, ten years after the start of the first American drug court, Australia initiated four different types of problem-solving courts. Among these was the first Australian drug court, launched in January 1999 as a two-year pilot program in Sydney, New South Wales (just one month after the start of Canada's first drug court). As the story goes, a New South Wales (NSW) barrister named Ross Goodridge took notice of American drug courts. After the courts attracted the interest of several NSW government officials, Jeffrey Tauber, who was president of the National Association of Drug Court Professionals (NADCP) at the time, was invited to Sydney in 1998 to talk with NSW officials about drug courts. Shortly after Tauber's visit, a delegation from the NSW parliament traveled to the United States. The delegation visited a number of drug courts and collected "a massive amount of literature." In keeping with an adaptation view of the importation process, a solicitor from the Sydney drug court recounts, "They came back to Australia and, from that research trip, designed a drug court for the Australian—the New South Wales—environment." The Drug Court Act, which determined the specific authority and parameters of the Sydney drug court, passed through the NSW parliament in December 1998. The Sydney drug court then began operations a month later. In 2000, three other Australian states—Western Australia, Queensland, and South Australia—started drug courts. All states but Tasmania now have some type of drug court in operation.[22]

Mental health courts are a second variety of problem-solving court to emerge on Australian soil. The country's first mental health court was initiated as a pilot scheme in Adelaide, South Australia, also in 1999.

When the pilot phase was completed, seven additional mental health courts were introduced in South Australia. Victoria introduced a program with some of the qualities of a mental health court in Melbourne in 2001. To avoid stigmatizing participants, the court is euphemistically referred to as an "Enforcement Review Program" or a "Special Circumstances" court, and it meets on the first and third Thursdays of every month. Queensland followed suit in 2005 when it proposed the establishment of a "special circumstances court" pilot program for mentally impaired offenders in conjunction with the initiation of a "Homeless Persons Court Diversion Program."

Inspired by domestic violence courts in both the United States and Canada, Australia initiated two domestic violence courts in 1999: one in Adelaide, South Australia, and a second in Joondalup (just north of Perth), Western Australia. These have been described as "inter-agency and community initiatives aimed at reducing the incidences of violence in families by integrating treatment into the court process." As in some U.S. and Canadian courts, then, offenders in Australian domestic violence courts "undergo intensive treatment and ongoing monitoring."[23] In June 2005, the Victorian government started family violence courts in two sections of Melbourne: Heidelberg and Ballarat, which, like American unified family courts and integrated domestic violence courts, hear both civil and criminal cases. Not long after, three additional scaled-down versions of family violence programs were initiated in downtown Melbourne, Sunshine, and Frankston.[24]

The ongoing judicial monitoring of defendants is not, however, part of the Melbourne family violence courts as it is for many American courts (though magistrates do tend to be more interactive with defendants than they are in a normal criminal court). More like in American courts, magistrates have the authority to impose a counseling program, even in civil cases, as part of what the Victorians call an "intervention order." As one magistrate explains, the imposition of such an order itself requires increased engagement with the defendant.

> There is a little bit more persuading that you have to do in the family violence division—particularly when you're going to be making a counseling order . . . you find yourself expanding your judicial role . . . you find yourself trying to explain to a man why this is going to be helpful, and why he's going to like it, actually, and get something out of it. So that's a bit of a difference. You don't do that in your normal judicial job.

The type of problem-solving court to find its way into the Australian criminal justice system most recently is the community court. The initiation of the Neighbourhood Justice Centre was a very public and high-profile case of legal borrowing, as was also seen in the exportation of community courts to England. In a ceremony attended by nearly four hundred people, the court was launched in the city of Yarra (in the northeastern part of the larger Melbourne area) on March 8, 2007. Like the Liverpool court, Victoria's first community court was directly inspired by the Red Hook Community Justice Center in Brooklyn. Staff from the Center for Court Innovation in New York led a seminar on community courts in Melbourne in 2004 that was convened by the Victorian Department of Justice. Australian officials visited both the Red Hook and Liverpool courts before launching the Neighbourhood Justice Centre.

Victoria attorney general Rob Hulls and Department of Justice secretary Penny Armytage both visited Red Hook and were impressed with what they saw of the project. Armytage said of her visit to Brooklyn, "What attracted me . . . is that it has a court engaged with the local community." She appreciated that the court "was not just about sentencing offenders but using the court as part of the network of services in the community. That sat very well with us."[25] Richard Wynne, who was Rob Hulls's parliamentary secretary at the time, recalls Hulls's return from his New York visit. "He was just beside himself about the opportunities that the Red Hook Justice Center represented in terms of the new wave of thinking about how you deliver justice at a community level." Hulls himself spoke of the "enormous privilege" of being able "to witness the Red Hook Community Justice Center in action," and how it "inspired . . . the small spark" that would lead the launching of the Neighbourhood Justice Centre in the city of Yarra.

In addition to community, family violence, mental health, and drug courts, a number of additional therapeutically inspired problem-solving schemes have been introduced into the Australian criminal justice system. In August 2001, for example, Michael King started the Geraldton Alternative Sentencing Scheme in Western Australia. The program addresses a range of "offending related problems," including drug and alcohol abuse, domestic violence, and gambling. Participants may be required to appear before the magistrate as often as once a week, and the court has used transcendental meditation techniques to encourage "stress reduction and self-development."[26] Magistrate Jelena Popovic runs a "Tuesday afternoon list" for prostitutes in Melbourne, Victoria. In 2006, the Victorian government allocated $17.1 million to fund the Court Integrated Services Program (CISP), a program "guided by the principles of therapeutic jurisprudence modeled within the problem-solving court framework."[27] Reflecting the sort of "going to scale" strategy found in New York, CISP functions within the existing magistrates' courts and aims to provide a range of services to help stabilize "repeat offenders with multiple and complex problems," in some cases using "judicial monitoring of the defendant's progress" when it is deemed "necessary and appropriate."[28]

Finally, like Canada, Australia has started a number of aboriginal courts, including Nunga courts in South Australia; a circle sentencing court in Norwa, New South Wales; aboriginal community courts in the Northern Territory; Murri courts in Queensland; the Yandeyarra aboriginal court in the Pilbara region of Western Australia; and Koori courts in Victoria.[29] The Koori courts in Victoria were started in a manner similar to that of the introduction of Gladue courts in Canada. That is, they were developed to comply with legislative directives (in this case, the Magistrates' Court [Korri Court] Act 2002 [Vic], s.4D), which—much like in Canada—were advanced over concerns about the high incarceration rates of indigenous people.

The first Koori court commenced operation in October 2002 in Shepparton, Victoria. Victoria now has six Koori courts, including a Koori children's court in Melbourne. While the Koori courts most closely resemble Toronto's Gladue courts, the Yandeyarra court in Western Australia functions more like the Tsuu T'ina court in Alberta, Canada. The sentencing court in Yandeyarra is actually held on the land occupied by the Yandeyarra aboriginal community. In a practice that commenced in September 2003, a Pilbara magistrate travels every four to six weeks to convene a circle court in a Yandeyarra community building. As with the Tsuu T'ina court, both justice officials and elders from the community work together in this synthesized version of an aboriginal court.

The first Australian aboriginal court of the "modern kind" was initiated in 1999 in South Australia. While the various Australian aboriginal courts are "insistently individual," they are also, as Kate Auty, the first magistrate of the Shepparton Koori court, puts it, "oddly uniform."[30] Auty, like Canada's Judge Van de Veen, sees therapeutic jurisprudence as among the uniform or common features of aboriginal courts. The Koori court, according to Auty, is "broadly and particularly representative of therapeutic jurisprudence principles for all involved in its operations."[31] Mark Harris, who wrote an evaluation of the Shepparton Koori court, agrees with Auty on this point: "Koori Courts embody many of the traits of problem-solving courts and . . . exemplify the main aspects of therapeutic jurisprudence."[32]

THERAPEUTIC JURISPRUDENCE IN AUSTRALIA AND CANADA

That Australian officials would wish to closely link aboriginal courts with therapeutic jurisprudence is indicative of a broader phenomenon in both countries: the embrace of therapeutic jurisprudence. Recall that in England, officials either have rarely heard of therapeutic jurisprudence or are openly dismissive of it. Particularly in the case of domestic violence courts, British court officials and analysts view therapeutic jurisprudence as an American feature of problem-solving courts not easily transferable to the British context. In glaring contrast, therapeutic jurisprudence deeply informs the theory and practice of problem-solving courts in Canada and Australia. It is a feature of the American version of problem-solving courts that has been consciously, deliberately, even enthusiastically included in the transplantation process.

In Australia, for example, from the very earliest days of importing problem-solving courts, officials have recognized therapeutic jurisprudence as a central feature of this new breed of court. In 2000, echoing the common refrains of Wexler and Winick, Judge Gay Murrell, the first judge of the Sydney drug court, wrote:

> The Drug Court endeavors to practice "therapeutic jurisprudence." Therapeutic jurisprudence acknowledges that, regardless of the outcome of litigation, the litigation process itself may be therapeutic or anti-therapeutic. . . . The role of the judge is pivotal to the achievement of therapeutic outcomes through a drug court.[33]

She reiterated this point in a later interview, asserting that in the Sydney drug court, "we are trying to practice therapeutic jurisprudence." By this she means, among other things, that the court tries to capitalize on the moment of crisis when someone finds himself or herself in the criminal justice system. It is at this point that "you might be able to achieve change," and in "achieving change the court's role can be a positive role or a therapeutic role." According to Murrell, "not only in its content but also in its structure," the court can be oriented therapeutically in a way that is "beneficial to people's recovery."

Judge Murrell is not the only Australian judge sympathetic to therapeutic jurisprudence. Indeed, most Australian judges working in problem-solving courts appear to align themselves with therapeutic jurisprudence. Consider several examples. Julie Wager, the first judge of the Perth drug court in Western Australia, says that "the drug court is a problem-solving court that uses therapeutic jurisprudence."[34] Tina Previtera, magistrate of the Brisbane drug court in Queensland, likewise says that "Queensland has embraced the notion of therapeutic jurisprudence, and there exist a number of specialist courts applying these principles."[35] Michael King, who has overseen two different types of problem-solving courts in Western Australia, notes the application of "principles developed in the United States . . . in therapeutic jurisprudence-based projects in magistrates' courts in regional Western Australia."[36]

Officials at the very highest levels of the state judiciary have observed the same. The chief judge of Western Australia, David K. Malcolm, for example, notes that in "the last decade or so, a series of specialized or problem-solving courts or court processes have evolved in Australia. These courts are based upon the principles of therapeutic jurisprudence." He credits the United States as the generative source of the problem-solving court movement and observes that because of "the tireless work of the leading scholars in this field—U.S. law professors David Wexler and Bruce Winick—the concept of therapeutic jurisprudence is cemented in the U.S. legal system."[37] That TJ has achieved so venerable and entrenched a status in the U.S. legal system is not so clear, but that Australians recognize and accept therapeutic jurisprudence as part and parcel of imported problem-solving courts is undeniable.

It is not just individual judges who point to therapeutic jurisprudence as the philosophical underpinnings of the new Australian problem-solving courts. Support for therapeutic jurisprudence appears widespread among state judiciaries. A survey of NSW magistrates conducted in 2003, for example, found that a majority of magistrates supported the concept of therapeutic jurisprudence.[38] Likewise, at their annual conference in November 2004, the Western Australian country magistrates unanimously passed a resolution to "endorse and adopt the principles of therapeutic jurisprudence."[39] According to King and Auty, the resolution was not just aspirational in nature. Rather, "it was a recognition that country magistrates already operate in diverse contexts in which they are often already applying therapeutic jurisprudence."[40]

Jelena Popovic, who runs several therapeutically oriented court programs in Victoria, invited David Wexler to Melbourne to speak to a large group of Victorian magistrates in 2002. According to Popovic, Wexler's teachings were well received, with some magistrates concluding that the theory only affirmed what many were already doing in their courts. Two years later, the attorney general of Victoria, Rob Hulls, issued an important strategic document, "Justice Statement" (2004), which endorsed problem-solving courts and acknowledged the central place of therapeutic jurisprudence in these innovative programs. This ten-year vision for Victoria's justice system anticipated not only that the government "will act to consolidate and extend the problem-solving approaches being employed in the courts," but also that, in the context of these courts, "therapeutic jurisprudence" has an important influence on "the design of court processes and sentencing options," including "the interaction between judicial officers and individuals in the court."[41]

Canadians have issued similarly broad endorsements of therapeutic jurisprudence. Perhaps the most significant is the influential document put out in 2005 by the National Judicial Institute of Canada, "Judging for the 21st Century: A Problem-Solving Approach." Like the various Australian endorsements of TJ, this document, written by Susan Goldberg, highlights the manner in which therapeutic jurisprudence "provides the underlying legal theory" for problem-solving courts.[42] Also like Australian publications, the document does not see TJ as limited to problem-solving courts. Rather, it holds that "therapeutic jurisprudence has applications in any court setting."[43] Natasha Bakht and Judge Paul Bentley make very similar points in another important paper written on behalf of the National Judicial Institute in Canada. Here, too, they identify therapeutic jurisprudence as the underlying philosophy of Canadian problem solving courts, arguing further that the "principles of therapeutic jurisprudence . . . can and should also be used beyond the borders of specialized courts in everyday trial processes and appellate courts."[44]

As in Australia, the relevance of TJ to problem-solving courts was recognized very early in Canada's efforts to import problem-solving courts. In one of the first published accounts of the Toronto drug court, for example, Judge Bentley described how drug courts "shift the emphasis of the court from legal to therapeutic."[45] Judge Van de Veen, writing four years later, expressed a very similar view regarding the theoretical foundations of Canadian problem-solving courts: "New problem-solving court developments . . . are founded upon principles which have come to be known as 'Therapeutic Jurisprudence.'"[46] That Judge Van de Veen, like Judge Bentley, sees TJ as applicable beyond new specialized problem-solving courts is evident in several instances. She has even joined with David Wexler to coauthor an article on the broader relevance of therapeutic jurisprudence to sentencing principles and practices in Canada.[47] Van de Veen and Wexler have also given a series of presentations "to the Canadian judiciary on emerging therapeutic jurisprudence principles in the area of sentencing."[48]

Consider, finally, a coauthored book on the development of mental health courts in Canada: *Mental Health Courts: Decriminalizing the Mentally Ill.* Richard Schneider, the first listed author, is a mental health court judge in Toronto (and is also, interestingly, a clinical psychologist). Schneider and his colleagues, Hy Bloom and Mark Heerema, identify therapeutic jurisprudence as "the theory that has animated the recent phenomenon of problem-solving courts within North America and has formed the theoretical underpinning of mental health courts."[49] Schneider and his colleagues, in fact, see "the creation of problem-solving courts" as "the most prolific example of a therapeutic initiative."[50] So central is therapeutic jurisprudence to the functioning of Canadian mental health courts that the authors argue that "no professional or worker from either the legal or mental health arenas should become involved in a mental health court unless he is philosophically oriented to a therapeutic outcome for the accused."[51]

Interestingly, the enthusiastic acceptance of therapeutic jurisprudence is coupled with an equally noticeable reserve about some of the courtroom practices commonly associated with this new legal theory.

CRITICAL REFLECTION AND RESTRAINT

As problem-solving courts continue to proliferate, Canadian and Australian academics and practitioners reflect in a critical, sometimes even worrying, manner about the consequences of TJ on courtroom practices. It is a kind of critical self-reflection that one rarely finds in the United States, where those involved in these court innovations (again, both practitioners and academics) can come across as uncompromising advocates, sales representatives, even religious zealots. One of the few American judges critical of this movement was invited to speak at a problem-solving court conference in New York. He admitted after the conference to feeling like "an atheist at a tent revival meeting." The kind of boosterism he experienced at the conference is much less apparent in places like Australia and Canada, where, again, one finds a greater willingness to reflect critically on the problem-solving court movement and the therapeutic ideals that inform it. Mark Harris of Victoria perhaps sums up this regional contrast best: "While there has been enthusiastic embracing of therapeutic jurisprudence in numerous areas of the law, this is not to suggest that it is accepted uncritically amongst either legal academics or practitioners."[52] Judge Schneider of Toronto offers a similar assessment of the advancement of TJ in Canada. Schneider says that the influence of therapeutic jurisprudence is "growing and certainly building momentum" in Canada. He adds, however, that TJ is not "something that people are intimately familiar with," nor is it something "that's been completely embraced even by those who do understand what it is all about." Still, he holds, interest is "definitely picking up."

Among the practitioners who express some reservations about problem-solving courts and therapeutic jurisprudence is Jelena Popovic of Victoria. She is a self-described practitioner of therapeutic jurisprudence who views the theory's aims as "laudable" and believes they should be "aspired to by all who serve in the courts."[53] Thus, she is anything but a skeptic or critic of the movement. Indeed, as noted earlier, Popovic was the one who invited David Wexler to speak to Victorian magistrates in 2002.

In spite of her championing of therapeutic jurisprudence, however, Popovic also worries that in all the enthusiasm of implementing and operating these new courts, something important may be getting lost.

She warns: "In the excitement to 'progress' the practice of therapeutic jurisprudence in our courts of summary jurisdiction . . . attention must be paid to basic principles of justice to ensure the rights of court participants are not eroded."[54] Popovic thus cautions her fellow practitioners to be sure "that we are not trampling on the rights of court users." In particular, she is concerned that "the overarching principles of open justice and natural justice" might be "sacrificed in our keenness for reform." She cites, for example, the practice (common in both Canadian and Australian drug courts) of pre-court meetings, or what she calls "case conferences," where the drug court team meets before court to go over the cases of participants who will be appearing in court that day. She is concerned that these "in camera" meetings, which do not include the defendants, may violate the principle of open justice.[55]

Popovic is also concerned about the informality of problem-solving courts. She admits that even in her "own practice of therapeutic jurisprudence," she has "to a large extent abandoned the 'arm's length' approach (and the protection it offers)," but she is not sure that such informality and flexibility "is in fact a good thing." She has even become a bit nostalgic for some of the advantages of greater judicial formality. For one, she believes a more formal court appropriately signifies the "solemnity and seriousness of what is occurring." It also helps to ensure a higher level of "predictability of the proceedings," so that "defendants know what to expect and are not taken by surprise." Moreover, according to Popovic, the kind of dressing-down that occurs in problem-solving courts may convey the wrong message. Instead of setting defendants at ease, as is often the stated hope for such practices, it may come across as "patronizing" and give defendants the "impression that they are second-class citizens" for whom it is not necessary to look the proper part.[56]

Judge Gay Murrell, the first judge of the Sydney drug court, has similar apprehensions about the kind of freedom and flexibility judges are given in the context of problem-solving courts, and she believes that judges need to be all the more cautious and restrained in light of these conditions. She observes, for example, that "the broad . . . discretions conferred on the judge and the absence of conventions governing much of the procedures of drug courts may be conducive to idiosyncratic conduct by the judge."[57] Given the kind of latitude permitted by such a novel courtroom environment, she believes the judge must "guard against inappropriate psychological interaction with participants" and "resist the temptation to make a personal emotional investment in the rehabilitation outcome for participants." Rather, the judge should strive to "maintain judicial impartiality and ensure that participants receive procedural fairness, despite a lack of protective conventions."[58]

Compare these sentiments with the views of an American problem-solving court judge, who instructs: "Be less the dignified, detached judicial officer. Show your concern. . . . Don't lecture the offender, but engage him or her in conversation. . . . Make a connection."[59] In notable contrast, Judge Murrell thinks:

> It is quite important to be a little bit restrained, because the judge does have such enormous power—not just in terms of things like sanctions or sentences, but in terms of emotional abuse of the person, if you'd like, in throwing their weight around generally. And I think the whole boundaries in which the judge operates [in this kind of court] are so blurred as compared to a traditional judicial setting that you've got to try to be aware of those boundaries. To that extent, restraint helps you not to transgress those boundaries.

Like Murrell, Tina Previtera, magistrate of the Queensland drug court, thinks the peculiar qualities of the drug court create a courtroom situation in which judges need to be extra cautious not to infringe upon defendants' due process rights and protections. For many generations, Previtera observes, defendants' rights have been "safeguarded" by "tradition and precedent" and a judicial commitment to such core values as "certainty, reliability, impartiality, and fairness." In drug courts, she notes, "there is no such history and experience upon which to draw." Given the relative absence of these protections, Previtera, like Murrell, believes it is incumbent upon the judge to vigilantly guard against violations of these rights. "We must charge ourselves with the responsibility therefore to ensure that therapeutic considerations do not over-ride long standing freedoms and rights."[60]

Some Australian judges offer still stronger criticisms of the application of TJ in Australian problem-solving courts. One magistrate with whom I spoke made several references to therapeutic jurisprudence as "the flavor of the month" and admitted that some of her fellow magistrates thought "the whole thing was a bit loony." She even made adjustments to courtroom practices after taking over the drug court from her predecessor. When she started, it was the common practice to clap when someone had a "clean urine." She noticed that some of the participants "cringed" and "winced" when they did this. She asked them about it and was told that they "didn't like the clapping." Subsequently, she eliminated clapping except when handing out certificates (i.e., when participants graduate from one of three phases in the program). Even in these instances, though, the ceremony is observably understated compared to practices in U.S. courts.

A magistrate overseeing a family violence court in Canberra goes even further. She does not believe the judge should be involved in case management of defendants at all. Like some domestic violence court magistrates in England, Magistrate Karen Fryar believes that "once a matter is final-ized (or an offender found guilty and sentenced), the court's role is fin-ished." She believes the case management should instead be left to correc-tive services (i.e., probation and parole). Fryar worries that her colleagues on the bench "tend to get carried away with the possible good that we can do," and she believes that they should resist straying into such "a difficult and dangerous area." Like a more traditional common law judge, she thinks the court should be "constrained by law and legislation," and that judges should remember that they are "not trained as social workers/ drug and alcohol counselors."[61] Recall that the Melbourne family vio-lence courts likewise do not engage in ongoing judicial monitoring.

Consider one final example of critical reflection offered by an Austra-lian judge. Speaking at a 2005 conference on therapeutic jurisprudence in Perth, Hal Jackson, a district judge from Western Australia, asked a number of pointed questions about TJ and problem-solving courts in a talk tendentiously titled "Changing Roles—The Way Forward or a Fog of Confusion?" His talk, pitched as "a plea for clarity . . . not an attack or an embrace," raised questions, first, about the very meaning of thera-peutic jurisprudence.

> What is therapeutic jurisprudence? What qualifies as coming within its content? Why is it different from what has gone before? And what are the problems it seeks to address? Is the name the problem, or is the name fashionable because it covers so many activities, and if so, is it appropriate for it to do so? Is it a state of mind, a process, or a result? Who is it for: offender, victim, community? Why do magistrates think they are an appropriate vehicle for its application?

Jackson raised additional questions about the relationship between thera-peutic jurisprudence and restorative justice, the appropriateness of allo-cating scarce public resources to courts rather than to other social agen-cies, the applicability of the TJ label to indigenous courts, and the degree to which therapeutic jurisprudence resembles the "mistaken" practices of the earlier rehabilitative era. He cited a refrain common among TJ schol-ars: that therapeutic jurisprudence represents the application of an "ethic of care." Straying from his prepared remarks, he then mused somewhat caustically: "Next time I sentence someone to eight years, I will tell them 'I really care.'"

Though less pronounced than in Australia, examples of critical reflec-tion and restraint are found in Canada as well. Kevin McNickle, with HomeFront in Calgary, for example, notes that in Calgary, not a few judges have been fairly skeptical of problem-solving courts and therapeu-tic jurisprudence and have asked the question, "Should judges be getting involved in that?" McNickle also points to some of the constraints placed on Canadian courts as a consequence of Canada's 1982 Charter of Rights. Civil rights explicated in this important document, McNickle explains, raise questions about whether it is "ethical or legal to mandate someone into treatment . . . or to subject an individual to random alcohol and drug testing if they have not yet been found guilty of an offense." Canadian judges have also debated whether it is fair to give "one class of crime [e.g., drug offenders] preferential treatment in the trial process," and they have questioned the equity of giving victims of domestic violence disproportionate assistance and resources. To some, according to Judge Pepler, the Calgary domestic violence court "looked like everybody was ganging up on the accused." As a consequence, the court was actually compelled to give HomeFront a less prominent place in the courtroom. Now, according to Pepler, "they're way back in the corner."

In terms of the behavior of Canadian problem-solving court judges, as in Australia, one does not find overly demonstrative behavior. In the Toronto mental health court, though participants regularly return to court for judicial monitoring, the judge only engages in a limited manner. Judge Richard Schneider, of the Toronto mental health court, observes that in U.S. courts there is "more involvement from the judiciary." His court, in contrast, is "a little more conservative." Schneider does not think it is necessary for the judge "to join in as one of the therapists." Instead, most of the hands-on work with clients is left to the court mental health support workers. Even in the Toronto drug court, which is less formal than the mental health court, the judge still maintains a more traditional sense of judicial reserve. As Bentley himself observes, "We're definitely more staid than an American court," though not "as staid as an English court." Thus, in terms of judicial behavior, as with other features of the drug court, Bentley sees the Canadian court as somewhere "in the middle" of American and British practices. Both Bentley and Judge Pierre Rinn also express concerns about violations of due process. Judge Rinn, for example, notes that both the Charter of Rights and the Criminal Code state that a person "should be tried and sentenced within a reasonable period of time." He observes that in the drug court context, "we're putting everything off for about a year or so," and he worries that "we don't have a higher court ruling on that."

Like Murrell, Popovic, and other Australian judges, Canadians recognize that the unique format of problem-solving courts opens the door for potentially problematic judicial behavior. Given the informality of problem-solving courts, therefore, judges are cautioned to tread carefully in this novel judicial context. Consider the following statement offered in a summary document from the First National Drug Treatment Court Workshop, held in Toronto in September 2001.

In spite of the informality and team spirit that dominates the process, the judge must maintain sufficient detachment. . . . One of the risks of a less traditional posture is that the boundaries between individuals can become blurred. Social service workers are trained in this as part of their professional education, but a judge is most likely not.[62]

Dawn Moore, from Carleton University in Ottawa, has also written about the manner in which practices in the Canadian drug courts "have concerning implications for questions of due process and the ethical treatment of court clients." She observes that procedures in Canadian drug courts "explicitly erase fundamental protections against abuse of power in the realms of both therapy and justice."[63] In particular, Moore highlights the way in which punitive practices, including incarceration, are given therapeutic classifications, a practice common in American drug courts. "In the treatment court, the notion of punishment is translated into the therapeutic goal of motivation." Yet, such sanctions as "increasing surveillance and the possibility of arrest and incarceration" are still, at the end of the day, "decidedly punitive."[64] A variety of sanctions are available to the Canadian drug court judge to encourage participants to comply with program requirements. As Judge Bentley explains, "Sanctions range from admonishment by the judge to increased court attendance, counseling, performing community service hours, or revocation of bail. In the latter case, offenders will be remanded into custody for a period not exceeding five days."[65] As Moore notes, such incarceration is sometimes referred to as a "therapeutic remand." Importantly, she also observes that community service orders are given "far more often than therapeutic remands."[66]

In fact, the Canadian drug court judge is disinclined to impose a sanction involving incarceration. As Bakht and Bentley note, "It is very rare for sanctions to be used in Canadian drug treatment courts. When they are used, it is typically only after an offender has been in the drug treatment program for a lengthy period of time and upon the advice of treatment providers."[67] This reluctance is indicative of a kind of judicial restraint not uncommon in Canadian problem-solving courts, particularly as compared to U.S. problem-solving courts. Thus, in both Canada and Australia, one finds a warm embrace of therapeutic jurisprudence in conjunction with a willingness to reflect critically on the therapeutic processes of problem-solving courts. One also finds a clear disposition to function within certain limits of judicial behavior. One factor that helps to explain the restraint evident in both Canadian and Australian problem-solving courts is the clear sense in which judges in both countries, like judges and magistrates in England, defer to the other branches of government—in particular to the legislative branch.

JUDICIAL DEFERENCE TO THE LEGISLATURE

As in England, problem-solving courts in the commonwealth countries of Australia and Canada were initiated in a more top-down manner than the grassroots manner more commonly seen in the United States. Amanda Coultas, a solicitor from the Sydney drug court, takes note of this clear difference. The Sydney drug court, according to Coultas, "is completely a creature of statute—so it wasn't a grassroots movement as it appears to be in the United States, but something that's been imposed from above." Similarly, in discussing the Perth drug court, David Indermaur et al. observe: "While U.S. drug treatment courts developed as part of a judicial 'grassroots' movement, in Australia their introduction came about through the activities of various senior bureaucrats and policy makers."[68] Cathy Lamble, a family violence court magistrate, notes the same difference between U.S. and Australian courts. She observes that in "the American experience these things are led by the judiciary." In Australia, contrastingly, "this is a policy decision of government. It is supported by legislation, and also by government funding." Though local initiatives have sometimes played a role in Australia and Canada, problem-solving courts have largely been initiated at the state (or provincial) and federal levels. Judicial deference to the legislative and executive branches of government has been notable, which helps to account for some of the limitations placed on problem-solving court judges. Judge Murrell of Sydney makes just this point:

> I think that the fact the court is legislatively based is significant. I think that leaves less scope for judicial idiosyncratic behavior. I think that judges here are probably more reserved and the whole atmosphere of the court is probably more reserved and less demonstrative than you would see in the U.S. courts.

In Australia, not only the Sydney drug court but also drug courts in Queensland and Victoria were established with specific legislation.[69] So was Australia's first community court in Melbourne, through the Courts Legislation (Neighbourhood Justice Centre) Act of 2006, and Victoria's Koori Courts, through the Magistrates' Court (Koori Court) Act of 2002. Even in Australian states such as South Australia and Western Australia, where drug courts were not initially established with new statutory law, judicial actors still strove to operate (sometimes with considerable difficulties) within the dictates of existing bail legislation. The case of Western Australia is of particular interest in this regard. It was expected that the Perth drug court would be given enabling legislation along the lines of legislation passed in New South Wales for the Sydney drug court. However, just two months before the opening of the Perth drug court, state elections altered the makeup of the Western Australia parliament, and the anticipated legislation did not materialize. As a consequence, the Perth drug court was forced to rely on existing legislation—namely, the 1982 Bail Act and the 1995 Sentencing Act—which significantly limited the scope and authority of the court. In particular, the court could not enroll serious offenders, only "participants who did not face immediate terms of imprisonment."[70] Moreover, the existing legislation limited the time a participant could be assigned to drug court to a maximum of six months, and in some cases only four months.

For Australians, the absence of specific enabling legislation in this instance was viewed as highly problematic. In their evaluation of the Perth drug court, Indermaur and his colleagues identified "the lack of a legislative base" as "the most serious issue affecting the legitimacy of the drug court."[71] Arie Freiberg and Neil Morgan likewise found it troubling that the court "had no legislative basis." Moreover, Freiberg and Morgan criticized the court's use of bail as a de facto sentencing mechanism and argued persuasively that "bail laws are designed mainly to ensure the smooth and effective running of the justice system with respect to the processing of past events, not a means of imposing positive obligations upon a person in order to provide a new basis for future decisions."[72] It is, therefore, not the purpose of bail "to impose stringent drug counseling and monitoring requirements or to embrace judicial case management."[73] The use of bail, as such, has a number of potential hazards, including the possibility of questionable "consents" to program participation, the imposition of disproportionately severe requirements for offenses that likely would not have resulted in jail, and the legal and ethical problem of imposing stringent restrictions on individuals who have not pled guilty or been convicted of a crime.[74]

Perth's first drug court judge, Julie Wager, also found the court's operational parameters, as determined by the existing legislative provisions, limiting and frustrating; to her, the "need for specific legislation" was crucial. Two and a half years after the start of the Perth drug court, legislation finally did pass through the Western Australia parliament that gave the court the authority to include more serious offenders through a pre-sentence order (PSO), which could last up to two years (rather than only four to six months). According to Judge Wager, the legislative adjustments "have totally changed the type of participant who is suitable for drug court and the way in which the drug court team interacts with that participant."[75] Though Freiberg and Morgan acknowledge that the new PSOs represent an effort to "place the Western Australia drug court on a firmer statutory footing," they are still concerned that even this new legislation may have "unfortunate consequences," including the potential for "net-widening and a reduction in procedural safeguards."[76]

The important point as it concerns the present analysis, however, is that Australians clearly worry about the statutory basis of their problem-solving courts. In spite of the notable enthusiasm for therapeutic jurisprudence and problem-solving courts, a "black-letter" legal disposition persists in Australian legal culture. According to Australians, innovation, though welcomed, should not circumvent "procedural safeguards," and expanded judicial action, though embraced by some, must still be justified on statutory grounds. Efforts to ensure a legislative foundation when starting a problem-solving court, judicial hand-wringing when it does not appear to exist, and an unwillingness to step beyond the boundaries of statutory law are all indications of a pronounced judicial deference to the other branches of government.

Even in courts that were initially established with specific legislation, officials remain cognizant of statutory requirements and continue to look to the legislation to guide their practices. This has clearly been the case in Sydney, as solicitor Amanda Coultas explains:

> We can always look to our Act to tell us whether or not we're on the right track, and in fact, in court that happens quite a lot. It's a pilot program, and it's been set up for two years—and that is stipulated in the Act. . . . The objects of the Act of the drug court are set up in the Act and they're quite clear, and again they're something that the drug court team goes back to over and over again to help us when issues arise as to whether or not we're taking the right approach.

Thus, as illustrated here, the judiciary accepts the checks placed on it by the other branches of government—the legislature in particular.

So pronounced is this judicial disposition that in 2000, magistrates resisted a policy initiative in Victoria directing them to carry out a new diversion scheme. In the absence of enabling legislation, magistrates were very uncomfortable instituting the initiative. Moreover, they feared that the diversion scheme would give too much discretion and power to police and would lead to net-widening. In the end, many magistrates actually refused to conduct diversion hearings. As Cathy Lamble recounts, "The diversion program wasn't supported by legislation, and a number of magistrates refused to participate in that program, because they didn't think it was lawful." Only after legislation was passed in 2002 in support of the initiative did reluctant magistrates agree to make orders placing defendants in the diversion program. Thus, as Lamble summarizes, Australian magistrates "think it's incredibly important" that judicial actions "are supported by legislation." In her view, this is part of what it means to "maintain our integrity as judicial officers."

Judicial deference to the legislative branch has not been quite as pronounced in Canada as in Australia. Rather, Canadian judges have been more apt to initiate new courts at the local level in the American style. That said, judicial deference to the other branches of government has been evident in several important respects. To begin with, though specific statutory laws (such as the 1998 Drug Court Act in New South Wales) were not introduced to support and guide the initiation of specialty courts, advocates of Canadian problem-solving courts often point to legislation passed in September 1996 as statutory justification for their innovative practices.[77] As Susan Goldberg notes, the 1996 legislation (and Supreme Court interpretations of it) "have incorporated some therapeutic aspects into the criminal justice system and have helped judges adopt a problem-solving approach to sentencing."[78]

Specifically, section 742.1 of the Criminal Code of Canada allows, in certain cases, for a conditional sentence in which "the court may, for the purpose of supervising the offender's behavior in the community, order that the offender serve the sentence in the community."[79] Two additional provisions were introduced as a result of this legislation. The first, section 718.2(d), asserts that "an offender should not be deprived of liberty, if less restrictive sanctions may be appropriate in the circumstance"—which is understood to give license to noncustodial programs typical of problem-solving courts. The second, section 718.2(e), holds that the court should consider "all available sanctions other than imprisonment that are reasonable in the circumstances." This latter statute directs the court to pay "particular attention to the circumstances of aboriginal offenders," which, as noted earlier, hastened the establishment of aboriginal courts in Canada.[80]

Two important Supreme Court interpretations of these provisions, *R. v. Proulx* in 2000 and *R. v. Gladue* in 1999, have given further support to the activities of Canadian problem-solving courts. In both instances the Supreme Court makes direct reference to restorative justice in its reflections on the new legislation. For example, in *R. v. Proulx*, the Supreme Court holds that the legislation was enacted to "reduce reliance on incarceration as a sanction and to increase the use of principles of restorative justice in sentencing" and concludes that "a conditional sentence will be better than incarceration at achieving the restorative objectives." Similarly, in *R. v. Gladue*, reflecting in particular on the language regarding aboriginal offenders in section 718.2(e), the Court holds that the statute was meant to "encourage sentencing judges to have recourse to a restorative approach to sentencing."

Judges point to this language as an endorsement of problem-solving court principles and practices. In the case of Gladue courts, however, it is important to note that the legislation did not just serve as a justificatory backdrop for the development of a problem-solving court; it was the direct impetus for their creation. More like the processes found in Australia in this instance, the courts were developed as an explicit effort to comply with the legislation. Judge Brent Knazan of Ontario asserts that Gladue courts were created "mainly in order to apply 718.2(e) of the Criminal Code in the way the Supreme Court of Canada directed in R. v. Gladue."[81] Toronto's Judge Bovard and Jonathan Rudin, with Aboriginal Legal Services, both argue that without this legislation, and the Supreme Court's interpretation of it, Gladue courts would not exist.

It is interesting to note, however, that in both R. v. Gladue and R. v. Proulx, the Court actually upheld lower-court decisions to incarcerate, and it did so based largely on the principles of fittingness. In R. v. Proulx, in fact, the Court makes no fewer than four references to fittingness and concludes that the lower court's original decision to incarcerate for eighteen months "was not demonstrably unfit for these offences and this offender." The offense in this case was a drunk-driving incident that resulted in a death and a serious injury. In R. v. Gladue, similarly, the Court, while encouraging courts to consider the unique conditions of aboriginal offenders, asserted that sentencing "must continue to be what is a fit sentence" and concluded that "for that offence by this offender a sentence of three years' imprisonment was not unreasonable." In this case, a woman pled guilty to manslaughter for fatally stabbing her common-law husband with a knife. Moreover, while the new provisions clearly do offer support for problem-solving approaches, section 718 actually highlights the relevance of a number of purposes for sentencing and states as its "fundamental principle" the classical notion of just deserts: "A sentence must be proportionate to the gravity of the offence and the degree of responsibility of the offender."[82]

Thus, the Supreme Court has not abandoned notions of desert in its endorsement of restorative justice principles, regardless of the manner in which these provisions have been appropriated in support of the therapeutic practices central to new Canadian problem-solving courts. What is of relevance here is that judges take pains to find legislative support for their practices, and they realize that even these provisions leave them shy of what they would prefer for the effective operation of their problem-solving courts. Like some of the Australian drug courts that were initiated without the guidance of specific statutory law, Canadian courts have had to rely on existing bail release guidelines rather than deferred sentence provisions. As one Canadian judge explained to me,

We have kind of slipped very carefully through our Criminal Code, because (a) we're postponing sentencing, which is not permitted in the Code, and (b) also a difficulty, we put people on a drug treatment court they want, and there's a question about whether we are using the bail provisions of the Criminal Code appropriately. Because what we did—we fashioned a bail and

we said: if you breach a term of the bail—which is not being honest, not showing up, etc., etc.—we can revoke your bail. Well, it [the bail provision] was
never meant to be revoked and then reinstated and revoked and reinstated the
way we do it here.

This judge anticipates the likelihood that someday someone will challenge
the process and take a case to the Court of Appeal, arguing that the practice has no legislative basis because the Criminal Code says sentencing
should be imposed as soon as practicable after conviction.

Not surprisingly, then, Canadian judges would prefer greater legislatively approved flexibility and authority, and hope such legislation is on
the horizon. Van de Veen and Wexler, for example, write: "It is expected
legislation will be forthcoming from the Parliament of Canada in the near
future to specifically permit judges to defer sentence in order to allow
treatment of an offender to take place prior to the determination of sentence."[83] In the meantime, practitioners operate according to rules they
believe are "inadequate to govern a legal process that focuses primarily
on therapeutic principles" and wish for a "legislative/regulatory scheme
to facilitate the imposition of creative sanctions and rewards in 'blended
legal/therapeutic' proceedings."[84]

Thus, even though they have strained to appropriate justificatory language within existing legislation, Canadian judges still demonstrate judicial deference to the legislature. As in England and Australia, Canadian
problem-solving courts have also depended upon government funding
and direction. This is especially true with Canadian drug courts. In Canada, drug crimes are regarded as a federal offense and therefore require
federal direction and support; other Canadian problem-solving courts operate mainly at the provincial level. Drug court advocates have often had
to wait patiently for government action in this regard. For example, after
much preliminary work and the submission of a proposal to the federal
government, personnel in Toronto had to wait months before government
funding finally came through. In June 1998, Judge Bentley described the
situation as it stood at the time:

We're now at the stage where we have put in a proposal to our federal government for money for a demonstration project in order to try to set up a pilot
drug court system in Toronto. We're waiting. We've been waiting for a few
months. They told us that funding is coming but we haven't seen it yet. I've
been to Ottawa last week and spoke to the people there and we're still waiting
for an announcement.

After six more months of waiting, an announcement finally did come. In
December 1998, Anne McLellan, Canada's minister of justice and attorney general at the time, announced the Canadian government's commit-

ment of more than $1,6 million to support the Toronto drug court as a pilot program for four years.

Though Canada's second drug court was launched three years later, it was not until 2005, seven years after the start of the Toronto drug court, that the federal government provided funds for additional drug courts. In June 2005, Minister of Justice and Attorney General of Canada Irwin Cotler announced the government's four-year commitment of $13.3 million to fund drug courts, including support for the initiation of four new drug courts in Edmonton, Regina, Winnipeg, and Ottawa. Therefore, though local interest may have played an important role, the courts did not begin until they had secured federal funding. Some areas, such as Calgary, wished to start a drug court but were not granted federal dollars (and therefore did not). The most recent Canadian drug court, in Oshawa, is the one exception to this basic rule. In this case, the court was started without any federal dollars. In general, however, Canadian drug courts, like similar programs in the United Kingdom, have depended upon federal funding.

To summarize, both Australians and Canadians have enthusiastically embraced problem-solving courts, though not without critical reflection and restraint. Judicial deference to the other branches of government is one example of judicial restraint, in this regard, and has played an important role in checking the proliferation of problem-solving courts in Canada and Australia. While judicial deference to the legislative branch is more pronounced in Australia, Canadians still seek to justify problem-solving court practices according to existing legislative directives. In the case of Gladue courts, the legislative foundation for the court is more direct and explicit. Moreover, similar to practices in the United Kingdom, the Canadian judiciary has had to appeal and wait for federal funding to roll out programs like drug court in a more widespread manner. Another defining characteristic of practices in both Australia and Canada that clearly sets them apart from the United States is their shared commitment to a treatment philosophy more like that found in the United Kingdom.

Harm Reduction

Canada and Australia share a harm reduction or harm minimization philosophy. That is, with respect to treatment and other matters, the courts in both countries stress the idea of reducing crime or, in the case of drug courts, reducing substance abuse. There is less certainty that the perennial problems addressed in these programs can be eradicated entirely. One even finds some who are reluctant to embrace the very concept of "problem-solving," preferring instead the more modest expression "problem-oriented." Writing in 2001, Australian criminologist Arie Freiberg noted that there was at the time "no generally accepted terminology" regarding these new court innovations.[85] His own preference was for the term "problem-oriented," which, as he put it, "is slightly less hubristic than 'problem-solving.'"[86] Australian criminologist John Braithwaite (as cited in chapter 2) also uses the term "problem-oriented," as does Susan Eley in her analysis of the Toronto K Court; she only qualifies this by noting that "problem-solving" is the nomenclature used "in the American literature."[87] In spite of this initial reluctance, "problem-solving" has now become the preferred term internationally. Nevertheless, the resistance, if only initial and short-lived, is still telling. Even if the commonwealth preference for the more understated terminology did not win the day, the basic harm reduction philosophy remains in place.

The notion of harm reduction has several applications. Among the more unusual is found in Melbourne, Australia. Magistrate Jelena Popovic views the Tuesday afternoon prostitution court as functioning within a harm reduction philosophy. She explains that there are actually three types of sex workers in Melbourne: the higher-class call girls, the prostitutes who work in brothels, and those who ply their trade on the streets. Many of those working the streets have serious drug addiction problems, and they are the ones who most often find themselves before Popovic in the Tuesday afternoon list. From a harm reduction perspective, according to Popovic, it is a positive step to move offenders from the streets to the brothels because the brothels pose fewer dangers as it concerns matters of health and safety. This does not represent an endorsement of brothels, to be sure—only an acceptance that reduced exposure to the hazards of life on the streets is a preferable situation and thus a worthy if modest goal.

With respect to drug control policy in a general sense, a harm minimization philosophy is often invoked to support needle-exchange programs, a drug control strategy practiced in both commonwealth countries. Catherine Rynne, the first treatment coordinator of the Sydney drug court, speaks proudly of Australia's "needle and syringe exchange programs," which, according to Rynne, "have left us with one of the lowest rates of HIV infection among injecting drug users in the world." Similarly, the Canadian cities of Toronto and Vancouver both have needle-exchange programs. In fact, Vancouver even has what it calls a "harm reduction hotel," where addicts are provided with a "safe injection site."[88] Starting in 2005, two cities in Canada—Vancouver and Montreal—initiated heroin prescription programs, a harm reduction practice that was for many years a central feature of British drug control policy.[89]

The most common application of a harm reduction approach in Canadian and Australian drug courts is the use of methadone as a central component of treatment. This is contrasted with the U.S. preference for a total abstinence approach—including, often, abstinence from alcohol, cannabis, and methadone. As Bakht and Bentley observe, "Unlike most U.S. drug courts, the Toronto DTC [drug treatment court] incorporates methadone maintenance as part of its treatment arsenal for heroin addicts. The abstinence model of most U.S. courts does not permit the use of methadone."[90] Also more like England, Canada and Australia have public health systems, which, according to Catherine Rynne, is directly related to a harm reduction approach. As she puts it, "harm-minimization really is a public health approach." Because both counties are "welfare states" and have "universal health care," according to Rynne, the courts are able to offer a range of services without requiring participants to pay for treatment, as sometimes happens in U.S. programs.

A harm reduction philosophy also affects perceptions of what constitutes success. In both Canada and Australia, reduced use or reduced crime is regarded as a success. As a consequence, program graduation requirements tend to be less restrictive. As Libby Wood, magistrate of the Perth drug court, explains, "We don't expect participants to be totally drug free. . . . We do tolerate some cannabis use. And we do tolerate some prescription drugs."

Requirements in Canadian drug courts are likewise less demanding, as determined by a harm reduction philosophy. Bakht and Bentley once again highlight this quality of Canadian courts in direct contrast to U.S. drug court practices.

> In the U.S. almost all drug courts either prohibit or strongly discourage the use of both illegal drugs as well as alcohol by drug court participants. By way of contrast, in Toronto where participants have achieved a positive lifestyle change, have stopped using crack/cocaine, heroin and other non medically prescribed drugs and have at least one marijuana free urine, they may be permitted to complete Phase I of the program at the discretion of the DTC team.[91]

COMMONWEALTH CULTURE

In Canada and Australia, then, we find two commonwealth countries in which the legal theory of therapeutic jurisprudence has been more fully embraced than it has in the United Kingdom. Indeed, it is arguably the key vector, particularly in Australia, driving both the development of specialty problem-solving courts and changes in the judicial system more broadly. Concerning the latter, both countries appear to be pursuing the "going to scale" strategy articulated by personnel at New York's Center for Court Innovation. Curiously, though these commonwealth countries are distinct from England in their acceptance of therapeutic jurisprudence, Canadian and Australian judges still demonstrate the kind of judicial reserve that is more common among British judges. Indeed, the top-down initiation of the courts, judicial deference to legislative directives, and a harm reduction treatment mentality are all features of commonwealth programs that render them more like UK than U.S. problem-solving courts.

Unlike in the United Kingdom, however, judges and magistrates in Australian and Canadian problem-solving courts have been given more authority and discretion. They can, for example, impose short stints in jail as a form of sanction. Moreover, judges and magistrates are more typically involved in the ongoing monitoring of participants in their court-based programs. This is, of course, in part attributable to the absence of lay magistrates, who are, as we have seen, so central to the British criminal justice system. Even with this greater power, however, Australian and Canadian judges have been reluctant to push the envelope too far. That is, there is still a kind of cultural reserve that prevents these judges from emulating some of the more demonstrative and theatrical behaviors of American problem-solving court judges.

Repeatedly, Australian and Canadian magistrates, judges, and other officials involved with problem-solving courts identify the greater reticence and reserve in their culture as a quality clearly distinguishable from American cultural proclivities and concomitant courtroom practices. They do not view themselves as given to the kind of emotionalism and "theatricality" of American problem-solving courts; they see a greater affinity with British culture in this regard. As this gets played out in the courts, then, there is clearly less theater in Australian and Canadian problem-solving courts than there is in the American courts. However, as noted earlier, some courts in both countries allow applause. In both the Toronto and Sydney drug courts, moreover, judges have given prizes, such as tickets to sporting events, as rewards for successful compliance with court requirements. Even these practices, though, were at least initially applied with some reluctance. As Colleen Subir, a probation officer in the Sydney drug court, recalls, "The concept of clapping in court and rewards has been fairly alien to a somewhat conservative Anglo-Saxon culture, and we were pretty hesitant about the whole thing at first."

Judge Murrell of Sydney, though certainly more engaged with participants than she would be in a normal criminal court, still ran her drug court in a relatively formal manner. Like other Australian judges, she had traveled to the United States to see American problem-solving courts in action. Though she acknowledged differences in the practices of individual American judges, she put forth as a general comparison that "it is not the Australian way to be as demonstrative as that." She added that the Australian judge "is not so much a Personality with a capital *P* as some of the American judges are." She attributes this contrast to basic cultural differences. In a statement consistent with the claims of a number of Australian and Canadian judges, Murrell observed, "I think it's just part of our culture; we're a bit more British, I think." Jelena Popovic says much the same thing. Commenting on the theatrical behavior of American problem-solving court judges, she says, "That's crossing the line. . . . We wouldn't do that. . . . We've probably still got some of that British reticence."

One interesting example of reserve in this regard concerns the practice of hugging. Judge Murrell noted that, at drug court graduation ceremonies, the judge will give a certificate and shake the participant's hand, and the registrar might take a picture. According to Murrell, however, behavior as informal and intimate as hugging would be unequivocally beyond the pale in an Australian courtroom. She finds the very idea of it "quite appalling," and she believes her opinion to be universal among Australian judges. "I could not bring myself to do that, nor could any other Australian judge, I don't think," she admitted. That Murrell's sentiments on this matter reflect a strong aversion to such practices among Australians more generally is further illustrated by a curious legal case in Victoria.

Jelena Popovic, who, as noted earlier, is a strong proponent of therapeutic jurisprudence and problem-oriented court practices, was once accused by an Australian journalist of hugging two "drug traffickers she let walk free."[92] So serious was this allegation that Popovic sued Andrew Bolt, the author of the article, and the *Herald Sun*, the newspaper that published it, for "malicious defamation."[93] Before the Victorian Supreme Court, Popovic argued that she "did not hug the two drug traffickers, but shook their hands when handing them certificates for completing a court drug rehabilitation program."[94] The court found that Bolt "had seriously defamed" Popovic and awarded her nearly $250,000 in damages.[95] As Popovic explained in a later interview, so outrageous do Australians find such behavior that to be accused of hugging in court is a serious defamation of character. Given the sort of cultural disposition illustrated here, it is not surprising that Canadians and Australians would find objectionable overly theatrical and emotive behavior in the courtroom.

Thus, Canadian and Australian problem-solving courts more closely model the type of reserve found in British problem-solving courts, even if the two commonwealth countries have embraced a legal theory that is clearly a product of American culture. A defining feature of Canadian and Australian cultures that distinguishes these from both American and British culture, however, is the important place of aboriginal peoples. In the case of Australia, not only are aboriginal courts among the fastest-growing types of problem-solving courts, but deferential statements and public gestures toward indigenous people are commonplace. The public launch of the Neighbourhood Justice Centre in Melbourne, for example, began with a "smoking ceremony" presided over by Joy Wanda Murphy, a Wurundjeri elder. Murphy was also among the first speakers to address those attending the public opening of the court. Likewise, in public statements at a therapeutic jurisprudence conference in Western Australia, several speakers opened their talks by acknowledging the aboriginal people of the region.

Not surprisingly, each session of the Shepparton Koori court likewise begins with the magistrate acknowledging the Yorta Yorta and Bangerang people. Like the Neighbourhood Justice Centre, the Shepparton court was launched with a smoking ceremony, and the building is decorated with aboriginal art. The magistrate even wears a tie with aboriginal designs on it. The entire format of the court is meant to convey to defendants that their aboriginal heritage is respected and welcomed.

The relationship between aboriginal courts, therapeutic jurisprudence, and restorative justice is a bit complicated. As mentioned in chapter 2, the practice of circle sentencing among indigenous communities is often cited as one of the original sources of the development of restorative justice. The kind of interaction that occurs between Koori elders and defendants in Koori court proceedings is, in fact, offered as an example of "reintegrative shaming"—a central theme, as noted earlier, of restorative justice.[96] A magistrate of the Shepparton Koori court specifically describes his court as a "shame court." As discussed at the start of this chapter, there are overlapping themes between aboriginal courts and therapeutic jurisprudence. However, there are also cultural sensibilities conveyed in aboriginal courts that seem rather singular and are not logically commensurate with therapeutic sensibilities.

The Tsuu T'ina people in Alberta, Canada, for example, place a strong emphasis on respect for elders. Ellery Starlight, the peacemaker coordinator of the Tsuu T'ina court, spoke personally of his great respect for his uncle, and he noted that this kind of respect for elders is a strong and defining part of Tsuu T'ina culture. Similarly, dominant themes emphasized in Victorian Koori courts include respect for elders and a commitment to place. Thus, defendants are commonly asked by elders in court, "Who are your people?" and "Where are you from?" The magistrate of the Shepparton court explains, "The elder wants to make the connection with the people first and the land next." Such inquiries make a connection. "And for Kooris that is like a lock. That gets their attention, and then demands their respect." The magistrate, therefore, often lets the elders do a lot of the talking.

At a Koori court session in Shepparton, an elder asked a male defendant whether he talks to his elders and urged him to show respect to his grandfather, who "as an elder should be respected. You young people have to show him respect." The same elder told another Koori defendant: "In the aboriginal community, we always look to extended family." He noted specifically that he knew the defendant's mother and grandparents: "You've got a great mother and I know her parents. They are good people, hardworking. They are community people." He then added, "Your grand-parents come from where I come from. It's the womb that we all come from." So important is the Koori sense of place that it was among the principles highlighted by Koori communities at the launch of the Koori court. The Aboriginal Community Code of Conduct includes such state-ments as "all Aboriginal people shall respect the land" and "all Aborigi-nal people shall take care [of] and nurture the environment."[97]

Such themes are not what typically come to mind when one considers the defining tenets of the therapeutic ethos, an orientation that tends in-stead to emphasize individual health and well-being and gives less atten-tion to such themes as respect for elders and sense of place. The aboriginal emphases on community and "reintegration" or "peacemaking," in this regard, more closely approximate restorative justice themes. As discussed in chapter 2, the neglect of traditional justice principles may be less likely in the case of restorative justice, as compared to therapeutic jurispru-dence. As such, there may well be a relationship between the flourishing of aboriginal courts in Australia and Canada and the checks against viola-tions of open and natural justice found in the problem-solving courts of these two commonwealth countries.

In other words, the pressing influences of aboriginal themes—along with greater reserve in the culture more broadly, deference to the legisla-tive and executive branches of government, critical reflection on innova-tive practices, and a harm reduction treatment philosophy—are among the features of the Australian and Canadian legal "accents" that perhaps help to prevent overt neglect of traditional due process concerns—or as the Australians put it, departure from natural and open justice. Whether such resistance can be sustained, particularly in light of these two coun-tries' comparatively warm embrace of therapeutic jurisprudence, remains to be seen. In the next chapter we turn to two areas of the world where therapeutic jurisprudence has received a much cooler reception.

Chapter Five

DEVOLUTION AND DIFFERENCE:

SCOTLAND AND IRELAND

> The Scottish system has used to great effect the evolutionary
> features of the drug treatment court, whilst studiously and
> rather cleverly leaving the revolutionary ones aside.
> —*Philip Bean*

W ITH an affinity similar to that found between the two commonwealth countries considered in the last chapter, Ireland
and Scotland are a natural pair. Both countries established
their first problem-solving courts in the same year, with the launch of the
Dublin and Glasgow drug courts in 2001. Six years later, both countries
announced plans to start community courts in the same two cities, modeled after community courts in New York and Liverpool. Problem-solving
courts in Scotland and Ireland have progressed at a pace slower than that
of the four other countries considered in this study. As of 2007 only a
handful of problem-solving courts were operating in Scotland, and only
one—the Dublin drug court—was operating in Ireland.

Moreover, these two small countries in the British Isles have often
looked to each other in the formation of their courts, recognizing that
they have similar cultures and legal habits. As an official with the Glasgow
drug court explained, "Ireland and Scotland have very similar cultures."
In her view, then, it made sense for Scottish officials to visit Dublin and
for Irish officials to visit Glasgow. In reference to such visits, she said,
"We learned a few things from Dublin, and I'm sure Dublin saw how we
did things and it affected their practice." She even held that, given their
similar cultures and legal practices, it made more sense for Scottish officials to go to Ireland than to the United States. "It'd be better and closer
to go to Dublin than to go across the Atlantic, where the culture is just
so different . . . and the laws are so different as well." Contrastingly, "laws
are going to be roughly the same between Scotland and Ireland," and the
cultures are "definitely very, very similar." Therefore, "it makes sense for
us to go there."

Thus, in Scotland and Ireland, as in Canada and Australia, one finds
something of a disinclination to borrow—or at least to be seen as bor-

rowing—a U.S. legal product wholesale. In the process of transplanting problem-solving courts, the influences of other countries besides (or in addition to) the United States are often highlighted, even while the U.S. origins of these courts are acknowledged (if sometimes only reluctantly). Another feature of Irish and Scottish problem-solving courts is not only a certain distancing from the United States, but a marked wariness toward England as well. Particularly in Scotland, where the spirit and institutional realities of devolution have had important political and legal consequences, one often detects a strong inclination to underscore the differences rather than the similarities between Scottish and English practices, legal and otherwise.

As with the other non-U.S. countries considered here, Irish and Scottish problem-solving court practices reveal a greater judicial reserve than is found in the United States. However, unlike the commonwealth countries examined in chapter 4, Ireland and Scotland have not embraced therapeutic jurisprudence as a guiding legal philosophy for the development of these courts. More like England, then, Ireland and Scotland have borrowed problem-solving legal practices from the United States but have not accepted the concomitant theory that so significantly informs courts in the United States, Canada, and Australia.

IRISH PROBLEM-SOLVING COURTS

What most obviously sets Ireland apart from the five other countries explored in this study is that as of 2007, Ireland had only one problem-solving court in operation: the Dublin drug court, which began as a pilot project in January 2001. As noted earlier, plans to launch a community court in Dublin were announced in April 2007. In both instances, the United States was the source of inspiration for the borrowing (or proposed borrowing) of these legal innovations. In the case of the Dublin drug court, the process of legal transplantation started in October 1997, when the Working Group on a Courts Commission, chaired by Irish Supreme Court judge Susan Denham, initiated a study of the American drug court model. As part of this study, several American officials, including Judge Patrick Morris of the drug court in San Bernardino, California, traveled to Dublin in January 1998 to discuss with Irish officials the possible exportation of drug courts to the Irish legal system. Then, in February 1998, the working group issued a report recommending the implementation of a drug court in Dublin.

The report made numerous references to the U.S. drug court experience, and included a letter sent by Judge Morris after his visit to Dublin. In the letter, addressed to Judge Denham, Morris suggested that the Irish choose their first drug court judge "with great care."[1] In a manner consistent with the activist qualities common among American problem-solving court judges, Morris advised the Irish to select a judge who is "willing to leave the bench and enter the community in order to educate and build public support for this new model of jurisprudence."[2] Morris also recommended that the judge and support team "travel to the United States for education and training"[3]—advice, in this instance, that the Irish followed. During the long planning stage of the Dublin drug court, Judge Gerard Haughton (who would become Ireland's first drug court judge) traveled to Judge Morris's court in San Bernardino. He also visited drug courts in Sydney and Perth, Australia. Another Irish judge, Desmond Hogan, visited Paul Bentley's drug court in Toronto. In addition to making these international visits to individual drug courts, Irish judges and drug court team members have, on a number of occasions, attended the annual NADCP conferences in the United States.

In his letter to Judge Denham, Judge Morris also recommended that the Irish move forward quickly and not let the planning process take too long.

> Don't let the planning process drag on. Set yourselves a tight planning time line and stick to it. I would suggest six months for planning and training, with a late summer or early fall start-up of your pilot drug court. The mantra of drug court judges in America is 'JUST DO IT!'"[4]

This advice the Irish clearly did not follow. Instead of taking six months (as Judge Morris counseled), it was another three years before the Dublin pilot drug court finally began. The delay was due in part to the careful and deliberative manner in which the Irish planned their drug court. A year after the 1998 publication of the working group's report, the Irish minister of justice, John O'Donoghue, established the drug court planning committee, made up of nearly two dozen representatives from a range of departments and agencies, including the judiciary, the police, probation, welfare, health, and education.

The size and complexity of the committee are indicative of the Irish view that it was important for the various stakeholders to have a voice in the planning and development of the court. According to Judge Desmond Hogan, who chaired the planning committee, each of the various representatives had "their own ideas," and "each fought their own corner and fought it hard and fought it well." To illustrate the difficulty of reconciling so many divergent views, Hogan joked, "It must be borne in mind that the definition of a camel is 'a horse designed by committee.'" After meeting for approximately six months, the planning committee reached a "working compromise" and, in August 1999, issued its own report. The report, among other things, recommended the establishment of a smaller steering committee to "plan the actual implementation of the pilot project."[5]

In addition to allowing for the lengthy planning processes of committee work, the Irish were also careful to secure commitments from the services that would be working with the court before moving forward. In other words, instead of adopting the American "just do it" style, the Irish took the time to ensure that the various contributing resources and agencies were in place before launching the Dublin drug court. As Judge Haughton asserted in 1999, "We are not prepared to start until we have the services that we need, because that would be a sure recipe for failure." Judge Hogan agreed that in spite of the "vibes that we are getting from America" to "start as quickly as we can," the Irish first "want the services to be there, so that we don't shoot ourselves in the foot and become self-defeating."

Even the pilot project, meant to last eighteen months, continued much longer than expected. After the project's launch in January 2001, it was not until February 2006 that the Irish Courts Service announced that the drug court would become permanent and be expanded "on a phased basis" to serve all of the Dublin metropolitan area.[6] Thus, five years after the launch of the pilot program, and nearly a decade after the working group's initial study of drug courts, Ireland's single problem-solving court became an established feature of the Irish criminal justice system. Contrast this with the United States, where, ten years after the establishment of the Dade County drug court, nearly five hundred drug courts were in operation. Clearly, the Irish proceeded in a slower, more cautious, and more deliberative manner.

Though they did not follow the American model in terms of the speed with which they implemented a drug court, the Irish nevertheless looked to the American experience for guidance throughout the process. When the steering committee began its work in 2000 it did so, as Judge Haughton recalls, "armed with the San Bernardino Drug Court Participants' handbook" and "a reasonable knowledge of the American drug court model as a starting point in our deliberations." American courts would also serve as the model for the planning of a second Irish problem-solving court.

In April 2007, Ireland's National Crime Council issued a report recommending the establishment of Ireland's second problem-solving court, a community court in Dublin. The process leading to the publication of this report again reveals a careful and deliberative style of legal innovation. Irish officials were first made aware of the community court concept in a presentation made by Julias Lang, of the Center for Court Innovation, to the Dublin City Business Association (DCBA). Tom Coffey, the chief executive officer of the DCBA, is also a member of the National Crime

Council, as is Michael Reilly, the Irish judge who chairs the council's Criminal Justice System Subgroup. Following Lang's presentation, Judge Reilly asked the subgroup to investigate the community court model and consider the feasibility of launching one in Dublin. The subgroup began its work in September 2006 and engaged in a thorough process of study, consultation, and deliberation.

This group's work included sending Irish officials to observe community courts in the United States. In 2006, a delegation of Irish officials visited community courts in Red Hook, Midtown, and Philadelphia. Two months later, they visited the Liverpool Community Justice Centre in England. In addition to observing court processes, officials asked "detailed questions in relation to the operation of the Court and other services of the relevant staff."[7] Following these visits and the analysis of additional related information, the subgroup carefully discussed the relevance and applicability of the community court model to Ireland. As described in the report, this "thorough deliberation process . . . allowed for the development and refinement of the subgroup's thinking and for the final proposals in relation to the introduction of Community Courts in Ireland to be agreed by the Council."[8]

Reminiscent of the extended prelaunch phase of the Dublin drug court, the council recommended the establishment of an "implementation group" and the hiring of a project manager to oversee and guide the introduction of Dublin's community court. The council recommended further that the court "be open within six months of the appointment of the Project Manager."[9] If the time required to introduce the Dublin drug court is any indication, the process is likely to last longer than six months.

SCOTTISH PROBLEM-SOLVING COURTS

Scotland's first problem-solving court—the Glasgow drug court—was launched in October 2001, nine months after the start of the Irish drug court. Less than a year later, in August 2002, a second Scottish drug court was started in Fife. The Fife drug court actually operates in two towns: Kirkcaldy and Dunfermline, located just north of Edinburgh, across the Firth of Forth. A single dedicated sheriff handles the drug courts in both locations. As in Ireland, the first Scottish drug court was started after a lengthy process of planning and deliberation. In December 1999, the Convention of Scottish Local Authorities (COSLA) submitted a report to the Scottish Executive recommending new approaches to handling drug offenders, including elements of the U.S. drug court model. Following this, COSLA cosponsored a conference at the Scottish Police College at Tulliallan Castle, outside of Stirling, in April 2000 to consider international experiences with drug courts. Among those invited to speak at the conference were Jeffry Tauber, then president of the NADCP, and Paul Bentley, Canada's first drug court judge.

After the conference, Justine Walker, COSLA's local government drugs officer, was commissioned to visit the United States to investigate and report on the U.S. drug court movement. Walker visited the United States in May and June of 2000, where she attended an NADCP conference in San Francisco, observed four California drug courts, and interviewed a number of U.S. drug court officials. The Central Research Unit of the Scottish Executive published Walker's findings in early 2001. Shortly after publication of the report, Iain Gray, then Scottish deputy minister of justice, established a working group to make proposals for the initiation of drug courts in Scotland. Like Ireland's working group, the Scottish committee was composed of representatives from a variety of disciplines and agencies.

The group met from February to April 2001. Using Justine Walker's report as a starting point, it also examined research and evaluations related to drug courts not only in the United States but also in England, Ireland, Australia, and Canada. The working group's report, issued in May 2001, recommended the establishment of a pilot drug court in Glasgow that could operate within existing legislation, including the UK-wide DTTO scheme considered in chapter 3 (the national rollout of which included Scotland). Scotland's DTTO pilot schemes, both of which began their first orders in 2000, were in fact located in Glasgow and Fife. The working group's report envisaged a Scottish drug court program that would use and build upon DTTOs, thus establishing them as an integrated feature of Scotland's drug courts.

It should be noted that, while England eventually abandoned DTTOs when their essential function was subsumed under the larger Community Order scheme in the form of DRRs, Scotland found DTTOs more successful and useful. More than once, Scottish officials highlighted Scotland's positive experience with DTTOs as something that set the country's work apart from the less successful effort of their English neighbors "down south." Not only were DTTOs used as a central component of Scotland's drug courts, but they were rolled out in all areas of Scotland in October 2003, the same year that Westminster passed legislation that would eventually scrap DTTOs in England and Wales. Recall from chapter 3 that DTTOs do not give the judiciary the authority to impose intermediate sanctions, an important difference between programs in England and those in the United States. Recognizing this limitation, the working group's report recommended passage of additional legislation that would enable the Scottish drug court to "impose an increased range of sanctions for positive drug tests and other compliance infractions whilst enabling the treatment order to continue."[10] Legislation allowing the imposition of interim sanctions finally did make its way through the Scottish parliament in 2003.[11] However, as will be discussed more fully later on in this chapter, Scottish sheriffs remain somewhat reluctant to use these sanctions.

As was the case in Ireland, the pilot phase of the Scottish drug courts lasted much longer than expected. Not until March 2006 did the Scottish Executive finally announce that the Glasgow and Fife drug courts would continue beyond the initial pilot period. In both Ireland and Scotland, then, the pilot phases of the first problem-solving courts—the Glasgow and Dublin drug courts—lasted a total of five years, illustrating the cautious and judicious nature of legal innovation in both countries.

A second type of problem-solving court was initiated in Scotland on October 18, 2004. The Glasgow domestic abuse court, like the Dublin and Glasgow drug courts, was launched after a comprehensive process of study and consultation. In fact, the planning and implementation of this particular court involved the preparatory work of *three* separate groups: a steering group, comprising representatives from the judiciary, prosecution (Procurator Fiscal), police, social work, and women's support services; a smaller working group focused on the practical implementation of the court; and another working group focused on "support to victims."[12] The steering group studied a number of programs internationally, including the Duluth model in the United States. The group paid particular attention to the first wave of domestic violence courts in England and Wales.[13] According to Sheriff Susan Raeburn, who chaired the implementation working group and was one of Scotland's first domestic abuse court sheriffs, the steering group was particularly impressed with the program in Cardiff, Wales.

Given this focus on other UK programs, it is not surprising that the Glasgow domestic abuse court would assume a more exclusively prosecutorial and less therapeutic orientation, especially in terms of its approach to defendants. In an apparent allusion to American courts, Scottish officials discovered in their preliminary research that some domestic violence courts "take a very specific therapeutic, problem-solving, preventive and/or restorative approach with perpetrators and victims."[14] However, this was not to be the focus of the Glasgow court. Instead, the program came to focus on a "streamlined and enhanced prosecution of cases," including such aims as increasing the number of guilty pleas and convictions.[15] As with the other UK domestic violence courts, most of the additional services provided in the multiagency approach are offered to the victims rather than to the defendants. In fact, £400,000 was made available to ASSIST (Advice, Support, Safety, and Information Services Together), the victim support agency serving the Glasgow domestic abuse court.[16]

Comparatively fewer resources have been dedicated to the rehabilitation of defendants. Any rehabilitative services for the accused have been provided, if at all, in the context of a probation order. An evaluation of the Glasgow domestic abuse court reveals that in its first two years of operation, 73 cases required attendance at CHANGE, a program aimed at "re-educating" domestic violence offenders.[17] This cognitive-behavioral program was itself developed through the study of three programs in the United States, including the Duluth program. With 332 total case disposals during this period, the 73 referrals to CHANGE represent only 7 percent of all disposals in the Glasgow domestic abuse court. Contrast this to the 18 percent (or 179 cases) that received straight prison sentences.[18] The absence of a more therapeutic orientation is also evident in the content of the CHANGE program, which, like programs in other parts of the UK, places more emphasis on a gender-based "power and control" model than on a therapeutic type of rehabilitation. Consider the following description of the essential focus of the CHANGE program:

> The perspective which CHANGE adopts on male violence is that it is intentional, albeit not always conscious, behavior that men use to maintain power and to control women in intimate relationships. It stems from the historic and cultural legacy of patriarchy whereby men are socialized into believing they are superior to and have rights over women.[19]

Even with only 7 percent of all disposals requiring participation in CHANGE, the court has had difficulty staffing these assignments. By the end of the two-year pilot period, offenders in the Glasgow domestic abuse court had to wait six months to participate in a CHANGE program.[20] Thus, both the content and limited availability of services for defendants reveal that the therapeutic rehabilitation of defendants is not a central priority of the court. As in England and Wales, more important is the speedy and successful prosecution of the accused and the provision of support and resources for victims. Also as with domestic violence courts in other parts of the United Kingdom, ongoing judicial monitoring is not a central feature of the program, though Sheriff Raeburn acknowledges that on occasion she will creatively include reviews for a defendant through a concomitant DTTO order or the deferral of a concurrent charge.

A third type of problem-solving court in Scotland, however, does involve more judicial monitoring. Scottish youth courts for sixteen- and seventeen-year-old (and in some cases fifteen-year-old) persistent offenders were introduced in two towns east of Glasgow—in Hamilton in June 2003 and in Airdrie in June 2004. As explained by Richard Simpson, deputy minister for justice, during parliamentary debate in June 2002, the idea for youth courts was inspired by the drug court model: "Drug courts are proving to be successful at the pilot stage, which is why we are considering their adoption as a model for youth courts."[21] Several months after Simpson's statement, a project group was established to "determine the feasibility of youth courts" in Scotland.[22] Like groups involved in the development of other problem-solving courts in Ireland and Scotland, the project group comprised some two dozen stakeholders from a variety of agencies who met between August and December of 2002 to explore, plan, and consider the implementation of new youth courts in Scotland.

In what appears to be a common practice among these sorts of groups in Ireland and Scotland, the committee studied related programs internationally, in addition to looking at the "formation and operation of the Glasgow and Fife drug courts" in Scotland.[23] The group also necessarily considered the proposed development of new youth courts against the backdrop of the Scottish Children's Hearing System, a diversion program for troubled youth under sixteen years of age, which was established in 1971.[24] Children's hearings share some of the features of problem-solving courts—and thus, on one level, represent something of a precursor to Scottish problem-solving courts. They are, for example, nonadversarial, informal in style, and aimed at addressing the needs and problems of "children in difficulty." However, as a diversion program run by panels of three laypeople, children's hearings do not fall under the direct purview of a judge or sheriff, and therefore do not alter (or threaten to alter) the format and style of criminal court processes. Interestingly, Scottish youth courts were initiated in conjunction with efforts to "fast track," and thus strengthen and make more effective, children's hearings for persistent young offenders.[25]

In any respect, the feasibility project group published its report in December 2002, and, as noted earlier, the first two Scottish youth courts were launched on a pilot basis in 2003 and 2004. Based on the "broadly positive" account conveyed in a 2006 evaluation of the Airdrie and Hamilton youth courts, the Scottish Executive decided to increase the number of youth courts. In November 2006, Justice Minister Cathy Jamieson announced plans to establish three more youth courts in Kilmarnock, Paisely, and Dundee.[26] Like Scottish drug courts, these youth courts include a multiagency approach, the availability of a range of resources, the potential use of a variety of disciplinary sanctions, and the possibility for ongoing judicial monitoring by the sheriff. However, as will be discussed more fully later on, sheriffs use the reviews in a more limited, less personal, and less therapeutic fashion.

Plans for the initiation of a fourth type of problem-solving court in Scotland were announced in 2007. In this case, one again finds a willingness to take the time necessary to set up the court in a careful and unhurried manner. The Scottish Executive indicated that it would likely start the Glasgow community court in 2009 and anticipated an initial cost of £5 to £7 million, plus another £1.5 to £2 million in annual operational costs. In this case, as in others, considerable preliminary research and discussion preceded the announcement. As noted in a March 2007 press release issued by the Scottish Executive:

> There are a number of community justice centres/community courts already in operation, including Midtown and Red Hook in New York and in North Liverpool. The project team members have studied research on these courts, met the judge from Red Hook and visited North Liverpool. The Justice Minister also visited Midtown Community Court in New York in 2004.[27]

This background information reveals not only that the Scottish government took time to study the community court concept, but also that it recognizes the United States as the source of inspiration for the model. However, here, as elsewhere, one finds the customary qualification: "The Glasgow centre will be based on both these [existing community courts] but adapted to suit the needs of the Scottish criminal justice system and local community."[28]

ADAPTING THE AMERICAN MODEL

In Scotland and Ireland, then, we again find that importers of problem-solving courts see themselves as adapting the transplanted program to suit their own local needs. Recall a prototypical example of this perspective cited in chapter 2. It was Judge Hogan, speaking of importing courts from the United States to Ireland, who explained that "in the natural order of things, you tailor the program to what suits you best"—that adjustments are necessary to "make the suit fit us." Dublin's first drug court judge, Gerard Haughton, similarly argued that the American model "needed to be modified to suit the particular circumstances in Dublin."[29]

The Scottish likewise view the American models as requiring important adjustments in order to work in Scotland. Discussions about drug courts in 1999–2000 Scottish parliamentary debates offer an interesting window into this perspective. The discussions reveal a cognizance among the Scottish not only of significant cultural differences between the United States and Scotland but also of devolution's important role in the development of problem-solving courts in Scotland. In fact, Scottish problem-solving courts have shown themselves to be integrally and interestingly related to devolution from the very beginning of the transplantation process. Moira Price, coordinator of the Glasgow drug court team, goes so far as to argue that "the very fact that we have drug courts at all is an element of devolution." Sheriff Matthews likewise notes that with "our own legislature, we can pass our own laws. With our own minister of justice . . . there is far more direct involvement of what's going on in the courts." Matthews regards this devolved arrangement as directly fostering (or at least speeding) the development of Scottish problem-solving courts: "So I think that the devolution process has helped us to set up these new disposals."

Following the electoral victory of Tony Blair's New Labour government in 1997, Scotland voted in favor of devolution, a process Blair had endorsed during his campaign. Elections to the new Scottish Parliament then took place in May 1999. As noted earlier, there was also at this time growing interest in the American drug court model among Scottish officials generally, including those in the Labour Party. However, the Scottish National Party (SNP), which has been a driving force behind efforts to achieve full Scottish independence, included an endorsement of drug courts in its election manifesto. Without specifically naming the United States, the manifesto observed that "drug courts have been successful in a number of other countries," adding that "we will adapt them to best suit our own legal system and social work structure."[30] The SNP endorsement of drug courts created a delicate political situation in which those outside the SNP became somewhat reluctant to speak favorably of drug courts (a reticence they gradually overcame after the elections).

Scottish members of Parliament eventually took up drug courts as a matter of policy interest in the new Scottish Parliament. It was Roseanna Cunningham, a member of the then minority SNP, who first spoke of "drugs courts" (in September 1999), noting that "the SNP has talked about drugs courts as a way of tackling drug-related crime."[31] Cunningham raised the issue of drug courts again in January 2000, when two government ministers were present (Angus MacKay, the Labour Party's deputy minister of justice at the time, and Iain Gray, then deputy minster of health, who would become deputy minister of justice in November 2000). This time she observed that drug courts "are beginning to spring up in many countries," including "the USA, Canada, and Australia." In an apparent effort to chide the Labour officials present, Cunningham added, "This particular minister [Angus MacKay] has apparently gone on record as saying that he believed that the American system could not be used in Scotland's current judicial set-up." Though MacKay attempted to rise when Cunningham spoke, it was Iain Gray who eventually responded to Cunningham. He explained that the Scottish Executive had looked at evaluations of American drug courts but felt that the DTTOs being piloted in Glasgow and Fife "strip out the most effective aspects of the drug courts in a way that is appropriate to our legal system."[32]

The Labour Party's reluctance to publicly endorse drug courts finally gave way later in 2000. This was in part attributable to a visit by Angus

MacKay to a New York drug court, where he had the opportunity to observe the court in operation and "discuss the working of the court with the presiding judge." In May of 2000, MacKay announced during parliamentary debate that "we, too, are now considering more noncustodial alternatives." In response, Cunningham could not help but point out that "the Scottish National Party has been arguing for such courts in Scotland" and was pleased to observe that MacKay had evidently become "a convert to that policy." Though perhaps a convert, MacKay recognized that the American model would have to be significantly adjusted to fit the Scottish context. He told the following story about his time in the New York drug court:

> Members will be interested to know that at the conclusion of one individual's 18 months in rehabilitation through the drug court, the judge left the bench in order, I thought, to shake hands with the woman concerned. Instead he gave her a large hug. There were many tears all around.

Taken aback by this behavior, MacKay added, "It is perhaps difficult to imagine Scottish judges and sheriffs engaging in such activity."[33] An important lesson that MacKay learned from his time in New York was that some elements of the American drug court would work in Scotland, and some clearly would not.

> I saw many things in the United States. I saw five or six excellent ideas and initiatives, not all of which can be replicated in the Scottish criminal justice system or in our other departmental set-ups, but the approach of the drug courts bears further examination, and we are actively considering how we can take the best elements of that system and incorporate them in our Scottish justice system.[34]

In November of 2000, during the lengthiest discussion on drug courts in the Scottish Parliament to date, the issue of adaptation was a central theme. Once again, Roseanna Cunningham led off the discussion. She communicated her delight that the Scottish Executive had publicly embraced the idea of drug courts at last, and she was careful once again to point out that the SNP had been championing the drug court model for some time—something she believed the Labour Party had not sufficiently acknowledged. In his belated support of drug courts, Iain Gray again underscored the need for adaptation. He maintained: "It would be too easy to believe that the American system could be picked up and transferred wholesale to Scotland—our legal system, traditions and culture must be respected."[35]

Another Scottish Member of Parliament (SMP), Lyndsay McIntosh, from the Conservative Party, made a similar point during the discussion. McIntosh had attended the COSLA conference held outside of Stirling in April. At the conference, NADCP president Jeffrey Tauber had played a number of video clips of American drug courts in action. The clips showed the graduation ceremonies, prize-giving, and courtroom applause for which the American drug courts are famous, as well as an ABC news story that included favorable testimonies about drug courts from actors Martin Sheen and Charlie Sheen. Recalling these videos, McIntosh said, "I do not know whether the minister has seen some of the material that is available on the subject, but I look forward with glee to the adjustments that he will have to make to take account of cultural differences. People who have seen the video tapes of U.S. drug courts will know exactly what I mean."[36]

RETICENCE AND RESERVE

Conveyed in McIntosh's statement is a belief that Scots would, unquestionably, regard the more theatrical and expressive qualities of American drug courts as inappropriate for their culture. In her view, a Scottish person need only see a video clip of an American drug court in action to immediately and intuitively recognize the need for cultural adjustment. Greater caution and reserve is, of course, a theme that also emerged in our examination of England, Canada, and Australia. In Ireland and Scotland, one finds similarities both in the ways the courts are set up and in the manner in which judges and other officials conduct themselves in the courtroom. What may distinguish Scotland and, to a lesser degree, Ireland from the other non-U.S. cases is a greater awareness of American cultural differences and of the importance of keeping the influence of those foreign elements at bay.

Irish and Scottish importers of problem-solving courts are particularly concerned with the behavior of American judges. Recall Australian judge Murrell's observations about the larger-than-life personalities of American judges. Officials from Ireland and Scotland observe the same propensity among American judges and note its contrast to what they regard as the more acceptable behavior of judges in their own countries. Dublin's Judge Hogan, for example, observes, "We don't have the idea of a judge going off on an ego trip here. It strikes me that there's perhaps the possibility for that in America." Moira Price likewise notes the way in which American problem-solving court judges "sit on the bench as personalities, almost personalities more than judges." She contrasts this with the Scottish drug court experience, in which the court is still "very much bound by the law and procedures," and sheriffs "are not imposing their personalities on the way the court is run."

Particularly in Scotland, officials see these differences in courtroom behavior as having everything to do with culture. As Moira Price puts it, "I
think it is mainly a cultural thing that sets it apart." Sheriff Hugh Matthews, one of Scotland's first drug court judges, explicitly argues that "the
manner in which the courts operate depends not only on the legal system
but on cultural factors."[37] Of Scottish culture more generally, Matthews
observes, "We don't have [high school] graduation ceremonies. We don't
throw our hats up in the air. We don't tend to discuss our feelings in
Scotland. We don't hug each other. It's just not part of our culture." He
notes further that the Scottish people are not nearly as expressive as
Americans. "Americans generally are much more able to express themselves than Scottish people are. . . . We're not very good at expressing our
emotions or our feelings."

Speaking specifically about the prospect of applauding clients for success in the drug court program, Matthews states unequivocally, "We don't
go in for that kind of thing." Again, they do not, according to this Scottish
sheriff, because it is not the type of people they are. "We're not overblown
in the way we applaud people or discuss feelings and make speeches. It
just gets embarrassing." Moira Price offers a similar assessment of her
home country: "We as a nation do not push ourselves forward. . . . We're
not personalities. We are all quite reserved." Scottish problem-solving
courts reflect this cultural disposition. In the courts, therefore, overly emotional behavior is viewed as beyond the pale. As Sheriff Raeburn puts it,
"I don't think there's really any room for any judge being emotional in
any part of their job. In my view, it's quite inappropriate." She sees this
emotional restraint as "one of the differences" between Scottish and
American problem-solving courts. Because the court has the power to
"send people to jail," she says it is important that it be "a formal court"
with "no nonsense in it." Raeburn's reflections here demonstrate not only
a certain cultural reserve, but also a concern about limiting state power
and protecting the rights of individual defendants—a consideration, as
we will see, that distinguishes Scotland not only from the United States
but from Ireland as well.

With respect to "nonsense" in the courtroom, Raeburn reveals what
she may mean by this in a discussion about rewards for successful participants. One reward used in the Glasgow drug court is a reduction in the
number of urinalysis tests the client is required to take. Raeburn contrasts
this with rewards offered in American drug courts. "They're not like
the sort of American award system, you know—getting money off your
drug court fees, or McDonald's vouchers, or teddy bears (as we know
about), or an extra hug from the judge," she explains. "We don't do any
of these things." In fact, the 2006 evaluation of the Glasgow and Fife
drug courts highlights the challenge to identify "culturally appropriate

rewards" and observes that such awards have been largely limited to shrieval "encouragement and praise" to communicate "the court's approval for progress made."[38]

Scottish cultural tendencies also directly affect drug court graduation ceremonies, or the lack thereof. Because Scots do not "tend to make a big deal of show about something," says Moira Price, graduation ceremonies are not as common or as important in Scotland as they are in the United States. As Price notes, "We've never had a graduation ceremony in the [Glasgow] drug court at all." Instead, when an order comes to a successful end, the sheriff will summarize the defendant's progress, thank him for his efforts, and wish him well in the future.[39] The 2006 evaluation of the Scottish drug courts offered the following as typical of a drug court sheriff's closing words: "I'm very pleased. I propose to end your Order today. You've worked very hard. Thanks very much for your efforts, they are appreciated."[40] Sheriff Matthews's closing remarks to a participant—who had earned an early revocation of his order in the summer of 2003—followed this basic pattern and tone. "Everybody is extraordinarily pleased with your progress," Matthews said. "You've been off drugs for fourteen months. You're an example to others that it can be done. You've earned an early revocation." The moment passed quickly. There was no applause, no fanfare, no tearful testimonies, no "overblown" ceremony.

Again, as Sheriff Matthews asserts, Scottish problem-solving court practices are determined by both legal and cultural factors. As such, even when the law may allow more activist and expressive actions by judges, cultural factors are still so binding as to prevent this type of behavior. Consider two further examples in this regard. As noted earlier, the initial working group for the Scottish drug court recommended that the court be given the power to impose intermediate sanctions—a judicial power common in the United States but absent in DTTO programs throughout the United Kingdom. Legislation was eventually passed in 2003 that gave Scottish drug court sheriffs the power to impose interim sanctions. The legislation specifically gave Scottish drug court sheriffs the authority to impose either a short prison sentence or community service as a sanction for noncompliance with an order. Interestingly, in both cases, the Scottish Parliament established upper limits for these sanctions: no more than twenty-eight days in prison or no more than forty hours of community service in *total* sanctions for an individual offender on an order.[41]

Even with this power, however, Scottish sheriffs have been reluctant to impose a short-term prison sentence. Nearly two years after the statute first authorized interim sanctions, a group of Scottish sheriffs said they had rarely used it. In fact, at that time, only one claimed he had imposed a prison sentence. Interestingly, he did not justify his imposition of a short jail term by employing therapeutic nomenclature (e.g., calling it "shock

therapy"), as sometimes occurs among American drug court practitioners. Instead, he described the action as a punishment that the defendant deserved. "It's just a judgment call," he said. "You feel that they
deserve punishment that will hopefully make them think, and they'll come
back in a better condition to deal with the order, but they need a punishment. They have just overstepped the mark."

Reasons offered for not imposing such interim sanctions are similar to
those offered for placing statutory limits on them. In explaining why the
prison sentences were limited to a total of twenty-eight days, one drug
court sheriff explained, "If there's no limit, I can end up giving the guy
his jail sentence, and at the same time giving him the alternative, and I
think it would be unfair." In such a scenario, he feared the defendant
would, in effect, be "punished twice for the same conduct." Limiting the
number of days of imprisonment prevents the possibility of such double
punishment. Other reasons offered by sheriffs for not imposing interim
sanctions include the expense of jail; the fact that participants are not
only exposed to drugs in jail but even targeted because they are known
to be on a drug court order; and the belief that because most of the offenders in the Scottish drug court are "high-tariff" offenders, jail is not much
of a deterrent anyway. Thus, for a variety of reasons, even though Scottish
sheriffs have been given legislatively approved authority to impose short
stints in jail, they typically resist using this power.

A second example of the manner in which judges show relative reserve,
even when they are legally able (or even encouraged) to be more active,
is found in the Scottish youth courts. Modeled on drug court processes,
youth court review hearings were envisaged to be a central part of the
new program for persistent young offenders. When Airdrie and Hamilton
were selected as sites for the new pilot programs, sheriffs were encouraged
to be more interactive with defendants in the context of reviews. The
sheriffs, however, were not particularly keen to engage defendants in this
way. A sheriff from the Airdrie youth court, for example, said that he did
not think it was "a terribly great idea" to get to know the defendants. He
noted that he had been encouraged to "be a bit more interactive with the
accused," but he was not entirely comfortable with such a style. "There
may come a day," he said, "when you have to send them to jail, because
they might not be cooperating. They might not be doing what they are
supposed to be doing." He reiterated that he did not think it was "really
part of the judge's job to get too close to the accused."

Given these sentiments, it is not surprising that an evaluation of the
Airdrie and Hamilton youth courts found that the reviews were rather
staid and formal in style. As indicated in the evaluation, sheriffs were
"keen to emphasize that the convening of reviews" was not to be "con-
strued as a mechanism to build rapport with the young person." Instead,

"communication between Sheriffs and young people was generally described by other professionals as minimal, with most business being conducted through defense agents." In the reviews, "young people spoke rarely and often appeared awkward in doing so."[42] In both the Scottish drug courts and youth courts, then, we find that though sheriffs are given legislative authority to act in a more engaged and proactive manner, a sort of reserve and restraint remains due to cultural sensibilities militating against such behavior.

A similar type of reticence can be found among the Irish judges. In reference to discussions about physical contact, for example, Judge Hogan said he would not even "raise the specter ... of people being hugged," adding that "we don't even hug each other, never mind hug the client." Moreover, as noted earlier, the Irish were among the most critical observers of the American judges' activist orientation. One area of judicial activity that struck the Irish as particularly unacceptable was the American judges' fund-raising efforts (undertaken to support their innovative programs). Judge Haughton questioned whether "it's proper for a judge to get himself involved in fund-raising," adding that he doesn't "think it's part of his function." Judge Hogan agreed that to introduce such an idea in the Irish context would "raise a great debate here." It would be "greatly frowned upon" for a "judge to get into that scenario." Both judges observed that judicial fund-raising could cause a "conflict of interest." As Judge Haughton put it, it would be only "a matter of time before somebody who has funded you appears before the court."

Scottish problem-solving court officials agree with this position. Moira Price, of the Glasgow drug court, even finds objectionable the idea of charging clients to help pay for treatment services, as occurs in some American drug courts. "I just think that anything to do with raising money should be kept quite separate from the criminal justice setting and from the court disposals," she explains. Such activity would simply be "alien to anything we would think about here." Again viewing it as a cultural impulse that is in some ways beyond explanation, Price repeats, "I just don't think that court disposals should be linked in any way to raising money. It just feels wrong intrinsically."

Another area of common ground for Ireland and Scotland is the essential treatment philosophy that prevails in both places. Here, as in the other non-U.S. countries, a harm minimization or harm reduction philosophy is favored. Irish and Scottish court officials recognize that a harm reduction orientation differs from the total abstinence mentality more common in the United States. Judge Haughton, for example, understands that "most American models are based on total abstinence from drugs and alcohol." He explains, however, that in Ireland, "the principal determining factor as to the success or otherwise of the drug court was whether or not there was significant reduction in crime," and the treatment service working with the court uses a "methadone maintenance program." Haughton concedes that "while total abstinence might be an ideal goal, it was unlikely to be realistic in many cases." The 1998 Working Group report expressed a similar sentiment. It acknowledged that "whereas total abstinence is the optimal object of a drugs treatment programme, the alternative of methadone maintenance should not be excluded."[43]

In fact, in both Ireland and Scotland, methadone maintenance has been a central part of the drug court program. In Ireland, participants can graduate from the program while still on a maintenance prescription for methadone. While participants may be encouraged to "come off the methadone," as a Dublin probation officer explains, it is not required to "graduate from the drug court program." The importance of methadone treatment in the Glasgow drug court is illustrated by the interesting story of a delegation of Russian officials who visited the Glasgow drug court. The visit evidently made it very clear to the Russians that the Scottish drug court was not transferable to a Russian context, and this was due in part to the court's use of methadone. Moira Price recalls the visit of the Russian delegation:

> We use methadone to a great extent here in our treatment, and methadone is an illicit drug in Russia. So . . . where we'd use methadone as an alternative therapy, they just could not use that at all. . . . They just could not get their heads around the concept of substitute prescribing as a way to deal with addicts. They seemed to think the way to deal with addicts was work therapy in prison.

IRISH AND SCOTTISH DIFFERENCES

Thus, one finds in Scottish and Irish problem-solving courts a number of common qualities. Both countries introduced problem-solving courts at the same time and have developed and planned their courts in a slow and careful manner. In the planning processes, working groups have looked not only to the United States but also to each other and to other countries experimenting with problem-solving courts. Practitioners in both countries, moreover, rely on a harm reduction treatment philosophy, are more reserved in terms of what is regarded as acceptable judicial behavior, and have expressed disapproval of some of the more demonstrative and activist orientations of U.S. problem-solving court judges. Along with these common features, however, one also discovers important differences between Scottish and Irish problem-solving courts.

To begin with, though both countries are reserved compared to the United States, one finds in Scotland greater concern about the preservation of court formalities and the due process rights of individual offenders. According to Sheriff Donald of the Fife drug court, this has been a feature of Scottish legal culture "throughout our history." He notes: "We've always been very, very cautious about the rights of the individual." Consider several examples. Gillian Oghene, coordinator of the Fife drug court team, demonstrates such concerns for offenders' rights in her reflections on U.S. drug court practices. Oghene "got the impression" from her visits to U.S. drug courts that "judges really can do just about whatever they want, and I was a bit leery as to people's human rights." Sheriff Raeburn, who has functioned as both a domestic abuse and drug court judge in Glasgow, says that in Scotland's problem-solving courts, "the procedural due process is very strictly adhered to." Moira Price says the same about Scottish problem-solving courts: "In Scotland these courts are still very much bound by the law and procedures, and we don't really deviate from that." Concern about due process, as such, was one reason that officials at the Glasgow drug court did not originally plan to have sheriffs attend pre-court meetings. They worried that it would be unfair for the sheriff to receive information about a defendant without the defendant present. Interestingly, officials from Dublin convinced Scottish officials to have pre-court meetings with the sheriff present. Consider Judge Haughton's recollections of this meeting:

> We brought about a radical change in their plans. They felt that the sheriff—the judge—should not, could not, attend the pre-court meeting, because he would be hearing things about a participant that may or may not be admissible in evidence. And they felt that that shouldn't be the case, and when we went over and spoke to them about their plans and how we worked and how we operated, we actually persuaded them to change their view on that. And the sheriff does attend, and they do have pre-court meetings.

One area in which the Scottish clearly differ from the Irish is with respect to the role of lawyers in the drug court program. British criminologist Philip Bean highlights this difference in his comparison of Irish and Scottish drug courts, observing that whereas in Scotland lawyers "have a part to play," in Dublin, "court lawyers were excluded from the outset."[44] Indeed, before the Dublin drug court was even launched, Judge Gerard Haughton made considerable efforts to ensure that lawyers would play a significantly reduced role. Based on his observations of courts in the United States and elsewhere, he became "convinced . . . that lawyers should not normally attend drug courts, as this places a third party between the accused and the court." Such interference, Haughton believes, "reduces the obligation on the accused to account for his own conduct." Thus, in the Dublin drug court, "neither the prosecution nor the defense lawyer appears."[45]

Like some Australian and Canadian courts, the Dublin drug court operates on a bail bond system. That is, defendants have pled guilty or been convicted of a charge. If defendants are deemed eligible for drug court, they are released on a drug court bail bond instead of a traditional sentence being imposed. If participants do not comply with the program requirements, they may have their bail revoked and be "placed in custody for a week/weekend" as an intermediate sanction. Haughton was concerned that defense lawyers, in particular, might not accept this practice, and he worried that they would "immediately resort to Judicial Review or Habeas Corpus." Anticipating such objections, he "organized a seminar in the Law Society under the aegis of the Criminal Lawyers Association" prior to the court's launching.

> I was quite direct in informing the lawyers that I did not see any particular role for them in appearing on a regular basis in the court and that on occasions defendants' bail may be revoked for a short period. Again, quite directly I conceded that such bail revocation orders could almost certainly be successfully challenged in the High Court. The result of such a challenge would be a fairly substantial fee earned from the State, the release of the client and his termination from the Drug Court Programme, none of which was of any long-term benefit to him. This has been accepted and once a participant is accepted in our Drug Court the lawyers (who do have a right to appear) step aside.[46]

According to Haughton, because lawyers "have the long-term interests of their clients at heart," he was successful in persuading them to "stay out of the court." As a consequence, "in the normal progression of the court [the accused] are not represented by lawyers at all." Instead, "it's one-to-one between the judge and the participant."

Contrastingly, lawyers do play an important role in the Scottish drug court. As clearly stated in the *Fife Drug Court Reference Manual*, "the legitimate role of the defense agent does not change in the drug court and includes that of advocacy, representing the interest of the client, and safeguarding the rights of the defendant."[47] Lawyers are welcome to attend the pre-court meetings, though they often elect not to. They are, however, present during the regular review sessions in court, and they typically speak first when a client appears before the sheriff.[48] A case in the Glasgow drug court illustrates the important role of the lawyer. During a pre-court meeting, the name of a particular client was presented to the group. The medical doctor, who spoke first, informed the group that this participant had been regularly coming up positive for cocaine and benzodiazepines. The doctor concluded, "I don't believe he is motivated to stop drug use." A social worker spoke next, adding that the client's attendance had been generally poor, and that he had missed his last three meetings. Another social worker said that the client had given false urine samples and had been engaging in "a lot of manipulation." The only really positive thing she could say was that his heroin use was down (though, obviously, it had been replaced with the use of cocaine and benzodiazepines).

Presented with this information, the sheriff intimated his inclination to revoke the order, but he wanted to wait until the court session, when the offender and his agent (defense lawyer) would be present. After the defense agent made her case during the court review session later in the day, the sheriff decided not to revoke the order and gave the client one more chance. In a later interview with the sheriff, he admitted that in the earlier session, he "was minded to impose a custodial sentence on him," but after hearing the agent's case, decided to "give him a further chance to do this." The sheriff cited the European Convention of Human Rights as prohibiting him from making decisions such as this without the defendant being present. Elsewhere, Sheriff Matthews has similarly stated that in the Glasgow drug court, "no decision adverse to the offender will be made at a pre-court hearing. Any such matter will require to be aired in open court."[49]

Another important difference between Scotland and Ireland concerns the use of jail as a sanction for noncompliance with program requirements. Recall that Scottish sheriffs did not originally have the authority to impose a short-term jail sentence; they lacked the statutory authority to do so. When the Scottish Parliament eventually gave them this power, sheriffs were still very reluctant to use it. The Dublin drug court, on the other hand, was launched without the passage of any new enabling legislation. Through use of bail revocations, interim sanctions of short-term periods in jail have been more frequent in Dublin than in Scotland. According to the 2002 evaluation of the Dublin drug court, one-third of all drug court clients have had their bail revoked, with stints ranging from two to forty days in jail.[50] It should be noted, however, that over time, the Dublin drug court has become increasingly less inclined to impose interim sanctions of incarceration.

The Dublin drug court differs from the Scottish drug courts in other ways. For example, Judge Haughton calls clients by their first names, whereas Sheriff Matthews maintains that he "will not be on a first-name basis with any of the offenders."[51] The Irish drug court will also include requirements on an order that at least some in Scotland find objectionable. Gillian Oghene, with the Fife drug court, for example, learned that Judge Haughton had "made a condition on somebody's order that the mother made sure the kids went to school." Oghene found this problematic. She said, "Look, this is a drug court order. It's not a social readdressing order or whatever. That is not the role of a judge to get involved in that." This would not happen in Scotland, according to Oghene, because "we are a bit more focused within the laws, which is a good thing."

The Dublin drug court also allows applause in the courtroom, issues certificates and awards clients with "small gifts" for achievements in the program, and holds graduation ceremonies for clients who successfully complete the program—all practices that Scottish officials eschew. In each instance, however, Irish drug court practices are more subdued than those one would find in an American drug court. As noted in the 2002 evaluation of the Irish drug court, though the court is "qualitatively different [from] other District Courts" and the "dialogue between the judge and the participant is both open and honest," the Dublin drug court "retains the formality and authority of the court" and "does not engage in the 'theatrics' associated with some drug courts operating in the United States."[52] For example, certificates are given to clients who graduate from one of the three phases in the program, but much like certificate-awarding in English DTTOs, the exercise is understated and the applause rather muted. A graduation ceremony typically involves a summary of the client's progress followed by comments from the judge and other team members. The judge then presents the client with a graduation certificate and shakes the client's hand (which is the extent of any kind of physical contact). As Judge Haughton puts it, "There's no hugging, but there's certainly handshaking." Court team members then join the client and his or her family for "tea and biscuits" after the ceremony.

Thus, the format of the Irish drug court allows for judicial action that is more like that of some American problem-solving courts. However, even with greater judicial leeway in this sense, Irish judges still tend to tread somewhat cautiously. Consider an example of such reticence I witnessed during one visit to the Dublin drug court. A judge who was new to drug court found some of the practices a little problematic. In a pre-court meeting, information was given by team members about a client who had apparently been involved in shoplifting. It was recommended that the judge deduct points for this behavior. In the Dublin drug court, clients are given "minus" points for noncompliance and "plus" points for successes. If someone on the program reaches seventy minus points, he or she will have to "spend seven days in custody." In this case, the judge felt uncomfortable discussing the alleged behavior in open court and then penalizing the client with minus points without giving the defendant a chance to challenge the charge in a more formal adjudicative process. Based on what the judge knew of the alleged shoplifting, he believed the defendant "probably would have gotten off."

Another discussion in a pre-court meeting centered on a drug court client who had twice gotten pregnant. Both pregnancies ended in miscarriages. A nurse on the drug court team encouraged the defendant to use contraception and suggested during the pre-court meeting that it would be helpful if the judge were to reinforce this recommendation. The judge, however, objected and refused to make such a recommendation in open court: "It's not the function of the judge to tell someone to receive contraception. I think it's an extremely good idea. But for her sake, I don't think it should be said in court. Besides, it could be misunderstood." He added, "I have always been a little unhappy about telling people what to do. It strikes me as a bit patronizing." In general, the judge said that he did not always like the basic structure of the program, which allowed him to have information about defendants (through the pre-court meetings) and then to "make judgments without hearing the defendants." In his view, this arrangement "creates a slightly patronizing tone" and "goes against a sense of natural justice." In this case, then, though allowed and encouraged to behave in a certain way, the Irish judge (like the Scottish sheriffs) was still disinclined to engage defendants in a manner that he viewed as condescending and outside the scope of proper judicial action.

TJ in Ireland and Scotland

Thus, in both Ireland and Scotland one finds a kind of instinctive judicial reserve and desire to maintain some of the formal qualities of a traditional court of law—an inclination that is more pronounced in Scotland than in Ireland. A final area, however, in which the two regions find common ground is the degree to which both places have (or have not) embraced therapeutic jurisprudence as a guiding legal philosophy. Recall from chapter 4 the significant extent to which therapeutic jurisprudence has informed problem-solving courts in Australia and Canada. In these commonwealth countries, numerous references have been made to the relevance of TJ to the development of problem-solving courts. TJ scholars, moreover, have been invited to give lectures and have coauthored articles with leading judicial officers in both countries. In Australia, magistrates have sponsored international conferences on the relevance of TJ to criminal courts. So pronounced is the influence of therapeutic jurisprudence in Canada and Australia that it sometimes seems that TJ, rather than problem-solving courts, as such, is the driving vector encouraging legal change.

In Ireland and Scotland, in stark contrast, one finds little sympathy with (or even knowledge of) therapeutic jurisprudence. The various working group reports and evaluations make virtually no references to therapeutic jurisprudence. Those importing and running problem-solving courts have rarely even heard of David Wexler and Bruce Winick and have little to no knowledge of therapeutic jurisprudence as a new legal theory. Even when they are aware of the concept, they play down its relevance and applicability to Ireland and Scotland. Sheriff Matthews of the Glasgow drug court, for example, said that therapeutic jurisprudence had not informed him "at all." Moira Price likewise asserted that she is "sure it didn't guide the thinking in Scotland or the introduction of the court." Price even questions the degree of its relevance to U.S. drug courts. "My impression was that the drug court movement had been doing what it was doing for a while, and then they [in the United States] found a handy label which they could attach to themselves to justify what they were doing." Because the Scottish do not see themselves as doing anything that is "particularly innovative in a legal sense," there is no need to "justify" the program "with another title."

Though they admit that the "label" has not been used in Scotland, other Scots believe that, as far as they understand it, the essence of TJ is reflected in what they are basically doing in these courts. Sheriff Donald of the Fife drug court appears to hold this essential view.

> It's a holistic approach dealing not with just cause-and-effect crime, but it is dealing with the whole background. . . . We're not just dealing with the offending behavior, but the housing problems, the family problems, the debt problems—everything that affects this guy and trying to find a solution, a major part of which is, of course, to prevent re-offending. But it is to help this guy to get his life back on the wheels, to get off the drugs, and that seems to me a therapeutic approach.

Judge Hogan of Ireland likewise says that the Irish do practice therapeutic jurisprudence, "except we don't call it that." What Irish judges do, according to Hogan, is to not immediately resort to jail in all cases but instead try to "help" the offender. As Hogan puts it, "You intervene, you bring in the probation service, and you try to help them. Isn't that the base of therapeutic jurisprudence?" Perhaps it is—but in a way that is certainly more scaled down than in American problem-solving courts, and in a manner that does not require such direct judicial involvement and role adjustment. In fact, the main examples Judge Hogan offers to illustrate this Irish version of TJ relate to greater use of probation and community service. Moreover, Irish practices are not linked in any fashion to the specific articulation of the TJ theory that emerged in the United States in the early 1990s (i.e., the theory propagated by Wexler and Winick), nor is it joined by the kind of revolutionary rhetoric that sometimes characterizes discussions of therapeutic jurisprudence in other places.

In addition to revealing a relative lack of knowledge about TJ, Irish and Scottish problem-solving court practitioners make very few references to acting therapeutically more generally. Evaluations of the Dublin drug court and the Scottish youth courts make no mention of acting in a therapeutic fashion. The only discussion of a therapeutic approach in the evaluation of the Glasgow domestic abuse court is, as noted earlier, a brief reference to what happens in some courts in *other* jurisdictions. The 107-page evaluation of the Glasgow and Fife drug courts makes only one reference to acting in a therapeutic manner. In this instance, the evaluation cites a drug court official's description of the review hearings, which is described as the point "where the legal side of things melds with the non-legal sort of therapeutic side of things."[53]

Again, the dearth of references to TJ, the basic disregard for a general therapeutic orientation, and the relative absence of overtly therapeutic practices in these courts are all indicative of fundamental cultural differences. In comments very similar to those offered by Susan Williams (the West London drug court judge cited in chapter 3), Moira Price, of the Glasgow drug court, identifies cultural differences as a central reason for the relative lack of sympathy toward a conspicuously therapeutic approach. According to Price, there "seems to be a much more counseling/therapy-based idea in America than here." In Scotland, she says, "we just don't have that. . . . It would never occur to us that people automatically need counseling [to] work through their issues." Thus, in Scotland, "I don't think we have a culture that necessarily thinks along the lines of always-needing-counseling."

Speaking specifically about such self-help groups as AA and NA—participation in which is commonly part of program requirements in U.S. drug courts—Price notes that such formats simply do not work in Scottish culture. "It's just hard to picture many Scots standing up in a group and saying all the things that you're meant to accept," she says. "And that can only be cultural; it's just that we're reticent." Also like Judge Williams, Price observes that the only way people would do such a thing would be if they were intoxicated: "We don't like speaking up, particularly in front of groups. I mean, I'd have to be drunk to stand up in a group and say I'm an alcoholic. I could only do it if I was drunk. If I was sober, nothing on earth would induce me to stand up among a crowd of strangers and talk about myself."

Gillian Oghene, with the Fife drug court, says much the same about the Scottish people. "In Scotland," she explains, such expressivism "would be very difficult. . . . People don't go to counseling. People don't go to group. And you don't stand up in group and tell people personal things." An addiction worker with the Fife drug court agrees: "That's a typical Scottish person. You know, they keep it in themselves. They keep it in the family." Oghene believes that the application of the American self-help model could, in fact, be damaging. Speaking specifically about such twelve-step groups as AA and NA—which are much less commonly found in Scotland than they are in the United States—Oghene notes that she has not been pleased with what use she had made of these programs for past clients. Were she to consider referring any future clients to such meetings, she "would want to make sure that it wasn't going to be more damaging." Speaking of therapeutically oriented groups more generally, Oghene worries that "if you are going to get people to expose themselves emotionally . . . we have to be careful that we don't damage them more than they already are damaged." She has "grave concerns" about such "heavy, intense, therapeutic groups." Instead, group work in the Fife drug court aims for a more "collective-learning and education" type of focus.

Oghene also has reservations about judicial attempts to act in a therapeutic fashion. As with other Scots involved in problem-solving courts, she thinks it is important that the court maintain a level of formality, because "it is a court of law" where "sanctions of the law can be imposed." It is important, in her view, that people "be reminded of that." She notes further that "sheriffs are lawyers," and they do not have the "specialist knowledge or understanding" of therapists. Therefore, she is not at all sure they "would get it right if they did take on a therapeutic role." She believes that such an attempt by a judge "to add to treatment already in place" would be "misplaced." Instead, the judge should "stick to what he knows . . . he does the law, we do the treatment."

In U.S. drug courts, where there are fewer scruples about a judge acting in a more therapeutic fashion, concerns about due process and defendants' rights sometimes fade to the background. Arguably, judicial preoccupation with engaging defendants therapeutically can foster neglect of traditional legal considerations, if only unwittingly. In her own observations of U.S. drug courts, Oghene notes, "There didn't seem to be any concept of punishment equating with crime." In Scotland, there is a much stronger sense that jail is punishment and that a person's punishment should be commensurate with a crime that has been committed in the past, even if it is imposed as an interim sanction for a problem-solving court client. Recall, for example, shrieval justifications for limits on interim sanctions, both statutorily and in practice. In the case of Scotland, then, we find the inverse of the American situation. Instead of a preoccupation with TJ leading in some instances to the neglect of due process considerations, we find demonstrable concerns about preserving due process rights positively related to a disregard for therapeutic jurisprudence.

Again, this appears to be the case in Scotland more than in Ireland. In Ireland, one finds more visible changes to traditional courtroom practices in the context of the Dublin drug court. As noted earlier, lawyers are generally absent at drug court review hearings, even in some cases when clients are remanded into custody. People applaud in the courtroom. Clients are given certificates and prizes, and graduation ceremonies are held when clients successfully complete the program. The Americanization of

the Dublin court may have reached a new level, when, at a 2006 graduation ceremony presided over by Irish drug court judge Bridget Reilly, the
Irish American comedian Des Bishop was invited to attend and address
the court. All such practices are still absent from Scottish courts.

Thus, there seems to be a greater openness in Ireland to move in the
direction of American-styled courts. Judge Hogan, for example, anticipates that "somewhere along the line . . . a judge in drug court is going
to have to be human. We are going to have to break down barriers."
While Hogan would reject out of hand such behavior as hugging, he observes that "little kindnesses are creeping in." He adds that "to make
the face of the court acceptable," Irish judges "must learn to drop the
barriers"—though he cautions that in so doing, "we must be careful not
to lose our authority." Speaking specifically about the therapeutically inspired disease paradigm that informs American drug courts, Judge Hogan
observes that the Irish are "not yet evolved [enough] in their thought
process to accept" drug misuse as "a disease." To assert such a view,
Hogan believes, would leave people with the impression that drug court
is a "soft option." Nevertheless, as the Irish continue to "evolve," he
"wouldn't rule it out"—the idea that eventually court practitioners would
be able to say that "it's a disease and we should treat it as a disease."

As it concerns the treatment of drug court clients in both countries,
however, one does not find much use of the sort of self-help therapeutic
approach common in the United States. Instead, the kind of treatment
services offered in conjunction with the Irish and Scottish drug courts
tend to be of a more clinical/medical variety, as is also the case in England.
Moreover, in problem-solving courts more generally in both Scotland and
Ireland, there remains a judicial reserve that is clearly distinguishable
from American practices. Developments in Ireland, in particular, however,
provide some evidence that legal imports inevitably lead to more cultural
transference than the adjustment view of legal borrowing would seem to
anticipate. That said, at least in these early years of the global problem-
solving court phenomenon, the clear difference between the American
version and the courts found in the five other common law countries considered here is pronounced.

Chapter Six

AMERICAN EXCEPTIONALISM

> Where the United States treads boldly, rapidly, and
> sometimes foolishly, Australia tiptoes carefully, slowly,
> and most times reluctantly.[1]
> —*Arie Freiberg*

HAVING now examined the development of problem-solving courts in all six common law countries, it is possible to organize and analyze the data according to several broader comparative themes. For example, we have found that the influence of therapeutic jurisprudence is more pronounced in the United States, Canada, and Australia than it is in England, Scotland, and Ireland. The structural limits of problem-solving courts in England—determined as they are by the unique qualities of the magistrate system—place these courts on one end of the spectrum; the greater flexibility and power afforded judges in American problem-solving courts locates these courts on the other end, with new court programs in the four other countries falling somewhere between these two extremes. Canada and Australia are also unique in their development of aboriginal courts, a phenomenon that has both influenced and been influenced by the broader advancement of problem-solving courts in both countries. One could imagine a variety of taxonomies to make conceptual sense of differences such as these.

While such distinctions are important, what stands out most profoundly is the degree to which the United States represents the exception in relation to the five other countries. That is, as revealed through an analysis of problem-solving courts, the American legal accent stands in singular contrast to the legal accents of the five other countries. Specifically, a comparison of the development process of problem-solving courts in the United States, England (and Wales), Scotland, Ireland, Canada, and Australia reveals an important difference between an American disposition characterized by enthusiasm, boldness, and pragmatism, and the contrasting penchant of other countries toward moderation, deliberation, and restraint.

ENTHUSIASM

Consider first the character of the American courts, beginning with the defining quality of enthusiasm. A visit to an American problem-solving court or a discussion with an American problem-solving court judge quickly reveals a great deal of commitment to and personal investment in these programs. Judges are "true believers," if you will, and they believe that what they are invested in is something of profound historical significance.[2] Not only are they committed to their own local court programs, but they are often proselytizers, wishing to spread the "good news" of problem-solving courts to their immediate judicial colleagues and quite literally to the rest of the world. Greg Berman, of the Center for Court Innovation, reflects the attitude of many in this community when he urges advocates to look "for every possible opportunity—PSAs [public service announcements], op-eds, public events—to spread the gospel of problem-solving justice."[3] Elsewhere, Berman and his colleague John Feinblatt again convey a religious-like commitment to problem-solving courts when they write of the "conversion narrative experienced by many problem-solving judges," and when they admonish supporters to "begin to preach to the unconverted."[4]

Such zeal for the movement is certainly evident in Phoenix, Arizona, where several problem-solving courts are in operation, including a drug court, a mental health court, a DUI court, and a domestic violence court. One judge, who was instrumental in the establishment of Phoenix's mental health court, describes the problem-solving court movement as "radical, revolutionary, the trend of the future." "It's the future of the law," he says. "It's the future of justice." This particular judge, while a student at the University of Arizona Law School, studied under TJ scholar David Wexler. Both Wexler and Winick, likewise, speak in effusive terms about the advancement of problem-solving courts. At an international conference in Edinburgh, for example, Winick spoke of the movement toward problem-solving courts as a "paradigm shift" and observed that "the courts are doing things they have never done before. . . . We all feel we are on the verge of serious systemic change." In their coedited book *Judging in a Therapeutic Key*, Wexler and Winick similarly assert: "In the past dozen or so years, a remarkable transformation has occurred in the role of the courts."[5]

The title of another edited collection, put out by the CCI, refers to the movement as no less than "a problem-solving revolution." Using similar language, a judge (and one of the leaders in the problem-solving court movement) has described the development as "nothing short of revolutionary." "What we are doing here," she said, "is no less than a complete revolution in jurisprudence." Still another U.S. judge, who describes herself as a "disciple" of the movement and who has actually served as a drug court judge, a mental health court judge, and a domestic violence court judge, says this of problem-solving courts: "I love it, I tell you. I mean, any place that we can expand it, we should." Someone had approached her about the possibility of starting a court for people over sixty years of age. Her response: "Do you want to start up a senior citizens' court? I'm your woman."

Judge Judith Kaye, another problem-solving court enthusiast, takes note of "how energizing a problem-solving court can be for judges"[6] and reports on the passionate commitment of judges presiding over New York's various problem-solving courts, even among those who were initially skeptical of these programs. For Kaye, "these firsthand evaluations from people I respect are compelling evidence from the front lines of the value and effectiveness of these courts."[7] Beyond citing the testimonies of individual judges, Kaye reports on her direct experiences visiting various problem-solving courts in New York. She recalls, for example, her attendance at a family treatment court graduation ceremony: "There were a lot of happy tears—including my own."[8]

Like others, Kaye sometimes uses a storytelling method in her advocacy of these courts. Consider the following promotion of problem-solving courts, which conveys not only Kaye's personal commitment to these courts but also the uniquely expressive flavor and tone of the American variety:

> As a veteran of drug court graduations—whether adult or family treatment court—I can tell you that these are very moving events. Typically, a lifelong drug addict who never before could complete treatment tearfully thanks everyone, including the judge, for giving her a chance to start her life again. Frequently I hear, "I wasn't just arrested, I was saved." Grown men report that for the first time in their lives they are able to have an apartment, a credit card. I heard a graduate in New York City say: "My head was bowed when I was brought before you in handcuffs, Judge, but today my head is high. I'm looking you right in the eye." . . . At family treatment court graduations, I have heard parents express gratitude for the opportunity to regain their dignity and self-esteem, reestablish connections with family members, and raise their own children. I have seen a child stand up in a crowded audience and proclaim, "Mom, I'm proud of you."[9]

As noted in chapter 1, U.S. problem-solving court advocates have even surveyed judges and presented evidence that problem-solving court judges have much higher rates of job satisfaction and feel better about themselves working in such a context. Judge Tauber, in presenting drug courts to an international audience in Scotland, highlighted judicial satisfaction as a selling feature of the courts. "I've talked to hundreds of judges who have done this work," he said. "I have not found a judge yet who has done this work for a significant period of time who hasn't said it is the most satisfying work that he has done in his career as a judge. I think that speaks volumes." Judicial enthusiasm, as such, is viewed as an asset to the movement. Laurie Robinson, former assistant attorney general in the U.S. Department of Justice, even argues that it is a feature of the movement that should be fostered.

> The energy, enthusiasm, and optimism embedded in the burgeoning problem-solving courts movement is a significant asset right now for the nation's beleaguered justice system, one that should be . . . nurtured.[10]

It is a feature of the American variety of problem-solving courts that individuals in the importing countries take note of, sometimes with trepidation. An Irish judge, for instance, observes that some might "be frightened by the great American enthusiasm and the almost evangelical approach" to problem-solving courts. This judge also believes that it is a feature of the American approach that importing countries are not likely to embrace. He says, for example, that problem-solving court advocates in the United States "might be slightly naive to assume that our sense of enthusiasm would match their sense of enthusiasm."

BOLDNESS

A second and related feature of the American version of these courts is a certain boldness in the actions of problem-solving court professionals, particularly the judges. In her book *A Nation Under Lawyers*, Mary Ann Glendon identifies two types of judges: what she calls classical judges and romantic judges. The classical judge is characterized by "modesty, impartiality, restraint, and interpretive skill," whereas the romantic judge is "bold, creative, compassionate, result-oriented, and liberated from legal technicalities."[11] While these are clearly ideal types in the Weberian sense, it is fairly safe to say that American problem-solving court judges tend toward the romantic, while judges in the five other regions tend toward the classical.

Judicial boldness, one of the defining qualities of Glendon's romantic judge, is apparent in the words and actions of American problem-solving court judges. American problem-solving court judges are activist judges. They are the leaders of the movement, directing initiatives both inside and outside the courtroom. As it concerns their actions in the courtroom, judges are bold in the sense that they recognize that the format of problem-solving courts affords them a great deal of power and discretion (beyond what they would have in a regular criminal court), and they are not afraid to use this increased power to "solve the problems" of the individuals who come before them.[12] In the problem-solving court context, courts are, as Bruce Winick puts it, "playing the bold role of problem solvers."

American judges are aware of the influence that is theirs in such a novel judicial context. Judge Judy Harris Kluger, who served as a community court judge in Midtown, reflects on the kind of authority given to the problem-solving court judge.

> I've found that we as judges have enormous psychological power over the people in front of us. It's not even coercive power. It's really the power of an authority figure and a role model. You have power not only over that person, but over their family in the audience, over all the people sitting in that courtroom.[13]

Judge Rosalyn Richter, another former Midtown community court judge, agrees with Kluger; she recalls a meeting at the Midtown community court in which "defendants said that having a judge monitor what they were doing affected them almost as much as having a sentence over their heads."[14]

Florida judge Cindy Lederman reflects more specifically on the substance of the new form of judicial monitoring. As a problem-solving court judge, says Lederman, "I'm not sitting back and watching the parties and ruling. I'm making comments. I'm encouraging. I'm making judgment calls. I'm getting very involved with families. I'm making clinical decisions to some extent, with the advice of experts." It is a role, she says that requires "courage" and a willingness to move beyond the role of "referee or spectator" and become a "participant in the process." Given this format, Lederman believes that the wrong type of judge could be a "disaster." That is, she concedes that potential harm could come from the increased discretion given the judge in the context of problem-solving courts. Contrasting her role with that of a judge in a conventional criminal court, Lederman acknowledges, "So I have much greater opportunities, I think, to harm someone than I would if I just sat there, listened, and said guilty or not guilty."[15]

As reflected in Lederman's comments, the kind of judicial monitoring found in problem-solving courts is often characterized by a personal and informal style of engagement. Physical contact between judge and clients is not uncommon. As we have seen, not a few American judges are comfortable with offering hugs. American judges, in fact, engage in a range of unusual judicial behaviors, including allowing clients to visit their chambers, arriving in court wearing acupuncture needles instead of the traditional black robe, and promising judicial cartwheels for ninety consecutive days of counseling. Thus, in a number of ways, problem-solving court judges boldly step beyond the parameters of their traditional roles. As one American problem-solving court judge put it: "We are the judges who get to color outside the lines."

Not all judges in new American specialty courts think that these boundaries should be so eagerly transgressed. A domestic violence court judge in Minnesota believes the "judiciary is backsliding in terms of what are appropriate boundaries." In reference to some of the actions of other problem-solving court judges, she says, "I do not want to be a chemical dependency counselor. I don't want to run AA meetings in my courtroom and sing 'Kumbaya.'" She makes it clear that she is not opposed to therapy: "I'm all for therapy. I'm all for treatment." It is just that in her view, it is not the role of the judiciary to function in a therapeutic capacity. As she puts it: "Judges need to be judges and need to have a certain distance from what's going on. . . . If we get too involved in cases, how do we fairly and impartially dispense justice? How do we maintain our credibility?" She adds that she is "all for society solving its problems," but she does not believe "the courts should be in the mix of trying to solve society's problems." In spite of her personal reservations about a therapeutic, problem-solving orientation, she recognizes that she is "clearly in the minority," that she goes "against the tide," and that, irrespective of her views, "the train has left the station."

Most judges involved in the movement, thus, are more willing to color outside the lines—which involves, among other things, employing a wider range of judicial options for dealing with clients. Freed from the sometimes frustrating constraints of mandatory minimum sentence guidelines, problem-solving court judges now have greater discretion. They can, as we have seen, impose a variety of sanctions, including community service, increased attendance at twelve-step meetings, involvement in "quality-of-life" groups, compulsory participation in anger management classes, and short periods in jail. As community court judge Rosalyn Richter explains, "Problem-solving courts have broadened the judicial horizon" and have "given judges more choices than [they] have ever had."[16] Comparatively, the United States is unique in the variety of sanctions that judges can impose in the context of problem-solving courts.

Given the missionary manner in which problem-solving court judges have advanced the movement and acquired these expanded powers, it is not surprising that problem-solving court judges—particularly the movement's early leaders—were described as "mavericks . . . dynamic individuals . . . free-thinking, charismatic, and well-connected," for whom "salesmanship" was a defining quality of their leadership.[17] In keeping with this orientation, Michael Shrunk, a district attorney in Portland, Oregon, seeks a certain type of person when recruiting new problem-solving court judges, as commissioned by his presiding judge. Among other qualities, Shrunk looks for a "risk-taker," someone who is "non-traditional," a "proactive judge rather than a reactive judge."[18]

The proactive nature of problem-solving court judges finds expression outside the courtroom as well.[19] In this sense, problem-solving judges are a far cry from the classical judge Tocqueville observed in early nineteenth-century America. Tocqueville identified as one of the "essential" characteristics of the American judge that "he cannot act until the cause has been duly brought before the court." Tocqueville described American judicial power as "devoid of action," in that the judge "does not pursue criminals, hunt out wrongs, or examine evidence of its own accord." Such action would "do violence to the passive nature of his authority."[20] The problem-solving court judge, in direct contrast, is full of action. Community court judges, for example, regularly meet with local residents and are often very visible in the community. Consider Alex Calabrese's description of his role as judge of the Red Hook Community Justice Center:

> I enjoy walking through Red Hook and talking with the residents about their concerns. I make a point of attending community meetings on a regular basis to hear residents' concerns about specific crime issues, such as drug dealing or prostitution at certain locations. . . . The meetings keep me informed about every problem location.[21]

Calabrese tells the story of the time when he was the "grand marshal of a local waterfront arts festival" and a local resident "whispered in [his] ear" about a candy store that was selling illegal drugs. With this information, he set in motion law enforcement action that led to the eventual closing of the "candy" store.[22]

Drug court judges are also activist judges. Actions of drug court judges outside the courtroom have included visiting clients at their place of work, lobbying Congress for funding, pulling together various resources to support the court's treatment and education programs, promoting the courts via the local media, and even raising funds to support their local programs.[23] The latter, as noted in chapter 5, is an activity that judges in other countries find particularly worrying.

National conferences are an important forum for the encouragement of such judicial activism. In reference to the infectious enthusiasm of the annual NADCP meetings, for example, Jeffrey Tauber recalls, "When [people] came to our conference, they felt they were part of a movement, something larger than themselves. . . . People felt so high after that, they'd go home and slay dragons."[24] Judge Peggy Hora likewise speaks of conferences as places where "those who see the law as a healing instrument . . . attempt to bring new sheep into the fold."[25] As such comments indicate, the American problem-solving court movement has been largely a grassroots effort led by practitioners within the judicial branch. The other countries, in contrast, have tended to rely on and wait for initiation and direction from the other branches of government. Problem-solving court officials in non-U.S. countries make note of this difference and sometimes try to explain it by pointing to the fact that many judges in U.S. state courts must stand for election. An Australian judge, for example, observed that because Australian judges are not elected, but have lifetime appointments, they see themselves "as part of the system rather than as competing for reelection." As a result, they don't feel the need to "stand out from other people"—whereas in the United States, because judges are elected, they "have to be a personality." A Scottish problem-solving court official similarly observed that because some U.S. judges are elected, they "almost need to have their unique selling points or something that will set them apart." Because of this, she sees U.S. judges as having "almost a dual role" of both politician and judge. In Scotland, on the other hand, judges "are just judges" who do not feel the need to stand out or "set up their own programs."

That the election of some American judges account for the kind of judicial boldness found in problem-solving courts is debatable. Even among American judges with lifetime appointments, there is evidence of increased boldness. Glendon's discussion of the romantic judge is, in the main, a discussion about the disposition of nonelected Supreme Court justices. As it concerns judicial boldness, Glendon also notes the relatively unique power of judicial review possessed by American judges. Both state judges and federal judges (who are not elected) have the power of judicial review, a power that is rare among liberal democracies. Even when compared to judges in the few countries that do have judicial review, American judges have "exercised their powers of constitutional review with much greater frequency and boldness than judges elsewhere."[26]

The increasing boldness of problem-solving court judges, then, is arguably reflective of a more widespread reality in the American judiciary. In the area of civil litigation, for example, observers note the manner in which new managerial practices give more power and authority to judges, thus fostering a more inquisitorial than adversarial form of adjudication.[27] In her discussion of these practices, the Italian sociologist Maria Rosaria Ferrarese notes a shift in the U.S. legal system from the "former image of the judge as 'supervisor of the trial'" to a situation in which judges are "too powerful . . . too intimate with the parties and too emotionally interested in the outcome of the controversy."[28] Along with increased judicial power, Ferrarese identifies a complementary feature of the American judiciary that is also evident in the American problem-solving court movement, namely, a distinctively pragmatic orientation.

Pragmatism

Oscar Chase, in a related discussion of American judicial managerialism, makes a similar connection between the complementary emphases on "efficiency and flexibility." Consistent with the broader social environment, according to Chase, court management of civil disputes reflected the same "technocratic efficiency-oriented" model of other twentieth-century business and government institutions. The courts "wanted to create a system that would be efficient and would be seen to be so," and "discretion was a necessary element of that vision because it enabled the relevant manager—the judge—to manage." Pointing to the direct influence of culture on this development, Chase argues that both efficiency and discretion were "in the air."[29] In the case of problem-solving courts, one finds the emergence of similar complementary tendencies. Not only are judges given increased judicial authority and discretion, but advocates repeatedly highlight the pragmatic qualities of problem-solving courts.

Laurie Robinson argues that problem-solving courts, along with other recent developments in the American criminal justice system, have been successful because of the general acceptance "of pragmatic, problem-solving approaches that look at bottom line impact and results."[30] In the same vein, Greg Berman describes the development of problem-solving courts, in particular, as "a deeply pragmatic movement." As noted in chapter 2, it is the feature of the courts he finds particularly appealing—a viewpoint shared by others in the movement. An American domestic violence court judge, for example, says that her commitment to problem-solving courts stems more from "practical than philosophical considerations." In sum, she says, "to me, if it works, do it." One rightly questions whether to be pragmatic is to eschew philosophy or theory. Recall Richard Posner's assertion, discussed in chapter 2, that legal pragmatism is, in fact, a theory. Regardless of whether problem-solving court judges recognize it as such, many operate within an essentially pragmatic frame of reference.

Problem-solving court judges repeatedly defend these programs on the grounds of program efficacy. So common is this defense that Eric Lane highlights "efficiency" as one of the "foundational premises on which problem-solving courts rest."[31] According to supporters, these courts save money because treatment is cheaper than jail, they reduce the recidivism rates of participants, and they more effectively address the underlying problems of offenders. Again and again, supporters argue that these courts work—that they are more effective than the alternative. Judith Kaye, in one of her first discussions of problem-solving courts, highlights the central place of efficiency in New York's court reform efforts. The focus of reform, she writes, "is to make sure that we do what we do efficiently." Of these efforts, she specifically states that "efficiency is a key value."[32] In a statement endorsing drug courts, President George Bush similarly highlights the central import of efficiency: "Drug courts are an effective and cost efficient way to help non-violent drug offenders commit to a rigorous drug treatment program in lieu of prison."[33]

This disposition is so pronounced that it sometimes seems that the efficacy and problem-solving capabilities of these courts outweigh other considerations. This is certainly reflected in Judge Stanley Goldstein's summary of the purposes of the courts. He once told a group of other American drug court judges: "As long as whatever you do is designed to get them off drugs and put them back out on the street in a position where they can fight using drugs, whatever you do to accomplish that is fine." Given this sentiment, I sometimes asked American judges whether the apparent departure from the more cautious restraints of the common law tradition bothered them at all. Many said, it does not. One New York judge, for example, said, "It was never a concern of mine." Why?

> We weren't making any headway and we are not stupid. So why don't we try different approaches? Our job is to make sure justice is done. Our job is also to punish, but what's the point of punishing if it doesn't work. . . . When they developed the common law, they didn't have these problems. . . . But we do now, so let's deal with it.

Ellen Schall makes a very similar argument. "The reason we got into problem-solving courts," says Shall, "is because it wasn't working for a judge to sit there and process." According to Shall, moreover, "the system from which the problem-solving courts have emerged was a failure on any count. It wasn't a legal success. It wasn't a social success. It wasn't working."[34] The central preoccupation with efficacy among American problem-solving court advocates has led some to warn against a departure from principles once more central to the aims of the criminal justice system. Timothy Casey, for example, reviews the common arguments that problem-solving courts are more "'effective' than the institutions they replaced," but he also warns that efficiency, as such, "should only be considered as ancillary to the primary objective of providing a fair and neutral method of resolving disputes."[35] Whether problem-solving courts are as effective as many advocates claim is another question. But that advocates think in such clearly pragmatic terms and justify the programs on these grounds is undeniable.

Maria Ferrarese rightly notes the extent to which "pragmatism," with its emphasis on "efficaciousness," is "a philosophy of markedly American inspiration."[36] While American problem-solving court judges do not typically cite the work of such philosophical pragmatists as John Dewey or Richard Rorty, or even legal pragmatists such as Oliver Wendell Holmes Jr. or Richard Posner, they do in important respects express views and experiment with judicial practices in a manner consistent with the ideas put forth by these thinkers.[37] If Posner is correct in his view that American judges are largely pragmatic and that, moreover, "in twenty-first century America there is no alternative to legal pragmatism,"[38] then problem-solving court practices represent only the most recent and visible manifestation of a legal orientation with deep roots in American legal culture. If, like therapeutic jurisprudence, pragmatism is a conspicuously American orientation, one wonders about the nature and extent of its transferability. Posner himself observes that both philosophical pragmatism and adjudicative pragmatism are essentially American dispositions that "may not travel well to other countries."[39] In the case of problem-solving courts, while there is certainly evidence (in some cases even increasing evidence) of pragmatism, the quality is still most pronounced in the United States. The other countries, in contrast, reflect a very different set of defining qualities.

MODERATION

As noted earlier, the first distinguishing feature of courts in the non-U.S. regions is moderation, which in certain respects represents a direct contrast to the boldness and enthusiasm of legal actors in the American courts. Whereas problem-solving courts are seen in the United States as a revolutionary panacea, in the other locations, individuals do not speak of these programs as a universal remedy to society's pressing social difficulties or as something that promises to transform or revolutionize the country's criminal justice system. Instead, problem-solving courts are viewed as one type of program, among others, that may be worth trying.

Judge Bentley of Toronto is clear on this point. His comments in this regard were offered in the context of a discussion about Proposition 36, an initiative passed in California in 2000 that mandated treatment for low-level drug offenders. Interestingly, most drug court judges in the United States initially opposed Proposition 36, because they saw it as a thinly veiled step toward drug legalization. They also saw it as undermining the coercive powers of drug court judges, because it would take away their ability to impose sanctions. Bentley found the strong opposition to Proposition 36 among American drug court judges a bit perplexing.

> I was never suggesting, and I was hoping they weren't suggesting, that this is *the* answer. If you think it's *the* answer, then of course what they've done in California is wrong. But if you don't think it's *the* answer, it's just *an option* . . . I mean, you have a whole spectrum of options. And drug courts can't possibly work for all people . . . you have to have all these other options.

Richard D. Schneider and his colleagues make a similar point about Canadian mental health courts. They expressly acknowledge that Canadian mental health courts "are not a complete solution, but rather a part of the solution."[40] Indeed, they see mental health courts as only a "bandage" response to the plight of a beleaguered mental health care system, and they would prefer the reinvigoration of mental health programs outside of the criminal justice system to the further proliferation of mental health courts. As reflected in these views, Canadian problem-solving court judges are more modest; they do not see problem-solving courts as a cure-all. Rather, they see them as one attempt among others to deal with a number of complex and difficult social problems.

Officials in other countries express similar views. The Scottish, for example, recognize that their more modest take on problem-solving courts stands in contrast to the celebratory disposition of American problem-solving court advocates. When she first began arguing in the Scottish Parliament in favor of drug courts, Roseanna Cunningham would qualify her support by making it clear that she did not regard drug courts as a panacea. In January of 2000, for example, she said that drug courts "are not the whole answer, but they are part of the answer."[41] She repeated this assertion in November of the same year: "They are not the complete answer, but they may be part of an answer."[42]

In the same parliamentary discussion, SMP Phil Gallie welcomed Cunningham's "point that the establishment of drugs courts" represents only "part of an answer," while SMP Bill Aitken, though a supporter of the initiation of a pilot drug court, cautioned, "We do not consider drugs courts to be the panacea that will change everything." Instead, said Aitken, "We should go ahead with the pilot, but we should do so with a degree of realism."[43] Gillian Oghene of the Fife drug court agrees that in defending drug courts, "you have to be realistic and honest," and she warns against creating a situation where "people expect too much." Moira Price of Glasgow makes a similar point: "You're setting yourself up for a fall if you claim that [drug courts] would work for everyone, since nothing ever will." Price continues,

> It can never work completely when it's in isolation from everything else. You have to do different things, helping people at different stages. . . . We're set up to deal with one particular problem, and we're not saying that we'll cure everything else. We can deal with what we're set up to deal with, and you need other things to deal with other problems.

The Irish are equally modest about what they believe problem-solving courts can ultimately achieve. The first major report on drug courts issued by the Irish government asserts: "Drug Courts are not a panacea, they are not a universal remedy for the drug problem."[44] Individual Irish judges express similar views. Judge Haughton, for example, makes clear that these courts are "not the answer to everything" but are "a useful part of the criminal justice system. . . . It has its place, but it's just part of the system." Judge Hogan likewise says that he does not "want to see drug court being built up as the savior of everything"—a not-very-oblique reference to rhetoric emanating from the United States, where "there's a tendency to do that." Hogan believes "that's a wrong tendency." In discussing the significant number of offenders assigned to the Dublin drug court whose orders were later terminated, Haughton puts forth a view consistently advanced by Irish officials: the "fact that the Drug Court approach is not a panacea for all drug misusing offenders."[45]

Moderation is also evidenced by the fact that those in the non-U.S. regions harbor fewer illusions that the perennial problems addressed in these courts will ever be fully solved. Recall Australian criminologist Arie Freiberg's preference for the "slightly less hubristic" term "problem-oriented" over "problem-solving" (which, as he explains, "signifies the effort rather than the result")—a viewpoint that he acknowledges "is slightly more pessimistic than [that of] American promoters of this concept."[46] Interestingly, Freiberg sets himself apart from the Americans in another sense when he writes that though he "can be identified as a supporter of the problem-solving experiment," he is "not messianic about it."[47] Jocelyn Green, in the United Kingdom, thinks Frieberg's preference for using the term "problem-oriented" to characterize these courts "is a good point" and notes that in England and Wales, "they're quite realistic about what they believe these courts can achieve." Compared to the United States, she thinks, "we're more realistic."

Another example of the contrast between American boldness and the relative moderation of the other countries is the differing treatment goals: total abstinence in the United States, and harm reduction or harm minimization in the other countries. Though this perspective is reflected in a number of initiatives (e.g., prostitution courts in Australia and needle-exchange programs in Canada and elsewhere), it is particularly evident in the operation of drug treatment programs in various problem-solving courts. As discussed in previous chapters, to graduate from a U.S. drug court, participants often must achieve a condition of total abstinence (including from alcohol), whereas in the other countries, the programs are satisfied with a reduction in use (and do not usually require abstinence from alcohol). Moreover, as we have seen, the other countries are much more likely to use methadone as a form of treatment, whereas in the United States, methadone maintenance is much less popular (and in many programs is strictly forbidden).

DELIBERATION

A second feature of the non-U.S. problem-solving courts is deliberation. In part, deliberation refers to the extent to which judges allow the formation of these courts to take place within the deliberative processes of the other branches of government. In the cases outside of the United States, problem-solving court programs are not typically initiated or advanced until there has been legislative approval, the establishment of an investigative working group, a long discussion among relevant parties, the establishment of a pilot scheme, and/or reevaluation based on the results of a pilot scheme. In the United States, problem-solving courts usually start at the local level, often without legislative approval or discussion.[48] Instead of boldness, then, problem-solving courts in the other regions are characterized by caution and deliberation—caution with respect to the extent to which judges are willing to act outside of legally defined and legislatively approved limits on their actions, and deliberation about whether to start the programs and/or expand problem-solving courts after they have been piloted for a specified period of time.

In all five non-U.S. regions, officials generally took longer to initiate courts, which were more typically established in a top-down rather than a grassroots manner. In some countries, the courts were established and/or given direction by the legislature. As a direct consequence, problem-solving court proposals necessarily passed through a deliberative body. Thus, one finds in places like Scotland and Australia considerable parliamentary discussion and debate about the merit, scope, and desirability of these courts long before a judge would ever sit as a problem-solving court judge. In other countries (e.g., England, Canada, and Ireland), direction and/or funding for problem-solving courts often came from the executive branch. In these instances, the judiciary had to wait for the government's initiative and financial support. In some cases, though there had been interest in starting a problem-solving court at the local level, without the government's support, plans for the new court were never realized. Calgary, for example, wanted a drug court and applied for federal support to start one. The federal government did not accept its proposal, and therefore Calgary did not get a drug court.

Processes of deliberation are also evident in the efforts of various working groups set up to explore the possibility of experimenting with problem-solving courts, particularly in Scotland and Ireland. As we have seen, these groups include representatives from a number of disciplines. With so many perspectives and interests involved, finding common ground and establishing program parameters acceptable to the various agencies often results in difficult and lengthy processes of deliberation. Recall, for example, the establishment of the Dublin drug court; not only did the various parties in the working group "fight their corner and fight it well," but also judges were unwilling to start the court until all the contributing services were in place—thus rejecting the American advice to "just do it" and move forward in a more hurried manner. It should also be noted that the working groups have typically studied related court programs in other countries to inform their analyses, an approach one does not often find in the United States (where the focus tends to be more specifically on what occurs in the United States).

Deliberation, moreover, does not end with the initiation of the court programs. A common practice in the five non-U.S. countries has been to establish pilot schemes before launching courts on a more permanent or widespread basis. The very notion of a pilot scheme (that is, testing before fully committing to a new program) is emblematic of the more cautionary approach typical in the other countries. Thus, Australia is not the only country that, compared to the United States, "tiptoes carefully, slowly, and most times reluctantly," as Aire Freiberg puts it. The continuation of the deliberative process is also evident in the manner in which the non-U.S. countries have made significant legislatively initiated adjustments to programs after they have been established. England's DTTOs were essentially scrapped six years after the launch of the first pilot programs. The Perth drug court was substantively altered through legislative action more than two years after it was initiated. Legislation directing the Sydney drug court has been amended several times—which is especially relevant in this instance, given that team members, as discussed in chapter 4, return to the legislation for guidance "over and over again." Recall also that Scottish sheriffs had to wait several years before the legislature gave them authority to impose intermediate sanctions (i.e., short stints in jail). As these examples make clear, processes of deliberation continue even after problem-solving courts have been launched.

In addition to the role that the executive and legislative branches continue to play in the non-U.S. countries, we also find ongoing deliberation and critical self-reflection within the judiciary itself. This is particularly pronounced in Australia, where magistrates openly worry about how therapeutic jurisprudence and problem-solving approaches might violate commitments to natural and open justice. Even without the pressures from legislative action, judges and magistrates have made certain adjustments to courtroom practices—sometimes in direct response to these concerns. Recall several examples. In Calgary, the domestic violence court eventually gave the victim support agency, HomeFront, a less prominent place in the courtroom out of concerns that the plaintiff/victim was being given an unfair advantage in court proceedings. A Western Australian magistrate disallowed clapping in certain instances after observing client disapproval of the practice. After running the Dandenong drug court in Victoria, Australia, for three years, Magistrate Margaret Harding decided to move away from review sessions with everyone in attendance to individual reviews. She found that "everybody was happy with that" and "seemed to prefer it." In particular, she found that participants were more open when meeting with her individually in court, and therefore decided to leave the new format in place.

This is not to suggest that one never finds such critical self-reflection and subsequent adjustments in the United States. American problem-solving courts have also, in some cases, been altered over time in light of related concerns. For example, many of the early drug courts were pre-adjudicative. As a consequence, clients were under intensive judicial monitoring and were potentially subjected to periods of incarceration, though they had never entered a guilty plea. Over time, the post-adjudicative model has become more common. Other courts have had to make significant revisions in response to net-widening tendencies, where drug court programs had become too large and unwieldy. These are no small adjustments. That said, the tone (or accent) of American problem-solving courts tends more toward a salesmanship and a "we-have-the-answers" orientation, which is very different from the more modest and self-critical tone common in the other countries.

RESTRAINT

This sense of caution and deliberation relates directly to—and will be further illustrated by—a final feature of the non-U.S. courts: the notion of restraint. Recall the opposing ideal types of romantic and classical judges. One of the features of the classical judge, in Glendon's typology, is restraint. She identifies three types of restraint: structural, interpretive, and personal.[49] All three are evident in the judicial mentality and practices among the non-U.S. problem-solving court judges. Consider examples from the comparative data to illustrate each.

Structural restraint refers to those limits placed on the judge by the other branches of government, by the federalist system (in the case of the United States), and by the court's place in the hierarchy of the judiciary. As we have seen in the other countries, the courts are clearly more deferential to the direction and guidance of the other branches of government. Court officials are reluctant to initiate programs independent of the executive and legislative branches. Structural restraint, as such, is perhaps most pronounced in England and Wales.

Recall, for example, that British domestic violence court judges and magistrates do not have the authority to bring defendants back to court for ongoing judicial reviews, which are typically a central feature of problem-solving court programs (even the less therapeutically inclined domestic violence courts in the United States). Those working in British domestic violence courts, however, are very clear that, even if they wished to implement this feature, such a practice could only be realized in their programs if granted by the legislature. As noted in chapter 3, according to a review of the Leeds domestic violence court, movement in this direction would require "legislative changes." It could only be achieved "through a new legislative framework." An official at the Leeds domestic violence court similarly states that the court cannot bring clients back for review because "there is no statutory basis for that." To add reviews or other forms of more proactive judicial engagement would "really need to be parliamentary driven."

Officials working with DTTOs and other drug court–like programs in England and Wales have likewise been largely deferential to the dictates of the government, clearly lacking the enthusiasm and entrepreneurial energy of American problem-solving court advocates. Recall the responses of officials working with the Croydon DTTO. With respect to the initiation of their program, one said, "We've been basically told to get on with it. Here's the legislation. Here are the Home Office guidelines. Work with it." On whether DTTOs should be introduced across the United Kingdom, another said, "It will be for the government to decide. . . . We are going to have to do what the government says." And when the government decided to scrap DTTOs altogether and introduce DRRs within the Community Order scheme instead, there were no strong public statements from magistrates or probation officers one way or the other in response. Instead, they simply followed the new legislative guidelines and "worked with it."

Deference to the legislature is also evident in Australia, where a variety of problem-solving courts have been created through acts of parliament. Judge Murrell makes very clear that the Sydney drug court is a "legislatively based court." The 1998 Drug Court Act, which passed on "a bipartisan basis," specifies in some detail the purpose, processes, and parameters of the court. For example, it spells out who is eligible for the program, it provides a legislative basis for rewarding and sanctioning participants, and it sets the standards for participant termination from the program. The act also specifies that any "final sentence" imposed on a participant "cannot be greater than the initial sentence"—which, again, according to Murrell, is clearly and specifically spelled out in the "statute under which I operate." Legislatively determined standards are important, according to Murrell, because, though she believes Australian judges exercise more personal restraint than do American judges, "it's desirable to have other restraints, which are not simply reliant on the personalities of each individual judge." Thus, for a number of reasons, Judge Murrell feels strongly that "the fact that it is legislatively based is significant."

In the early years of the Toronto drug court, Judge Bentley expressed some envy of the type of judicial authority and flexibility found in American drug courts and in the Sydney drug court. "I wish that I had as much leverage as the American judges," said Bentley. "We don't have that flexibility." Elaborating on this point, Bentley compared what happens in American courts to his powers in the Toronto court. "I know in some American jurisdictions you can give them the sentence beforehand and say, 'I'm going to suspend the sentence,' but then you impose a little bit of it. Well, I can suspend the sentence, but then I can't keep on bringing them back." According to Bentley, "they'd have to change the legislation" for him to be able to "keep bringing them back." He cited Judge Murrell's court in Australia as having "more flexibility" because it is a "legislative court," and he believes if the same were the case in Toronto, he also would have more leverage and flexibility. However, without the enabling legislation, Bentley concedes that he cannot deal with clients in this manner: "legally, I cannot."

Recall also how in Scotland, sheriffs would not impose intermediate sanctions until given legislative authority to do so. Until June 27, 2003, participants on a Scottish drug court order or DTTO could not be sent to jail as an intermediate sanction for noncompliance with an order. To send a participant to jail would be to terminate the order. Sheriffs did sometimes find ways to impose what were, in effect, short jail terms while a participant was still in the program. If the offender had several charges, the court would in some instances hold the participant on concurrent orders. Therefore, if the offender violated the terms of the order, he could be terminated from one order, sent to jail for a short period of time, and then returned to the court for supervision on one of the remaining orders. However, this was not a common practice, could only be applied to participants with multiple charges, and still technically complied with existing legislation.

The second type of restraint—interpretive restraint—refers to those limits required by judicial deference to constitutional precepts, statutory law, and legal precedent. Consider several examples of interpretive restraint from non-U.S. problem-solving courts. In Britain's first community court, Judge Fletcher has considerable authority and discretion. However, he recognizes the limits within which he must operate. Like other British judges, he realizes that he is "hidebound by maximum sentences," and he can only "use the tools that government" gives him. As with magistrates and judges in other British problem-solving courts, he is limited by statutory law in terms of his power to impose intermediate sentences. Thus the observation of one Liverpool official who said, "Judge Fletcher is very limited on what he can actually impose."

The ongoing interpretation of statutory law is also evident in Australia. Not only were courts set up by the legislative and executive branches of government, but judges continue to consult the particularities of statutory law as they attempt to run their programs. Recall how officials in the Sydney drug court describe going back to the Drug Court Act "over and over" to make sure they are "on the right track." The first judge of the Perth drug court had to work within existing bail legislation, which in her view seriously limited the court's effectiveness. Only later did the Parliament of Western Australia give the court greater discretion and leverage. Such judicial deference to the dictates of statutory law is also found in Victoria, where, as discussed in chapter 4, magistrates essentially refused to send offenders to a certain diversion program because, according to their interpretation, statutory justification for such action did not exist.

In Canada, the very genesis of aboriginal courts can be traced to the 1999 amendment to the Canadian Criminal Code, section 718.2(e), and the two Supreme Court interpretations of this legislation. Officials make clear that without section 718.2(e), the Gladue courts in Toronto simply would not exist. And while other problem-solving courts in Canada did not come into being as a direct result of parliamentary acts, problem-solving court judges have made considerable efforts to justify new initiatives through reference to existing statutory law, and many hope for the eventual passage of legislation that would expand problem-solving court powers.

The final type of restraint identified by Glendon is personal restraint, which refers to the limits the judge places on herself in her efforts to be fair, impartial, objective, and dispassionate. Arguably, this is the type of restraint that, when exhibited, most clearly reveals the habits of mind of a local legal culture. As we have found, problem-solving courts give judges greater power and discretion. In some places—such as England—this expanded authority is limited by structural restraints, e.g., the strength of probation and the limitations of the magistracy. Both in England and in other countries (where such limitations do not exist), however, judges and magistrates still intentionally hold themselves in check, even when they could, if they wished, act with more discretion.

Given the expanded parameters of problem-solving courts, in fact, some even recognize that personal restraint, as such, is all the more important. This kind of understanding is particularly evident in Australia, where judges both acknowledge and worry about the potential for a blurring of boundaries inherent in the problem-solving court format. Australian judges may agree with American judges that problem-solving courts provide a setting in which judges can "color outside the lines," but they believe that precisely because of this freedom, judges should be all the more careful to curb their own artistic license (pushing this metaphor a bit further) so that the final "drawing" is still recognizable as a court of law.

As noted in chapter 4, problem-solving court officials in both Canada and Australia express this basic view. Judge Gay Murrell, for example, says that "despite a lack of protective conventions," in problem-solving courts, judges must strive to "maintain judicial impartiality and ensure that participants receive procedural fairness."[50] Tina Previtera of Queensland similarly observes that the "evolving nature" of problem-solving courts means that the "richness and history" that previously "safeguarded" a "defendant's legal protection" is not as available to a judge in this context. Without the binding influence of "tradition and precedent," says Previtera, "we must charge ourselves with the responsibility therefore to ensure that therapeutic considerations do not over-ride long standing freedoms and rights."[51] Jelena Popovic likewise admonishes fellow practitioners to "strive to ensure that we are not trampling over the rights of court users."[52] Recall also the summary statement issued by conferees at a problem-solving court conference in Toronto, which noted that "one of the risks of a less traditional posture is that the boundaries between individuals can become blurred" and thus warned that "in spite of the informality . . . the judge must maintain sufficient detachment."

In Australia and other countries, we have observed judges who, though given license to stray beyond the boundaries of traditional judicial practices, nevertheless maintain what they understand to be appropriate judicial reserve. Judge Richard Schneider of the Toronto mental health court, for example, believes that the judge should guard against too much familiarity. "By becoming too intimate with the procedure," says Schneider, "you lose that distance and therefore the impact that you have when you do get involved. The closer you get, that sort of impact I think is reduced." Similarly, recall how Scottish sheriffs who were given the authority to impose intermediate sanctions still hesitated to use this power and worried about imposing what could, in effect, be sanctions disproportionate to the offenses committed. Also in Scotland, we found youth court judges who, though encouraged to relate with clients in a more personal and interactive manner, resisted such engagement, believing that it is not "really part of a judge's job to get too close to the accused."

Recall also how an Irish judge who was encouraged to speak to a client in open court about certain matters ultimately refused, believing such interaction to be patronizing and unfair to the accused. We have also seen that judges in all five non-U.S. regions, with only a few exceptions, resist engaging in the expressive, theatrical, and emotive form of courtroom behavior one finds in many American problem-solving courts. Not only do nearly all non-U.S. judges considered here find the prospect of hugging clients "appalling" behavior for a judge, but many are also against clapping in the courtroom, holding graduation ceremonies, interacting in an overly personal manner, or even expressing emotions. Judicial reticence to engage in this manner, again, often has more to do with cultural dispositions than it does with any kind of formal legal and structural restrictions. Many non-U.S. problem-solving court judges simply see such behavior as nonsensical, beyond the pale, inappropriate, and unbecoming of a judicial officer.

Such perceptions of American practices revealed here may well reflect more general attitudes toward the United States. As we have seen, some judges actually speak of American cultural imperialism and try, in some instances, to downplay the American genesis of problem-solving courts when advocating these courts in their own country. Curiously, we have also seen that officials recognize and sometimes highlight the American inspiration for problem-solving courts. One might label such apparently contradictory dispositions as a kind of ambivalent anti-Americanism which, like other comparative features of problem-solving courts considered in this chapter, is indicative of broader legal and cultural realities. In the next chapter, we turn to a fuller exploration of the kind of anti-Americanism found in the international problem-solving court movement, and consider how this relates to global attitudes toward the United States more generally.

Chapter Seven

AMBIVALENT ANTI-AMERICANISM

> Opinions about the U.S. . . . . are complicated and contradic-
> tory. People around the world embrace things American and,
> at the same time, decry U.S. influence on their societies.
> —*Pew Global Attitudes Project*

AT A 1999 NADCP conference in Miami, an international panel,
comprising representatives from Canada, Scotland, Australia,
and the United States, was assembled for the purpose of discussing the establishment of international standards for drug courts. In
addition to the panel members, others participating in the discussion included representatives from Ireland and England. Concern about "American cultural imperialism" was among the topics addressed during the session. The Scottish panelist, who had by his own account been promoting
drug courts in Scotland for three years, offered the following anecdote to
illustrate the anti-American attitudes that had sometimes frustrated his
promotional efforts:

> I was meeting with a director of social work, who has responsibility for the
> probation service and the second largest authority in Scotland. He says, "I'll
> meet you in Starbucks down in Glasgow," and he came in with these Nike
> trainers and his Levi's jeans and the rest of the American designer gear, and he
> said to me, "Of course, American ideas just don't work in Britain."

The irony of the Scottish social worker denouncing American ideas while
at the same time fully embracing American products is indicative of a
larger social reality. That is, globally, one finds a kind of ambivalent anti-
Americanism, where citizens in other countries say they do not like American ideas and the incessant infusion of American culture into their societies, yet they simultaneously admire and cannot seem to get enough of
American technology and cultural products.

This finding was among the most interesting of the Pew Global Attitudes Project, which issued its first major report in 2002. The 2002 survey
of citizens in over forty countries around the world found that Americanization, or the spread of "American ideas and customs," is overwhelmingly viewed as a negative development.[1] Not surprisingly, this view is

particularly pronounced in the Middle East, where a majority in every Middle Eastern country sees the spread of "American ideas and customs" as "bad." Those who view favorably the spread of things American number as low as 2 percent in Pakistan and 6 percent in Egypt. Concerns about the processes of Americanization, however, are also widespread in Western Europe and Canada, where at least 50 percent of those surveyed in each country of these regions in 2002 viewed the spread of American ideas and customs in their countries as a bad thing.[2]

In the five years since the 2002 survey, such concerns have only intensified. The 2007 Pew Global Attitudes survey reported that in thirty-seven of forty-six countries, over half of those surveyed viewed the processes of Americanization negatively.[3] As it concerns countries considered in this comparative analysis (which were included in the Pew survey), negative views about the spread of American ideas and customs increased between 2002 and 2007, from 54 to 67 percent in Canada and from 50 to 67 percent in Britain.[4] Survey findings reveal growing anti-Americanism in a range of other areas as well. For example, between 2002 and 2007, "favorable ratings" about the United States decreased in twenty-six of thirty-three countries (for which such longitudinal data are available).[5] The 2007 survey also found that majorities in all but a handful of African countries believe that U.S. policies increase the gap between rich and poor countries.[6] Majorities in most countries dislike American ideas about democracy and believe that the United States promotes democracy to serve its own interests.[7] Thus, it seems that many would agree with the perspective of the Scottish social worker that American ideas do not work (or are not welcomed) in their country.

Also like the Scottish social worker, however, negative views about the spread of American ideas and customs do not necessarily translate into a rejection of American cultural products. The same surveys find that a majority of people in most countries around the world like American popular culture and admire the United States for its advances in science and technology. This is particularly the case in Canada and Western Europe. As reported in the 2002 survey, 77 percent of Canadian and 76 percent of British respondents said they "like American music, television, and movies," and approximately the same percentages said they "admire the United States for its technological and scientific advances."[8] Though decreasing slightly, these numbers remained nearly as high for Canada and Britain in the 2007 survey.[9]

Thus, the survey report offers the following paradoxical conclusion: while "large proportions in most countries think it is bad that American ideas and customs are spreading to their countries," there is also "near universal admiration for U.S. technology and a strong appetite for its cultural exports in most parts of the world."[10] In a number of interesting ways, importers of American problem-solving courts exhibit the same contradictory attitudes toward the United States. That is, they worry out loud about American cultural imperialism, even while they simultaneously import and embrace what is undeniably an American-grown legal product. Such a paradoxical juxtaposition creates an interesting sort of tension for advocates of problem-solving courts in the non-U.S. regions. While they wish to introduce new court programs in their respective legal systems, they also sometimes appear compelled to play down the American origins and the more conspicuously American features of the legal innovations. Advocates of problem-solving courts outside of the United States employ at least three different strategies for resolving this dilemma.

THE ANTI-AMERICAN PITCH

The first of these strategies is to sell the court programs in almost anti-American terms. This is the approach that Paul Bentley has sometimes taken in his efforts to promote problem-solving courts in Canada. As noted in chapter 4, he is very cognizant of anti-American sentiments in Canada. "We get your culture bombarding us day in and day out," says Bentley. He sees the infusion of American culture into Canadian society as particularly concentrated because "we're so close." As a consequence, "we pick up all your stations, TV, radio, magazines, it's unlimited." Navigating between the zeal of Americans on the one hand and Canadian concerns about "American cultural imperialism" on the other has sometimes proved challenging for Bentley. Like the Irish, he finds that some American judges "get a little impatient" with the speed at which the movement is advanced outside of the United States. He rightly notes that in Canada and Europe, things develop "much slower and with more hesitancy" than in the United States, where "things grow exponentially." In Canada, because "people are more cautious," they resist the entrepreneurial and proselytizing zeal of their powerful neighbors to the south. There is an attitude in Canada, according to Bentley, that "just because Americans are doing it doesn't necessarily mean it's right."

Canadians' "love-hate relationship with the U.S.," therefore, is something with which Bentley has had to contend. Recall how Bentley advocated the introduction of drug courts in Canada by highlighting "what a mess" the Americans made of their system before they finally discovered drug courts. Thus, he endeavored to sell drug courts to Canadians by, in essence, proposing a program that would avoid the mistakes made by the Americans. In addition to contending with skeptical Canadians, Bentley has also had to deal with the overeagerness of American judges in the movement—judges who not only want to see the more speedy development of problem-solving courts outside the United States but also are sometimes insistent about what the courts should look like in practice. Having participated in a number of international conferences with representatives from Ireland, Scotland, Australia, and elsewhere, Bentley observes that practitioners in other countries are, like him, not entirely comfortable with American boldness, enthusiasm, and rigidity.

The rigidity, according to Bentley, refers to the American attitude that "it's our way." Bentley and his counterparts in other countries have found that some American judges "don't seem to be open to the fact that in Scotland, they may want to do it a different way. Or in Vancouver, they want to do it a different way. Or what have you." Instead, he has sometimes experienced an American attitude that says, "this is how drug courts work, and this is the way you will have your drug court work." According to Bentley, American judges sometimes demonstrate "a resistance or a difficulty accepting that other communities and other jurisdictions want to do it differently." In response, Bentley has been careful to emphasize that each country's experience with problem-solving courts will vary. As he told an international audience in Scotland, "The Canadian experience is not the American experience, and the Scottish experience is not the Canadian experience."

Mary Hogan, another Canadian drug court judge, is likewise aware of a general wariness of the United States among Canadians. "We see ourselves as a different sort of society than the U.S.," says Hogan. She notes, in particular, that Canadians "see the U.S. as more imperialistic" and highlights important differences between the United States and Canada in a number of policy areas, including gun control and health care. Because of differences such as these, according to Hogan, "a lot of us see ourselves as more European than American." As for herself, she "would never want to be part of the U.S.," and would never wish for Canada to "operate the way the U.S. does." Nevertheless, like Bentley, she notes that, "unfortunately," because Canada is "so close we are in a lot of ways Americanized." As it specifically concerns problem-solving courts, Hogan notes the "fervor" of American judges and describes the development of problem-solving courts in the United States as "almost a religious movement." In contrast, she sees Canadians as "much more low-key" and not always receptive to the eagerness and enthusiasm of American judges. Hogan, for example, is sometimes bothered by the "do this, do that" nature of "all these e-mails I keep getting from the NADCP."

From the very early years of Scotland's exploration of the drug court concept, there has likewise been resistance to the proselytizing efforts of American problem-solving court advocates. Justine Walker, for example, while in the process of setting up the conference outside of Stirling, said, "We don't actually want people to come over and do a sales pitch." Instead, she said that the Scottish were looking for descriptive information about drug courts in the United States, and she noted in particular some skepticism regarding U.S. claims of program efficacy. She found the evaluation studies to be "very, very weak," and doubted that, if presented to Scottish officials, the data "would have sold anybody" on drug courts.[11] As in Canada, Walker also spoke of a general attitude among the Scottish of not wanting to simply follow what the Americans were doing. "There is a real reluctance within the Scottish system to follow everything America is doing," Walker says. "We're different." She adds, "There is quite a strong feeling" among the Scottish that "we don't want to just follow in their footsteps."

AFFINITY WITH OTHER COUNTRIES

A second strategy to avoid being seen as directly emulating American practices is to highlight related developments in other countries. Thus, though Walker invited Americans to the conference in Scotland, she also invited representatives from Canada and the United Nations Drugs Control Programme in Austria. In fact, the title of the conference, "Court Intervention with Drug Using Offenders: An International Perspective," intentionally emphasized the international nature of the movement and even managed to avoid use of the American-generated term "drug court." Importers of problem-solving courts show interest in other countries for several reasons. First, as noted earlier, highlighting developments in other countries gives the appearance that problem-solving courts are not just an American but an international phenomenon. Second, in keeping with the deliberative orientation of the other countries, looking elsewhere allows officials to assess the scope and success of problem-solving courts in a more careful and comprehensive manner. Third, outside of the United States, it is a fairly usual practice more generally to consider laws in other countries, whereas learning from foreign legal systems is less common in the United States.

Indeed, when a few U.S. Supreme Court justices recently ventured to cite foreign laws in several controversial decisions, they met with a strong backlash. For example, in *Atkins v. Virginia*—a 2002 case in which the court ruled that it was cruel and unusual punishment to execute mentally retarded criminals—Justice John Paul Stevens observed in a footnote that such a punishment was "overwhelmingly disapproved" of "within the world community" and specifically cited a brief for the European Union in support of this observation. In his dissenting opinion, Justice Antonin Scalia responded indignantly: "[I]rrelevant are the practices of the 'world community,' whose notions of justice are (thankfully) not always those of our people."[12] As a result of exchanges like this, discussion about the relevance of foreign laws to U.S. constitutional law has developed into a broader public debate. Justice John Roberts, for example, was even questioned on the topic during his Senate confirmation hearings. He responded by expressing several reservations about the citing of foreign laws by Supreme Court justices.

Judges outside of the United States have fewer scruples about borrowing from other countries.[13] What one finds in the case of problem-solving courts is that judges in the five other regions considered here frequently look elsewhere, and they are at times keen to highlight the influence of countries other than the United States. Interestingly, such a reluctance to adopt (or to be seeing as adopting) laws from the United States can also be found in the area of constitutional law. Anne-Marie Slaughter, for example, observes the disproportionate influence of Canadian and South African constitutionalism on developing democracies. Slaughter explains that "their influence may spring from the simple fact that they are not American." Because of this, the legal reasoning in these countries is seen as "more politically palatable to domestic audiences in an era of extraordinary U.S. military, political, economic, and cultural power and accompanying resentments."[14] In a discussion of legal transplantation, Frederick Schauer likewise observes that "in some political quarters, avoiding American influence just because it is American often appears to be a driving force." As an example, Schauer observes that the Supreme Court of Canada "relies less heavily on American precedents than one might have predicted"—this because of Canadian worries about "being perceived as the 'fifty-first state' of the United States."[15]

In the legal transplantation of problem-solving courts, one finds a similar tendency to highlight the influence of and affinity with countries other than (or at least in addition to) the United States. Recall, for example, Moira Price's discussion of legal and cultural common ground between Ireland and Scotland. Price also speaks of the influential role of Canada, which, in her view, has a "much more similar culture" to Scotland than does the United States. Sydney's Judge Murrell similarly believes Australia is culturally closer to Canada and Ireland than it is to the United States. In discussing a visit of Irish officials to Australia, Murrell recalled that the Irish "felt very much at home in our drug court, as opposed to the U.S. drug courts." By way of explanation she added, "I think they identify with the more reserved and less personal role of the Australian judge." Murrell observes similarities between Irish and Australian cultures more generally, especially in Sydney, where there has been a "strong sort of Irish influence." Moreover, both Ireland and Australia "derived from the same judicial system" and are thus much "closer to the common law traditions in Britain than the U.S." In this regard, recall finally Murrell's expressed affinity with the United Kingdom as it concerns judicial reserve in Australia: "It's just part of our culture; we're a bit more British."

In setting up problem-solving courts in England, officials have also consistently looked to other countries besides the United States. While developing England's first community court, for example, Judge Fletcher visited a number of countries, including Australia, and, as Jonathan Monk at the Ministry of Justice explains, "He brings things back that he can then begin to utilize here." In planning Scotland's first community court, project team members studied community courts in both England and the United States, met with the Red Hook judge, and visited the Liverpool community court. Judges from Ireland have visited courts in all the countries considered in this case study. "I think the more information you have about what's going on," Judge Haughton explains, "the better you are able to set up your own model." For these judges, then, the legal practices of the "world community" are regarded as anything but "irrelevant."

Reports assembled by the various working groups also consistently consider developments both in the United States and in other countries. In its first study of drug courts, the Irish working group considered programs in Germany, Sweden, Australia, England, and Wales, in addition to the United States. A study of problem-solving courts commissioned by the Ministry of Justice in England extensively examined community courts, drug courts, domestic violence courts, and mental health courts in Australia, Canada, and the United States—an examination that was itself preceded by a more general Internet review of developments in the United States, Ireland, Scotland, Australia, New Zealand, Canada, South Africa, the Cayman Islands, and Bermuda. The study was conducted "with a view to informing current and proposed initiatives in this country."[16] Similarly, a working group investigating drug courts in Scotland "considered detailed reports on the establishment and operation of drug courts in America, Canada, Australia, and Ireland."[17] When the Scottish National Party first endorsed drug courts in its 1999 party platform, it did not even name the United States, but referred to the success of drug courts in "a number of other countries."[18] Thus, time and again, officials in the five non-U.S. countries look to and highlight their affinity with programs in regions outside of the United States.

In contrast, the United States does not often look to other countries to inform its legal decisions or the development of legal programs. Again, this is a tendency one finds at the level of the U.S. Supreme Court as well. Justice Ruth Bader Ginsburg, for example, has observed, in contrast to the practices of judges abroad, that the "same readiness to look beyond one's own shores has not marked the decisions of the court on which I serve."[19] In the case of problem-solving courts, one does encounter references by Americans to legal developments overseas, not so much for the purposes of informing practices in the United States, but as a way of demonstrating the movement's success and growing influence. Robert Wolf, from the CCI, for example, argues that one way to determine an idea's success is "to measure how far the concept travels."[20] He highlights the center's work internationally to illustrate how, according to this measure, problem-solving courts have been "highly successful."[21] Another report from the CCI observes that between 1996 and 2006, visitors from over fifty countries toured such projects as the Red Hook and Midtown community courts. According to the center, "The impacts of these visits can be seen across the globe."[22] The center also boasts that it has "counseled jurisdictions around the world in the development of groundbreaking justice experiments."[23] This international influence thus contributes to the movement's own legacy and standing. As the center "spreads the word about New York's innovations," it helps to solidify "New York's reputation as an international leader in justice reform."[24] Again, focus on work in other countries serves not as a way for Americans to learn about— much less from—other societies and cultures, but as a kind of "feather in the cap," underscoring the significance and genius of their own innovations. Thus, the center sees as its "most lasting legacy" the notion that it "sits at the fulcrum of an international movement."[25]

Visits by U.S. officials to other countries for the purposes of observing and learning, as opposed to instructing and spreading "the gospel of problem-solving justice," have been comparatively rare. An official from Scotland's first problem-solving court says that her court has had a number of international visitors, including representatives from Ireland, Norway, Russia, and Macedonia, but no visits from any U.S. officials or practitioners. Moreover, when the Scottish have presented as a panel at annual NADCP conferences, they do not typically get much interest from U.S. conferees wanting to learn about the Scottish experience. Instead, some who have attended their sessions "were planning a vacation to Scotland and wanted to get tips from the panel." The Scottish are not necessarily bothered by this lack of interest. With notable modesty, as one official explains, they would, in fact, "be surprised if someone chose to come all the way over the Atlantic to a small country when they [the Americans] have got so many [problem-solving courts] on their doorstep." This official asks: "Why would they specifically come to what is, in relative terms, a very small country?" Less forgiving, a Scottish sheriff observes a lack of interest in things foreign among Americans in a more general sense. He notes that some Americans "are completely unaware of what is going on in the rest of the world. I mean not only are they unaware, but they don't care. They're not interested."[26]

This observation parallels other findings from the Pew Global Attitudes survey, in particular the results from a question about foreign policy. In the 2007 survey, respondents were asked if they thought the United States takes into account the interests of other countries in making international policy decisions. Significantly, respondents in Canada and Western European countries overwhelmingly felt that the United States did not take into account the interests of other countries.[27] The survey reports that 83 percent of Canadians, 74 percent of the British, 89 percent of the French, and 91 percent of the Swedish hold such a view.[28] Obviously, this question has more to do with foreign policy initiatives such as the U.S. invasion of Iraq than it does with the borrowing of local court innovations. In both cases, though, what one finds is a perceived lack of concern on the part of the United States in learning about the interests, practices, and cultures of other places, and a preoccupation among Americans with spreading their own ideas and practices.[29] In contrast, the five other countries explored here consistently show a wider interest in practices outside of their own countries and typically investigate these practices as a way to inform and guide their own efforts, as well as to show that they are not "slavishly adopting" an American-made legal innovation.[30]

EMPHASIZING ADAPTATION

Perhaps the most common strategy employed by importers of problem-solving courts to avoid conspicuous emulation of American programs is to emphasize the process of adaptation. That is, those adopting the U.S. problem-solving courts will acknowledge the American genesis of the innovation (though sometimes reluctantly), but will stress the extent to which the programs must be adjusted or tailored to fit local circumstances. According to this strategy, importers can express open disdain for the overtly American features of a particular problem-solving court while also arguing for the relevance of the program to their local legal system.

Recall, for example, how an Australian judge referred to American judges as having a "Personality with a capital *P*"; how an Irish judge worried about the American judicial propensity to go off on an "ego trip"; how a Canadian judge contrasted the "low-key" style of Canadian judges with the "fervor" and religious zeal of American problem-solving court judges; how an English magistrate concluded, after observing the expressivism of an American problem-solving court, that it would be difficult to "envisage such emotional events taking place in the courts in this country"; and how a Scottish Member of Parliament anticipated with "glee" the adjustments that would have to be made to the American model "to take account of cultural differences." In each instance, officials identified a peculiar inflection in the American legal accent that deviates from the tone of their own legal culture.

Because of these perceived differences, importers emphasize the need for adaptation. In each of the countries outside of the United States, we have repeatedly seen importers of problem-solving courts emphasize the need for adjustments in the transplantation process. Consider several examples by way of review. An Irish judge argued that the American model "needed to be modified to suit the particular circumstances in Dublin."[31] When the Scottish Executive announced in 2007 that it would launch a community court, it stressed that, though it would look to community court models in other countries, the new Glasgow community court would be "adapted to suit the needs of the Scottish criminal justice system and local community."[32] An Australian solicitor recounted how, after a delegation of Australian officials returned from a visit to the United States, they were determined to start a drug court "designed . . . for the Australian—the New South Wales—environment." David Indermaur and Lynn Roberts, in their evaluation of the Perth drug court, noted the tendency of a number of English-speaking countries to "import the best and worst of American criminal justice innovations" and warned against "adopting American models that may not be suited to an Australian environment."[33] Though the United States served as one of the models for the development of domestic violence courts in England and Wales, these courts were, according to an evaluator, "always modified according to local conditions." The first Canadian drug court judge began the process of starting a drug court "with the purpose of developing a model that fit the Anglo-Canadian criminal justice system." As he told Americans at the time: "We want to use what you've done well, ignore what you haven't done so well, and adapt the model [to] our own local use."

Emphasizing adaptation, then, allows importers to identify what the Americans "haven't done so well." Often signifying at least a subtle form of anti-Americanism, importers openly denounce those features of the American courts they wish to avoid. As we have seen, officials in other countries speak against the theater, emotionalism, and physical contact found in American problem-solving courts. They also, in some cases, denounce overwrought graduation ceremonies, prize-giving, clapping, a total-abstinence treatment philosophy, and judicial fund-raising. In other cases, they "ignore" therapeutic jurisprudence, a rehabilitative orientation toward domestic violence offenders, acupuncture, and the self-help group format of some treatment models. Importers of problem-solving courts believe they can pick and choose elements of the American model, employing what is useful and applicable to their local situation and jettisoning what is not. The comparative differences described in chapter 6 provide some evidence that the courts have, at least initially, been successful at resisting the importation of unwanted elements of the American model.

That importers see themselves as adopting only that which fits their local situation calls to mind the various reflections on globalization and legal borrowing first introduced in chapter 2. Is the legal borrowing of problem-solving courts best understood as contributing to homogenization, heterogenization, or some kind of synthesis of the global and the local? If the borrowing is contributing to a kind of synthesis, are judges who see themselves as domesticating or indigenizing problem-solving courts importing more into their local legal culture than they either realize or would wish for? If so, is the impact of the imported legal program best characterized as a further step toward full convergence with American ideas and practices, or as that which will evolve into something altogether new and unexpected in the receiving legal culture? A variety of interpretations of legal and cultural borrowing—all of which take into account contradictory anti-American attitudes—aim to make sense of the manner in which U.S. global exports are handled.

MODELS OF BORROWING

In keeping with the perspective of many importers of American problem-solving courts, British criminologist Philip Bean sees selective borrowing as a general pattern in the British importation of American drug control policy for a good part of the twentieth century. Bean's analysis underscores the sort of ambivalent anti-Americanism discussed here. For example, he writes that American influence on British drug control policy is limited because of the perceived "extreme nature of the American criminal justice system." With its retention of capital punishment and initiation of "three-strikes" policies, the American system, he notes, strikes many British observes as "wretchedly inhumane." This perception creates a "barrier, producing a measure of distrust that limits the wholesale transfer of ideas."[34] At the same time, however, Bean cites numerous examples of ongoing British interest in U.S. drug control policy throughout the twentieth century. For example, he characterizes policy initiatives in the early 1980s as follows: "It was not a question of the United States imposing ideas on a British Home Secretary; it was that a certain type of American idea was eagerly sought, and transported back to the United Kingdom."[35] Much the same could be said of the more recent transplantation of problem-solving courts to the United Kingdom.

Therefore, as in the case of problem-solving courts, the transatlantic transfer of drug control policies has been complicated, revealing both an interest in and mistrust of things American. Bean also identifies differences in legal cultures that parallel findings from the present analysis. For example, he notes an interesting contrast between "the American 'can do' culture" and the British way of being "more slow-footed and less able to change."[36] As it specifically concerns drug courts, Bean views the early DTTOs as an example of British slow-footedness. In keeping with the sort of ambivalent anti-Americanism discovered here, Bean also notes that, though the American drug court served as the essential model for DTTOs, British officials were reluctant to admit this publicly.[37] Bean sees the translation of American drug courts into British DTTOs as indicative of a more general pattern of Anglo-American borrowing. As he puts it, "What one can see is that where American policies have been imported they have been changed to fit British experience and made to fit British culture . . . Britain will accept some and bend them to its own view."[38]

The bending process in the case of British DTTOs has, in Bean's view, been rather substantial, so much so that he describes DTTOs as "a very weak form" of drug court. In the final analysis, he offers a sort of pick-and-choose model for describing the process of borrowing and adaptation. "What is clear," says Bean, "is that there is a willingness in Britain to accept some American ideas and a reluctance to accept them all. Some are worth taking on board, some are not."[39] He is particularly complimentary of the Scottish importation of drug courts in this regard. That is, he believes the Scots effectively took "on board only as much as [could] be accepted within the legal and cultural norms of the country." In so doing, they left behind the "revolutionary" and "more extreme ideologies attached to the American drug court system." By softening, modifying, and diluting the American model, the Scottish successfully adopted the "evolutionary" while rejecting the "revolutionary" features of drug courts.[40]

Evidence presented in chapter 5 would support this conclusion. However, Bean's use of the term "evolutionary" to describe the Scottish court is instructive. It conveys not only a sense of moving forward in a slow, deliberative, and incremental fashion, but also the sense of an innovative program that is still in process. In other words, the story of Scottish problem-solving courts is not over. Have the Scots truly indigenized the model to "fit existing legal demands"? Or will the Scottish model continue to evolve in such a manner that the unwelcome revolutionary features might become more evident over time, though perhaps in new and unexpected forms? Interestingly, officials in other countries have also invoked the notion of evolution to depict the importation process. Judge Desmond Hogan of Ireland anticipates that though the Irish have not yet accepted a disease paradigm for understanding drug addiction, they might eventually "evolve" toward such an understanding. With more foreboding, Tina Previtera of Australia likewise speaks of the "evolutionary nature" of problem-solving courts, warning her fellow jurists to guard against the potential erosion of defendants' traditional legal protections.

That the imported courts continue to evolve necessarily complicates an understanding of the importation process: it is not simply a matter of choosing what works in the receiving country and rejecting what does not. While such a model is helpful for making sense of the manner in which officials themselves experience the transfer, it may not fully convey the difficulty importers have with (a) discerning which parts of the model are fitting for their local legal culture and which are not, and (b) determining whether it is even possible to disentangle the agreeable from the disagreeable parts of the legal innovations.

As it concerns the first matter, Jonathan Freedland, in his comparative analysis of British and American political cultures, believes that the British have actually done a poor job of picking and choosing. Offering several colorful metaphors to depict British failures of this sort, Freedland says that in terms of importing from America, the British "are shipping in junk and leaving behind gold."[41] As it concerns British interest in American exports, Freedland, like Bean, highlights the ambivalent nature of British anti-Americanism, referring to the "screaming contradiction of our attitudes towards" the United States.[42] "We simultaneously disdain and covet American culture," says Freedland, "condemning it as junk food even as we reach for another helping—a kind of binge-and-puke social bulimia."[43] He offers a telling anecdote to illustrate this contradictory attitude, one that calls to mind the scenario of the Scottish social worker described at the start of this chapter. Freedland recounts a television documentary produced by British broadcaster Melvyn Bragg in which Bragg essentially declares the end of his "personal love affair with America," a country in which he now sees "only greed, commercialism, and a grotesque gap between rich and poor." For Bragg, "there is nothing left to envy about America." Freedland, however, highlights the irony of the documentary's broadcast in the United Kingdom, which was immediately followed by three television commercials advertising American products: "dream holidays in Florida," a favorite vacation spot for Brits; Tropicana orange juice, "made with real American oranges"; and the American Express card.[44]

To resolve the contradictions inherent in Britain's "love-hate relationship with our colonial offspring," Freedland advises greater discernment regarding what is imported from the United States. As Freedland puts it, the British need to more carefully examine the "cultural traffic" coming across the Atlantic and more critically decide "what to let in and what to keep out."[45] Arguing against a sort of deterministic Americanization, he believes a more critical selection process is possible. He writes: "We *can* choose what we want from America; we just have to start doing it."[46]

Thus, like Bean, Freedland notes a general ambivalence in attitudes toward the United States, observing that the British denounce even while they insatiably "lap up" American culture.[47] Unlike Bean, however, he would say that the British have not been very careful or discriminating consumers of things American. With more careful accounting—a sort of "audit" of American cultural traffic—he believes the British could do better at importing the gold and rejecting the junk, rather than the other way around. His "audit" model, however, only addresses the first issue raised earlier: the ability of importing countries to identify imports that are culturally fitting. Freedland's analysis does not really address the second matter. That is, is it even possible to disentangle the agreeable from the disagreeable? Are not singular American ideas and products so deeply woven into the broader fabric of American culture as to make such disentangling impossible?

A third model put forth by Arie Freiberg moves toward addressing this question. Though interested in and generally supportive of the Australian adoption of problem-solving courts, Freiberg also displays the same sort of ambivalent anti-Americanism as other importers of problem-solving courts. For example, Freiberg is careful to point out that his account of problem-solving courts is not meant to be "a panegyric to problem-oriented courts or an uncritical endorsement of all that emerges from the criminal justice system of the United States."[48] Indeed, he has argued strongly that "Australians should be extremely wary of following every American sentencing trend and fashion."[49] In his analysis of these transplanted programs, however, Freiberg is a bit more pessimistic regarding the possibility of careful selection, and he conveys a more deterministic view of Americanizing processes. He actually sees Australians as having resisted disagreeable aspects of American legal culture. That is, in Freedland's terms, they have selected carefully. However, in light of larger global realities, Freiberg anticipates that such resistance cannot be sustained. Freiberg's discussion is offered in the context of an analysis of changing sentencing practices in the Australian criminal justice system. He notes the impact of Americanization on both Australian law and Australian culture more broadly: "Australia, as a net importer of ideas, has been particularly exposed to" the "influences . . . of the United States, whose language and ideas . . . tend to permeate and possibly eclipse local cultures, including legal and sentencing regimes and practices."[50]

In spite of this influence, however, Australians have been, at least in the short term, successful at retaining distinctive elements of their legal culture. Specifically, Australia has resisted "a return to capital punishment." Australians have also, according to Freiberg, "not embraced boot camps, we have kept imprisonment rates at a comparatively low level, rejected numerical sentencing grids and guidelines, and kept the number of mandatory sentences to a minimum."[51] Moreover, in Australia, "proportionality still remains central to sentencing practice, especially in retaining some upper limits on sentences."[52] Nevertheless, as Freiberg sees it, these specific policies do not stand alone; they are not isolated from broader global currents. Freiberg ultimately worries that the resistance, though commendable, is likely to be short-lived because of unremitting global influences on "the mood, sensitivities, and sensibilities of the public, legislators, and judges."[53] In other words, though it may not be immediately evident, the ongoing " 'carpet bombing' of culture" will continue to shape the sensibilities of Australians in such a way that American criminal justice practices—which are themselves deeply influenced by dominant currents in American culture—will increasingly appear less foreign and will thus become more easily accepted.

Therefore, Freiberg ultimately anticipates greater cultural homogenization over time. "In an age of global communications, franchised merchandise, and transnational corporations," he writes, "national differences diminish in the face of a homogenization of culture, commerce, and law." Given such a process, Freiberg questions whether careful selection will, in the long run, keep the less fitting features of American exports at bay. "Resistance may not be useless," says Freiberg, "but it is difficult." He seems to suggest that a full Americanization of Australian legal culture is almost inevitable: "From baseball to boot camps, from Macy's to macing, the process of Coca-colonizing Australian criminal justice, while not a fait accompli, has more than a little commenced. In the new Australian fashion, we could say, it has just got to first base!"[54]

LEGAL IRRITATION RECONSIDERED

Bean, Freedland, and Freiberg thus offer different ways of making sense of the processes of legal and cultural borrowing. Bean says that importers of things American pick and choose. Freedland says that they do not do this, but should, and in a more careful manner. Freiberg says that, at least in the case of Australia, even though borrowers have been careful and selective, in the end the broader processes of Americanization and globalization will likely overshadow this limited resistance. Freiberg understands that specific legal imports are only one part of a broader influx of cultural influences. That is, global connectedness is so advanced that even successful cases of resistance will ultimately be rendered futile by the ongoing "'carpet bombing' of culture." What Freiberg's assessment does not convey—at least as put forth in this particular discussion—is that perhaps *within* programs like problem-solving courts, which have been imported and ostensibly indigenized, there lie features of American culture that will themselves contribute to a fuller Americanization, or a significant and unintended alteration, of the Australian criminal justice system. Such a view, of course, brings us back to the sort of ideas advanced by Hiller, Legrand, and Teubner, who reflect more explicitly on the cultural dimension of legal transplantation. Recall Hiller's argument that, because law and culture are so fully intertwined, to transplant a law or legal program is to necessarily bring along with it defining elements of the culture from which the law originated. Therefore, when Australians or Canadians import a problem-solving court—adjustments notwithstanding—they also bring on board some of the basic assumptions about the world that determined and shaped the program in its country of origin.

Consider, as a simple example, what these courts are called. Freiberg initially tried to label them "problem-oriented" courts. However, as noted in chapter 4, "problem-solving" has become the preferred term internationally, even in Australia. Freiberg, however, rightly understands that embedded in such a label are particular cultural predilections. "Problem-solving" reflects the ambitious, optimistic, even hubristic nature of the American "can-do culture." It is an obvious institutional manifestation of a form of consciousness endemic to a modern technological society. As Peter Berger puts it, "Problem-solving inventiveness" or a "generally tinkering attitude" is a form of consciousness directly fostered by encounters with the productive processes of modern industrial capitalism.[55] It is also a form of consciousness that gets carried over to other aspects of modern social life, including, as Berger observes, education and politics. Here we see it carried into the realm of law and criminal justice.

Freiberg's effort to put forth the more modest, cautious, and understated term "problem-oriented," which arguably carries a very different set of cultural understandings, ultimately failed. The American term, in this instance, triumphed. Thus, when the attorney general of Victoria published his ten-year strategic *Justice Statement* in 2004, he spoke of the government's commitment to "consolidate and extend the problem-solving approaches being employed in the courts."[56] The acceptance of a label, as such, may seem innocuous enough. However, for the court to be about *solving* problems, rather than delivering justice or adjudicating offenses, portends a rather significant—indeed, revolutionary—redefinition of the central aims and purposes of the criminal justice system. "Problem-solving" is culturally determined nomenclature more in keeping with the boldness and pragmatism of the American courts than the moderation and restraint of courts in the other countries. To adopt a legal program along with its defining terminology is to adopt elements of American culture. In this case, then, one could argue that Americanizing influences were smuggled into Australian society not so much through the broader impact of American popular culture, but through the importation of a legal program and the culturally laden terminology attached to it.

Perhaps more profoundly, we have also seen American features of these courts become more pronounced over time in certain countries where, initially, there was resistance to at least some elements of the American variety of problem-solving courts. The example of England and Wales is instructive in this regard. In the early years of transplanting problem-solving courts, England was arguably the most resistant to the American model. DTTOs and the early drug courts were such a "weak form" of the American model that many did not view the British versions as drug courts at all. The early domestic violence courts were likewise very clear about their rejection of therapeutic jurisprudence, ongoing judicial reviews, and a rehabilitative orientation toward offenders. More recently, as discussed in chapter 3, one finds in new British problem-solving courts more evidence of American traits. The Liverpool community court judge is an activist judge who interacts directly with clients in the courtroom and regularly meets and engages with a variety of stakeholders in the North Liverpool community. There is even a sense that the judge's strong personality, in this instance, is critical to the court's effective functioning.[57] Judge Philips, of the West London drug court, moreover, is as demonstrative and charismatic as any American drug court judge. Some recent domestic violence courts, additionally, have begun to experiment with judicial reviews of offenders, a practice conspicuously absent from the earliest British domestic violence courts.

In England, then, problem-solving courts have indeed evolved, and they have evolved in such a manner that previously rejected qualities of the American courts have become more evident in recent iterations. How do we make sense of this evolution? Freiberg might say that the larger forces of globalization and Americanization have ultimately overshadowed or superseded the instances of limited local resistance. In England, then, one could point to broader cultural changes—such as the more open expression of emotions that followed Princess Diana's death—as evidence of cultural change that would facilitate legal change. In horticultural terms, the more prepared the cultural soil, the more likely a transplant will survive in its new environment.

However, Hiller and Legrand, also sensitive to the influence of broader cultural forces, propose a slightly different understanding of the borrowing process. The transplanted product brings along with it certain cultural entanglements. These entanglements themselves then affect their new environment. In Hiller's terms, the imported law "will 'skew' the receiving culture in profound ways."[58] The transference process induces change that impacts not only the new cultural setting but the imported law as well. Thus, in Teubner's words, the imported law "irritates." However, Teubner's analysis, linked as it is to an autopoietic understanding of legal systems, focuses on legal "rules"—and on the altered understanding of a given rule fostered by the new social context, but as reconceived within the discourse particular to the legal community. The degree to which we can understand a transplanted law to be reinterpreted strictly within the bounds of the new legal system, however, makes less sense when the unit of analysis is a legal *program* rather than a legal *rule* or even a reasoned opinion in a legal decision.

In the case of problem-solving courts, as we have seen, there is sometimes no actual change in the written law. Moreover, problem-solving courts involve more than just legal actors. Directly involved are treatment providers, doctors, educators, victim support workers, and so on. In this case, then, law's integration with its societal context is more obvious than it is in the case of a legal rule or written legal decision. Given the team-oriented nature of the programs, it is difficult to envisage the transplantation as a strictly legal one. For this reason, legal anthropologist John M. Conley sees in problem-solving courts a useful example of a more socially integrated (and Malinowski-inspired) understanding of law. In his own ethnographic work on U.S. courts, Conley finds that "ordinary people expect the law to interact with family, religion, work and other social institutions," and that "citizens come to the law seeking a holistic response to their social problems."[59] This is not to deny the social embeddedness of legal *rules*. As Legrand argues, "A rule is necessarily an incorporative cultural form."[60] It is to suggest that law's social integration is simply made more obvious in programs like problem-solving courts, if only because of their multidisciplinary format.

Consider the example of the West London drug court. Judge Philips's court is different from the magistrate-run DTTOs that preceded it in several ways. First, the program is clearly a collaborative and team-oriented effort, as discussed earlier. The impetus for the court stemmed not only from Judge Philips's research of American drug courts but also from the education he received from a drug counselor friend named Erol. Judge Philips explains that Erol "taught me about drug rehabilitation. . . . Almost all the work I do is based on what Erol has taught me." In a very direct way, then, this new program was introduced into the British criminal justice system with the influential input of a nonlegal actor. Unclear, then, is the boundary between the law and other social institutions. The West London drug court also represents a departure from DTTOs and the early West Yorkshire drug courts in that it is, as Judge Philips puts it, "very much a judge-run court." Yet it still operates within a system where, unlike in the United States, the probation service has considerable power and authority. As a result, one of the observable features of the new court is the very apparent tension between the judge and the probation service.

A judge-run program in a probation-empowered legal culture is aptly characterized as an irritation.

One finds another sort of legal irritation in the case of Scottish problem-solving courts. A defining feature of most problem-solving courts is, of course, ongoing judicial reviews and the sanctioning and rewarding of clients in the program. When the Scots imported the American drug court model, they brought with it certain expectations about how offenders should be rewarded and sanctioned. These are expectations with which Scottish sheriffs have had to contend. For example, the Scots are clearly not comfortable rewarding clients in the style of American drug courts and are fairly clear about what they do not like. They do not like graduation ceremonies, they do not like prize-giving, they do not like hugging, and they do not like applause. Regarding misgivings about applause, Sheriff Matthews explains: the offender "is not supposed to be doing drugs, and he's not supposed to be offending anyway, so while staying clean is a good achievement for him, he's only doing what he is supposed to be doing anyway." Many other people, Matthews adds, have avoided offending all their lives—so "why the hell is he getting applause. . . . In many ways it's applauding him for keeping out of trouble for a year to eighteen months, which, in the grand scheme of things, is not a big deal for most people."

Recall also Sheriff Raeburn's thinly veiled contempt for such American practices as hugging, awarding McDonald's vouchers, and the like. And yet the Scots wrestle with the expectation that they should offer some sort of reward for successful clients. Glasgow drug court staff struggle to identify "culturally appropriate rewards."[61] In Scotland, the "most common vehicle for communicating the court's approval of progress made" has been shrieval "encouragement and praise." Even this more tempered practice of rewarding, however, does not come easy in the Scottish setting. Scottish youth court sheriffs were encouraged by the Scottish Executive to be more interactive, but still had strong reservations about being too warm and friendly with defendants. As noted in chapter 5, one sheriff explained that it is not "really part of the judge's job to get too close to the accused." Thus, as reported in an evaluation of the youth court, the interaction between sheriff and youth is minimal and directed mostly through defense agents. Moreover, given the continuing formality of the court, defendants "spoke rarely and appeared awkward." The same sort of discomfort has been found among drug court clients in Fife, who likewise "were often unable to respond to the sheriff's questions and reported feeling awkward about the public nature of the exchanges."[62]

Yet the expectation to interact, to reward, and to sanction remains; these practices are arguably endemic to the program. In fact, two years after the start of the Scottish drug courts, the Scottish Parliament passed legislation allowing for the imposition of intermediate sanctions, including short stints in jail. Even here, though, aspects of the legislation seem to be more of a burden than a relief, given that sheriffs have only very rarely imposed short jail terms. As expectations to include these sorts of practices have persisted, however, Scottish officials appear to have gradually made some minor adjustments. When a client finished a DTTO program just prior to the start of the Fife drug court, for example, Sheriff Donald interacted in a more informal matter, discussed family matters, and even asked after the client's new baby boy (whose name he remembered). When the reviews in youth court were temporarily suspended in 2005, sheriffs reportedly "lamented" the loss; they had evidently come to believe that reviews provided an effective means of encouraging ongoing compliance with the program.[63] So, while not entirely comfortable with the sort of interactions expected of sheriffs in the problem-solving court format, Scottish officials have struggled to find rewards, sanctions, and styles of interaction that are fitting in their culture.

Thus, just as a judge-run program irritates a legal system with a powerful probation service, so expectations that sheriffs will interact, reward, and sanction irritate a more traditional and reserved judicial setting. In both cases, however, these are tensions generated from within the imported model rather than from the outside influences of the broader cultural environment. This is not to suggest that such sources of change are mutually exclusive. Broader cultural influences may, in fact, make internally driven change more acceptable. Several people with whom I spoke actually observed such a connection. For example, in a discussion of the comparative formality of British courts, Paul Hayes referred to several videos of American drug courts he had seen. He thought the more informal "interaction between the offenders and the judges would be inconceivable" in an English court—not just for the judge, but for the client as well. That is, both the judge and the offenders "couldn't do it." Anticipating possible changes, however, Hayes also acknowledged, as discussed in chapter 3, a shift in British culture; in reference to the impact of American television, he observed that though the British are not yet as good at it as Americans, they are becoming more accustomed to expressive and confessional discourse. Approximately six years after Hayes made this observation, the *Evening Standard* described Judge Philips's behavior in the West London drug court as follows: "Judge Philips presided over Court Eight in shirtsleeves and without a tie. There is no dock in the courtroom. . . . With a disarmingly informal style, he coaxes, cajoles, and threatens addicts into quitting."[64] In reference to more expressive discourse in British problem-solving courts, Jonathan Monk of the Ministry of Justice notes that "more displays of sentimentalism in British public life" may "lead the way" to changes in the courts.

Legal Borrowing and Anti-Americanism

Thus, one can speak of two types of Americanizing influences: the broader influences of cultural "carpet bombing" on the one hand, and the more subtle impact of cultural entanglements that accompany legal imports on the other. These two separate yet related influences parallel, in certain respects, the distinction found in the global surveys on anti-Americanism. Citizens of countries outside the United States say they regret the spread of American ideas and customs, and yet they like and admire American-grown products. In the case of problem-solving courts, importers express general anti-American sentiments, yet they willingly import what is clearly an American-grown legal innovation. In both cases they are adopting products closely linked to a culture about which they express strong reservations.

One could imagine several explanations for this contradiction. One possibility is that importers of American products have more affection for things American than they care to admit. Another possibility is that importers and consumers of American products really do not like the United States and its international influence, but they view appropriation of its cultural exports as a separate matter altogether. Law and culture scholars would say such a parsing is naive. American-grown products, legal and otherwise, are themselves the very expression of American culture. Because "law," as Hiller puts it, "is a product of culture,"[65] to import an American-grown legal product is to import American culture. This is the essential point made by Peter Berger, as cited in chapter 2. When "Mexicans eat *hamburguesas*," writes Berger, they are "consuming whole chunks of American values 'in with, and under' the American hamburgers."[66] The same could be said of problem-solving courts. It is as naive to believe that a process of domestication will fully extricate Americanism from imported problem-solving courts as it is to think that placing a McDonald's restaurant in an old Tudor building will somehow negate the unseemly qualities of American fast-food culture.

One wishing to resolve this sort of contradiction might offer one of two possible solutions. First, one could propose that importers admit to their undivided affection for things American, and thus free themselves to more fully imbibe of what they truly thirst for anyway. In this regard, importers could heed with abandon the offer made by Mayor Bloomberg to Lord Falconer: "You're welcome to take all of our ideas and copy them." Alternatively, one might advise a more consistent rejection of Americanization. If American ideas and customs are not welcomed, then local consumers should more consistently reject American exports. However, there is little evidence that consistency, as such, is a valued virtue, and therefore there is little likelihood that either solution would be regarded as a plausible option. Instead, an ambivalent anti-Americanism seems likely to persist, and elements of American culture are likely to continue to infiltrate foreign legal systems, even as importers lament the spread of America's growing global influence.

A final feature of the American variety of problem-solving courts to find its way into other countries is the manner in which the courts are defended publicly. That is, a common justification for these courts, as we have seen, is the promise they offer to restore public confidence in the criminal justice system. At least in the United States, the pragmatic, problem-solving, and therapeutic features of these court innovations are put forth as qualities that offer to re-engender confidence in a criminal justice system whose legitimacy is somehow in question. Curiously, this justificatory rhetoric has, in some instances, also been transplanted. The relationship between popular expectations and public justifications for legal programs represents an important nexus for analyzing the relationship between law and culture. Therefore, we turn in the last chapter to a consideration of how problem-solving courts are justified, and how these justificatory strategies themselves represent a curious type of international transplant.

Chapter Eight

BUILDING CONFIDENCE,

JUSTIFYING JUSTICE

> Across the globe, many criminal justice practitioners are
> grappling with similar problems: . . . dissatisfaction with
> the results of traditional punishment . . . and lack of
> public confidence in justice.
> —*Robert V. Wolf*

A S DISCUSSED in chapter 1, new specialty courts promise to address problems at three different levels: the problems of individual offenders, the problems of a troubled criminal justice system whose relevance and legitimacy is somehow in question, and the problems of society at large. These are, of course, not unrelated categories. To solve the problems of individual offenders is also to address, at least in small measure, society's problems on a broader scale. As it concerns the legitimacy of the judiciary itself, advocates of problem-solving courts in the United States regularly describe the American criminal justice system as suffering from eroding public confidence and offer problem-solving courts as a remedy to this perceived ailment.

One reason for the lack of confidence in the criminal justice system, advocates claim, is the public perception that the courts and the judges running them are irrelevant and out of touch. Judge Veronica McBeth, presiding judge of the Los Angeles Municipal Court, makes just this claim: "The reason there is diminishing confidence in judges generally is because judges have isolated themselves from the communities they serve." Judges do not, says McBeth, "go out into the community and listen to what their concerns are."[1] Some fear that unless judges work to make themselves more relevant, the public will increasingly view the judiciary as meaningless. Addressing a large audience of drug court professionals, Massachusetts judge Thomas Merrigan warned, "If we don't change what we are doing in the next few years, and if we don't change how we go about serving the community with more relevancy, with more meaning, we are going to find that in 25 years we have become irrelevant in the minds of the public. They will no longer consider us meaningful." Accepting this diagnosis, advocates of problem-solving courts are, according to Berman and Feinblatt, "united by the common belief that courts need to reassert their relevance in society."[2]

That the courts need to be relevant is itself a singular proposal. Interestingly, one finds the perceived need to be relevant in other social institutions in the United States—a preoccupation that has led to the acceptance of ideas and practices not dissimilar to those found in problem-solving courts. Consider religion, for example—an institution in which relevance, as such, has not always featured as its primary raison d'être. In his analysis of the "seeker church" movement—one of the fastest-growing developments in contemporary American Protestantism—Kimon Sargeant identifies the quest for relevance as central to what these churches are all about, even to the extent of shaping the theology in the movement. One image of God presented, in this regard, is of a judge who is "eager to doff his robes and give you a big heavenly hug."[3]

As we have seen, problem-solving court judges, in their own efforts to be more relevant, have sometimes assumed a very similar posture. Whether it is a matter of irrelevancy or of judges somehow being out of touch with the community, defenders of problem-solving courts often claim that the judiciary does not enjoy very much public trust, and that what confidence remains is quickly eroding. Rottman and Casey, for example, note "considerable dissatisfaction with the accessibility and relevance of the courts and the low levels of trust and confidence in the judiciary."[4] The Center for Court Innovation, in a document celebrating its first ten years of operation, likewise observes that public opinion clearly demonstrates that "there has been a marked erosion of public confidence in the justice system and those who work in it."[5] Berman and Feinblatt go so far as to assert that declining confidence in the American judiciary outpaces the loss of public faith in other institutions. "No civic institution," they claim, "has experienced a greater loss of public faith in recent years."[6]

Interestingly, though references are made to public opinion surveys in these discussions, no specific surveys are actually cited. When one considers the available data, it is not entirely clear that such a precipitous erosion of confidence in the judiciary has actually taken place in the United States. A question asked in an annual Gallup survey between 1993 and 2007 (see figure 1) shows that confidence in the criminal justice system has actually risen slightly during the past fifteen years. In 1993, the first year the survey question was asked, 17 percent of respondents said they had a "great deal" or "quite a lot" of confidence in the criminal justice system. In 2007, the confidence level was at 19 percent and had been as high as 34 percent in 2004 and 25 percent in 2006. Confidence levels at these percentages hardly represent a ringing endorsement of the criminal justice

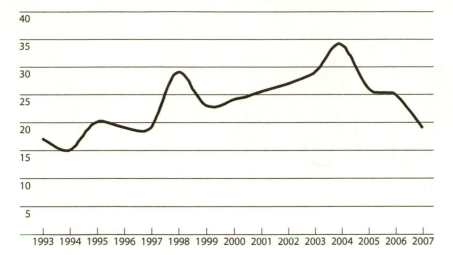

Figure 1. Confidence in the American criminal justice system. Percentage of respondents reporting "a great deal" or "quite a lot" of confidence in the criminal justice system. Gallup Poll Surveys, 1993–2007.

system. However, it is difficult to conclude from this evidence that there has been a "marked erosion" in the judiciary, much less that the "judicial branch" has experienced a greater loss of confidence than any other civic institution.

Indeed, at least some data indicate just the opposite. Since 1974 respondents to the General Social Survey (GSS) have been asked about their confidence in a number of social institutions, including the American presidency, Congress, and the Supreme Court (see figure 2). Levels of confidence in the executive branch, while undulating considerably over the years, have generally declined (from 29.9 percent in 1974 to 14.5 percent in 2006). The same essential pattern is observable in the case of Congress (with confidence levels declining from 24.1 percent in 1974 to 10.8 percent in 2006). However, public confidence in the Supreme Court not only has been consistently higher than in the other two branches of government, but also has remained relatively steady during the thirty-two-year period. In 1974, 32.6 percent of respondents said they had "a great deal of confidence" in the Supreme Court, and in 2006, 33 percent said the same. Meanwhile, as with the criminal justice system more generally, a variety of voices have expressed worries about the legitimacy of the Supreme Court during this period.[7]

In their comparative work on levels of confidence in criminal justice systems around the world, Mike Hough and Julian Roberts see the relative stability of confidence in the U.S. Supreme Court as interesting, particularly because "levels of trust have been declining" in other areas

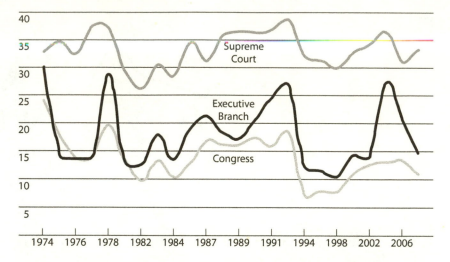

Figure 2. "A Great Deal of Confidence" in Government Institutions. General Social Surveys, 1972–2006 (Cumulative File), Inter-University Consortium for Political and Social Research.

of U.S. public policy.[8] For example, the number of Americans expressing trust in government has steadily declined during the last half century. In 1958, over 70 percent of Americans said that they trusted the government to do the right thing, a level of trust that dropped to 47 percent by 2004 and was as low as 21 percent in 1994.[9] In 1998, the American Bar Association conducted a national survey in which it repeated questions asked in a 1978 Yankelovich national survey. A comparison of the two surveys reveals an increase in levels of confidence in three different areas of the judiciary.

Those responding that they were "extremely confident" or "very confident" in state and local courts increased from 23 to 28 percent between 1978 and 1998; in federal courts (other than the Supreme Court) from 29 to 34 percent; and in the Supreme Court from 36 to 50 percent. In contrast, levels of confidence in other institutions—including public schools, Congress, and the media—declined during the same time period, and by 1998, were below confidence levels for all three areas of the judiciary.[10] In light of this kind of data, it is difficult to conclude that confidence in the judiciary—in comparison to other civic institutions—has declined so sharply, as supporters of problem-solving courts assert. Nevertheless, the erosion of public confidence in the judiciary is the conventional wisdom, and advocates of problem-solving courts repeatedly offer new specialty courts as a solution to this perceived lack of public trust.

Consider several examples of this basic position. Greg Berman asserts that problem-solving courts not only solve the problems of individual offenders but also "improve perceptions of the quality of faith in government and justice."[11] One way in which the courts achieve this, as discussed in chapter 1, is by increasing job satisfaction among judges. When judges "are feeling productive and positive," so it is argued, these attitudes carry over into the court, which then "affects the public's trust and confidence in the court."[12] One reason the Conference of Chief Justices and the Conference of State Court Administrators adopted resolutions in support of problem-solving courts both in 2000 and in 2004 was the expectation that these courts would "advance the trust and confidence of the public."[13] Such expectations have served as an important justification for the initiation of individual problem-solving courts at the local level. Support for a community court in Austin, Texas, for example, was generated in part by the belief that such a court "would promote confidence in the justice system."[14] Advocates claim that these anticipated benefits have been realized. Berman notes that "independent evaluators" of the Midtown community court "found that the court had helped to restore a measure of judicial legitimacy and public trust and confidence in justice."[15] Laurie Robinson makes a similar claim: "New research shows that problem-solving courts are making a difference in . . . spurring greater community confidence in the court system."[16]

Such a view is not limited to assessments of the situation in the United States. "Across the globe," says Wolf of the CCI, "many criminal justice practitioners are grappling with similar problems," including a "lack of public confidence in justice."[17] Whether other systems suffer from the same ostensible lack of public trust is debatable, but that officials speak of such a condition as a defense for the initiation and advancement of imported problem-solving courts is clear. In some cases, in fact, the transplantation of this justificatory strategy has been as pronounced as the transfer of the courts themselves. However, appropriation of the strategy has varied among countries, which is itself suggestive of defining cultural differences.

BUILDING CONFIDENCE: INTERNATIONAL COMPARISONS

Defending problem-solving courts on the grounds that they will restore public confidence in the judicial system has been most evident in the transference of courts to England, Canada, and Ireland, principally as it concerns the development of community courts in each country. In the case of England, however, such rhetoric has been applied more generally to defend other types of problem-solving courts as well, including drug courts and domestic violence courts. The idea is even emblazoned on the sign situated in front of the Liverpool community court: "Community Justice Centre, North Liverpool, Reducing crime, building confidence." Lord Falconer has spoken of building confidence in the judiciary numerous times in his public statements of support for the introduction and spread of problem-solving courts in Great Britain.

As in the United States, officials expect that these courts will help to restore confidence in the judiciary. A discussion of the "key principles" of community justice in the United Kingdom, for example, anticipates that community courts will strengthen the "connections between the court and local people," which should, "in turn, raise public confidence in the work of the court and the wider criminal justice agencies."[18] A comparative study issued by the Ministry of Justice likewise states that "specialist courts have the potential to play a significant role in increasing public confidence in the justice system."[19] The study, moreover, views "increased public confidence in the justice system" as one measure upon which the success of these courts should be evaluated.[20]

When Ireland's National Crime Council issued its endorsement of a community court for Dublin, it looked to both the United States and England to formulate its proposal. When the Irish delegation visited the Red Hook community court, its members were told by Red Hook staff that "improved public confidence in the criminal justice system" was one of "the benefits brought about by the Court."[21] Similarly, when visiting Liverpool, Irish officials learned that North Liverpool was selected as the site for the first community court in England and Wales "because there was a low level of public confidence in the criminal justice system" in the area.[22] In light of these findings from abroad, the Irish anticipate that a Dublin community court will "bring a range of benefits," including "renewed confidence in the criminal justice system."[23] Without citing data indicating low levels of trust in Ireland's criminal justice system, the Irish appear to have accepted both the stated problem of declining public confidence in the judiciary and the solution promised in the establishment of a community court.

One finds very similar justifications for the initiation of the Vancouver community court in British Columbia. As in the Liverpool and Dublin cases, Canadian officials were aided by advice from the CCI. Like their English and Irish counterparts, the Canadians identified declining confidence as a central concern and used it as a justification for taking action. The British Columbia Justice Review Task Force, which issued the report recommending the establishment of the Vancouver community court, argued, "Failure to change our current approach will cause a continued decrease in the quality of life in Vancouver and a further erosion of confidence in the justice system."[24] The task force recommended the initiation of a community court, believing that such a court would "help restore the public's confidence in [the] justice system."[25]

In all three cases (Liverpool, Dublin, and Vancouver), then, importers identify low and eroding public confidence in the criminal justice system as a reason for the initiation of new community courts in their respective countries. This, of course, begs the question of whether confidence in their judicial systems is in as precarious a condition as importers seem to believe. The Canadian report specifically cites public opinion polls to document these assertions. Interestingly, the data indicate that, in fact, levels of confidence in the judiciary are notably higher in Canada than they are in the United States. The report itself cites a 2003 survey of Canadians that used the same basic language that was used in the U.S. Gallup surveys represented in figure 1. The Canadian study found that 57 percent of the respondents said they had "a great deal" or "quite a lot" of confidence in the Canadian justice system,[26] compared to 29 percent of Americans who in 2003 reported the same. Nevertheless, the Canadian task force report asserts that "public confidence in the criminal justice system is low," and a community court will help to increase "the public's confidence in the system."[27]

In England and Ireland, similarly, some evidence indicates that confidence levels are not as low as commonly believed.[28] For example, a 2003 MORI survey found that 55 percent of respondents were "very confident" or "fairly confident" in British magistrates; 54 percent were confident in judges; and 51 percent were confident in the courts.[29] As it concerns comparative data, a 2001 international survey of European countries likewise employed the same language used in the U.S. Gallup surveys. As in Canada, the results of this survey show that levels of confidence in both the Irish and British justice systems are higher than those in the United States. In the United Kingdom, 49 percent of respondents said they had a "great deal" or "quite a lot" of confidence in the justice system, and in Ireland 55 percent reported the same.[30] Again, this is considerably higher than the 25 percent confidence level found among American respondents in 2001 (see figure 1). Still, in both the United Kingdom and Ireland, officials speak of low confidence in the justice system as one reason for starting new community courts.

While there is not the same breadth of longitudinal data available elsewhere as there is in the United States, additional evidence calls into question the common assumption about *declining* levels of confidence. For example, 27 percent of British respondents in a 1996 survey indicated that magistrates were doing an excellent or good job. In 2003, 26 percent of respondents felt the same. Public ratings of judges' work over the same time period increased from 20 percent in 1996 to 25 percent in 2003.[31]

In light of data like this, Hough and Roberts conclude that "there seems no evidence to believe that confidence in the British criminal justice system is declining, despite the public view that matters are worsening."[32] Roberts argues essentially the same for Canada. Here too respondents have been asked over time to rate the job performance of the courts. Data spanning the sixteen-year time period between 1988 and 2004 reveal a "picture of relative stability," says Roberts, with ratings of the courts "no less positive in 2004 than in 1988."[33]

Thus, it almost appears that British, Canadian, and Irish importers of problem-solving courts (especially in the case of community courts) borrow not only the court programs but also the concomitant justificatory rhetoric found in the United States as well, even when the available data in their own countries do not always comport with repeated assertions about low and declining levels of confidence in the judiciary. One British problem-solving court judge with whom I spoke was somewhat skeptical of this new development. As she put it:

> There's a great deal of talk about a lack of confidence in the judiciary. This is a relatively new development. If politicians say often enough that the public has no confidence in the judiciary, then you will create a perception that the public has no confidence in the judiciary. . . . And what do you mean by "having confidence in the judiciary?" . . . It's one of those platitudes bandied about, but when you examine it and break it down, you can't figure out what people actually mean by it.

In certain respects, it reminds one of the strategies advanced by some pharmaceutical companies that essentially pathologize certain human behaviors that were once regarded as normal, like shyness, and then offer a pharmaceutical remedy to the socially created problem.[34] Thus, Paxil is offered as a remedy for "social anxiety disorder." In the same way, officials generate the perception of low public confidence in the judiciary and then offer problem-solving courts as a solution. Yet, both the diagnosis and the proposed solution beg certain questions. Are confidence levels really eroding, either in the United States or in the receiving countries? Is a lack of relevance really an issue about which the judiciary should be concerned?[35] Even if the answers are yes to these questions, do problem-solving courts represent the best remedy to the perceived problem of eroding confidence in the judiciary?

Results from a series of surveys—conducted in North Liverpool in the first eighteen months after the start of the Liverpool community court—suggest that perhaps too much weight has been given to the promise that community courts will build confidence in the criminal justice system. Three "waves" of surveys (conducted in North Liverpool in the summer of 2005, the summer of 2006, and the winter of 2006–7) found that levels of confidence actually declined slightly during this period. The percentage of respondents who said they were "very confident" or "fairly confident" that "the criminal justice system is effective in bringing people who commit crimes to justice" declined from 35 percent in the first survey to 30 percent and 33 percent, respectively, in the next two. Confidence in the treatment of witnesses, interestingly, declined more significantly—from 40 percent in the first survey to 29 percent and 28 percent in the second and third surveys.[36] Satisfaction with the criminal justice system to deal with antisocial behavior also declined during this period, from 37 percent in the first survey to 27 percent and 28 percent in the next two.[37] Such data—though admittedly preliminary and hardly conclusive concerning the long-term impact of the Liverpool community court—cast some doubts on the often-asserted promise that these courts will build confidence in the judiciary.

Interestingly, in Australia and Scotland one does not find the same tendency to buy into this promise or to speak of declining confidence as a justification for these programs. In his lengthy discussion of problem-solving courts in the United States and Australia, Andrew Phelan, in fact, notes the absence of this way of thinking in Australia. Phelan observes that in the United States, "Community confidence . . . is an essential goal," especially in the case of community courts. He notes further that similar concerns "have begun to be reflected in United Kingdom court reforms," but have not "yet been reflected in Australian courts to any similar degree."[38] Still, the idea was at least introduced to Australians in an October 2004 forum in Melbourne led by Julius Lang and Chris Watler of the CCI. In their advocacy of a community court for Victoria, Lang and Watler argued that the establishment of a community court would "make a difference in the local community, improving public safety and bolstering public confidence in justice."[39] Three months later, David Fletcher, the presiding judge of the Liverpool community court, also visited Melbourne. Australians learned from him that one of the central aims of the Liverpool court is to "to increase the legitimacy of the court."[40]

However, as Phelan notes, this type of justificatory strategy has not taken hold in Australia as it has in England, though there are occasional instances of its usage.[41] In Australia, what one finds instead are very different understandings about what will sustain public confidence in the judiciary. Recall from chapter 4 Magistrate Jelena Popovic's concern that Australians, in their enthusiasm for new therapeutically oriented courts, might compromise their commitments to natural and open justice. According to Popovic, one of the reasons that open justice is so important is because "it promotes and maintains public confidence in the judicial process."[42] She also worries that the greater informality of specialty courts might undermine the dignity of the court and send the wrong message to defendants. In her view, then, it is not a therapeutic or problem-solving orientation that builds confidence, but rather it is protecting the principles and practices of open justice—even against the potentially harmful effects of therapeutic jurisprudence—that will sustain public confidence in the courts. As Popovic argues, "It is easy to fall into the trap of sidestepping open justice in favor of practices designed to expedite hearings and make them more therapeutic."[43]

We have also seen that Australians remain concerned that court programs rest on a legislative foundation. For Australians, judicial activities that depart from legislative directives pose a threat to the court's legitimacy. As David Indermaur and his colleagues note in their evaluation of the Perth drug court, among the "most serious issues affecting the legitimacy of the drug court" was its "lack of a legislative base."[44] Without "a clearly defined set of guiding parameters from legislation," they saw the Perth drug court as operating within a format that threatened "the credibility and legitimacy of the drug court."[45] Australian jurists, in keeping with this attitude, are very reluctant to stray from specific legislative directives. For Australians, then, the legitimacy of the judiciary is linked to ensuring a solid legislative foundation and maintaining open and transparent court processes.

The Scottish also associate judicial legitimacy with preserving open justice. Scottish sheriffs, for example, point to the "transparency" of review hearings "held in open court" as a feature of Scottish drug courts that is "valuable to maintaining public confidence in the drug court."[46] Officials at the Glasgow drug court also point to the "transparent and clear view" of the court's "aims and objectives," as put forth in the working group reports, as contributing to "public confidence" in the new court.[47] Whether it is building confidence or making the courts more therapeutic, Scottish officials do not feel a need to adopt new justificatory strategies, because they do not believe what they are doing is substantively different from what is practiced in a conventional criminal court. Recall Moira Price's reflections on this point: "I don't think what we are doing is particularly innovative in the legal sense, in that we're still very strictly following the rules of law and procedure, as we always have been. So I don't think we're doing anything that's greatly innovative that would need to justify itself with another title."

These limited discussions of confidence building in Australia and Scotland, then, tell a different story. Confidence is not renewed or restored through the initiation of new problem-solving courts. Rather, public confidence is preserved by ensuring that the courts are legislatively based, are open and transparent, remain dignified, and observe due process. Given the findings considered in chapters 4 and 5, it is not surprising that both Australia and Scotland would be less likely to accept wholesale an

American-inspired justificatory strategy that essentially redefines the basis of judicial legitimacy. As we have seen, both places are concerned with preserving the dignity of the court, protecting due process, and ensuring that court processes rest on a legislative foundation. Maintaining the legitimacy of the courts, then, has more to do with sustaining these long-held traditions than with introducing revolutionizing changes. Thus, an Australian magistrate says, "We must take care to ensure that therapeutic considerations do not over-ride long-standing freedoms and rights,"[48] while a Scottish official maintains, "there's a comfort in tradition."

JUSTIFYING JUSTICE

Represented in these various discussions about building confidence, then, are two different visions for establishing or maintaining the legitimacy of the courts. One vision argues that therapeutically oriented problem-solving innovations will help restore the legitimacy of the court. The second holds that protecting the due process rights of defendants and maintaining the dignity, fairness, transparency, and formality of courtroom processes will sustain the legitimacy of the court. According to this second vision, problem-solving courts may even represent a potential threat to the court's legitimacy. The second vision is certainly the understanding of legitimacy put forth in Jerome Bruner's discussion of legal storytelling. As Bruner sees it, legal legitimacy rests on the principles of procedural fairness, judicial neutrality, and ritualism.[49] The latter, according to Bruner, refers to the "steadying role" of the court's solemnity and traditions. In Western courts, for example, the judge's "priestly black robe" signifies the judge's "metaphoric elevation beyond the contentiousness of everyday life."[50]

Invocations of legitimacy call to mind David Beetham's trenchant analysis of the concept. In his revised formulation of Max Weber's work on legitimacy, David Beetham argues that there are three important components of legitimation in any political or legal order: justification, the manner in which laws are justified according to dominant cultural sensibilities; validity, the exercising of power based upon written laws and rules; and consent, the extent to which individuals agree with or consent to the exercise of state power. "These factors," says Beetham, "successively and cumulatively, are what make power legitimate. To the extent that they are present, it will be legitimate. To the extent that they are absent, it will not."[51] Discussions about confidence, then, have mainly to do with matters of consent. That is, reported levels of confidence can be viewed as one measurement of the degree to which citizens of a given country willingly accept and consent to state authority. The manner in which advocates defend problem-solving courts, on the other hand, has more to do with what Beetham means by justification.

Because justifications, as put forth by advocates of problem-solving courts, are essentially appeals to dominant cultural values and sentiments, they represent an important nexus of the law/culture relationship. In other words, the particular basis upon which public officials defend or justify new legal programs says much about the specific culture within which the proposed law or legal program is situated. The justification discussed thus far in this chapter centers on the notion of building confidence. As we have seen, not all importing countries accept the proposition that confidence in the courts is declining or that problem-solving courts will restore confidence in the judiciary. Nor have all accepted the various other justifications that have been offered to defend problem-solving courts more generally.

Included among the other types of justifications put forth in defense of problem-solving courts is the argument that specialty courts *work*. That is, it is argued that these courts are more effective and more successful than conventional criminal courts. Justifications of this sort typically cite evaluation studies showing reduced recidivism rates among participants, reduced costs to the state, and so forth. Problem-solving courts are also defended on the grounds that they are therapeutic. Specialty courts are said to be more humane, holistic, caring, and responsive to the needs and problems of individual offenders and victims. Therapeutic jurisprudence and, to a lesser extent, restorative justice, as we have seen, are sometimes invoked as the theoretical basis for this justification. Finally, the courts are also defended on the grounds that they are tough on crime. It is sometimes defensively asserted that problem-solving courts are not a "soft-option," but are instead much tougher than the alternative. As noted earlier, "tough" and "therapeutic" are not mutually exclusive categories but can often work in a complementary fashion.[52] It has become commonplace in the United States, for example, to argue that coerced treatment is as effective as voluntary treatment.[53] Thus, the courts are at the same time, tough, effective, and therapeutic. It is this combination of justifications that gives problem-solving courts, at least in the United States, their broad appeal. As Eric Miller puts it, problem-solving courts "appear all things to all people."[54]

These, anyway, are the types of justifications one finds in the United States. If, as noted earlier, justifications are offered in accordance with dominant cultural sensibilities, then we should expect to find particular cultural inclinations reflected in these justifications. A number of indicators, in fact, point to the pervasiveness of therapeutic and pragmatic tendencies in American culture. To cite just one example, in their important work, *Habits of the Heart*, Robert Bellah and his colleagues found expressive and utilitarian individualism to be the defining languages of modern American culture. Thus, therapeutic jurisprudence and legal pragmatism are theories that, like their practical and legal applications, fit the American cultural context. The fact that legal scholars can assert with credibility that the law should be made more therapeutic and more effective—while offering little explanation for why this should be the case—suggests that the assertions are made in a cultural context where therapeutic and pragmatic orientations are taken for granted.

If justificatory strategies are culturally rooted, then we would expect certain justifications to be more readily embraced in some cultures than in others. David Nelken observes that concerns with efficiency are less pronounced in Italy than they are in England or the United States. Because of this, according to Nelken, Italians are not so alarmed by their country's notoriously long delays in legal trials (e.g., in 1999, the first stage of civil case trials in Italy took five years on average and the appeal stage over nine years). Italian views on trial delays, as discussed at a 2003 conference in Padua on the topic, are revealing in this regard. At the gathering, Italian jurists spoke derisively of "utilitarianism, managerialism, and pragmatism," and they "greeted with laughter" the "mention of some trials in Denmark taking no more than twenty-three days."[55] In Italy, efficiency is not sacrosanct. Indeed, Italians believe a preoccupation with efficiency would "sideline questions of ideal aims into sordid questions of costs and benefits." Italian jurists "see it as a pre-eminent task for law not to compromise its ideals and procedures."[56] Given this attitude, it is not surprising that there are far fewer measurements of recidivism rates in Italy than in the United States or the United Kingdom. In fact, an international literature review of the outcomes of "quasi-compulsory treatment of drug dependent offenders" (including U.S. drug courts) found no systemic studies of outcomes for such programs in the Italian literature.[57]

Given this cultural predilection, it would make little sense to approach an Italian judge or politician about problem-solving courts on the grounds that the innovative court programs would help to make the Italian system more efficient. Why is efficiency, the Italian might respond, so important for a justice system? Justifying legal programs on the grounds of efficiency might make more sense in other common law countries—though, as we have seen, views about what constitutes success vary between countries. However, we have also seen that some countries essentially reject therapeutic justifications for these programs. As it concerns the defense of these courts on the grounds that they will restore confidence in the judiciary, we find that some countries reject this rationale and some accept it (even when it is not entirely clear that the diagnosis is accurate or the proposed remedy warranted).

In the cases where the "building confidence in the judiciary" strategy is not accepted, the court's legitimacy is instead associated with protecting due process rights, natural and open justice, a solid legislative foundation, and the traditional ritualism of courtroom practices. It is even feared that problem-solving courts might, if only unwittingly, undermine traditional protections. Interestingly, several recent critiques of U.S. problem-solving courts raise similar concerns.[58] Among these, Timothy Casey's work is of particular interest, in that he reflects on problem-solving courts and the protection of due process rights in the context of a discussion about legitimacy. In so doing, Casey offers a perspective more in keeping with the views of the Australian and Scottish officials cited earlier.

Casey argues that the court's legitimacy rests not on the court's therapeutic or problem-solving promises, but rather on the court's commitment to and demonstration of such foundational principles as "neutrality, procedural justice, fairness, and ritualism."[59] Casey questions whether problem-solving courts actually protect these traditional judicial values in practice. As it concerns the larger legitimation equation, he addresses matters that David Beetham would refer to as validity—the exercise of power in accordance with written rules and codified laws and procedures. He rightly notes that in the United States, most "problem-solving courts are the creation of judges. There is no enabling legislation or mandate: courts simply open shop."[60] As we have seen, this tendency is more pronounced in the United States than in any other country considered in the present case study.

Because the U.S. courts are, in the main, not legislatively based and because they do not typically emphasize such traditional judicial concepts as neutrality, fairness, impartiality, and so on, they are, according to Casey, riding on "borrowed legitimacy." Casey, therefore, accepts neither that courts are suffering from low public confidence nor that problem-solving courts are the obvious antidote to this ostensible condition. In keeping with the second proposed vision discussed earlier, he does not believe that problem-solving courts will restore legitimacy in the courts. Rather, problem-solving courts "rely on the existing cache of legitimacy held by the court." As in the case of the juvenile delinquency courts of the first part of the twentieth century, Casey believes the illegitimacy (i.e., lack of validity) of problem-solving courts will eventually become evident.

> This "borrowed legitimacy" is not based on the problem-solving court's current action. Instead, the problem-solving court has authority because it is a "court." As soon as the smoke clears, however, the problem-solving courts will have to justify their exercise of authority without reference to the traditional courts. This will be a difficult, perhaps impossible, task. The problem-solving courts change the basic nature of the courts. They demonstrate none of the

characteristics that would ordinarily add to the rational basis of legitimacy. They are not fair. They are not neutral. In some instances, they are not legislatively enacted. Without a rational basis to exercise authority, the tradition of following the authority of the court, merely because it is a court, will deteriorate. The problem-solving courts are headed for a crisis of legitimacy.[61]

Thus, Casey believes that, as occurred with the earlier juvenile courts, problem-solving courts' lack of validity will eventually become evident. The smoke will clear. Rather than restoring legitimacy, then, problem-solving courts threaten to undermine the legitimacy of the judiciary. However, Casey also notes that problem-solving courts change the "basic nature of the courts." This is a crucial point. If the court system is so fundamentally transformed by a problem-solving orientation (as many advocates hope), and the transformation is in keeping with dominant cultural values, then on what grounds will people object to problem-solving courts? Casey observes that U.S. problem-solving courts, informed as they are by therapeutic pragmatism, introduce into the court system a new paradigm—a paradigm that invites a very different set of evaluative criteria.

> Treatment is judged only by efficacy. For example, a treatment is not judged by whether it is fair, or deserved, or proportional. When a child is immunized, there is no discussion about whether she deserves the pain from the needle's prick. The inquiry is only whether the vaccine is effective in preventing the disease. Ideas of liability, fault, guilt, and fairness are irrelevant in a treatment regime. Accordingly, the imposition of the same fifteen to life term perceived as unfairly disproportionate would be fitting if it were deemed part of a "treatment" and not a punitive "sentence."[62]

"Fitting" may not be the best choice of word here in that it suggests the notions of proportionality and desert. Rather, one could say that treatment (and all that occurs under its aegis) is viewed as more acceptable or plausible simply because is it called treatment. Casey notes further that because "problem-solving courts operate primarily on the treatment model," they are open to the criticism that they are "unfair." However, if cultural sensibilities are commensurate with therapeutic pragmatism, then why would anyone wish to challenge the courts on the grounds of fairness? In other words, if the courts appear to operate in accordance with the same ideals that are regarded as commonsensical in the broader culture, then on what grounds will people find them objectionable? In a time and place characterized by the predominance of therapeutic pragmatism, reasoning based on such notions as fairness and desert become increasingly irrelevant—both in the culture and in the courts.

As we have seen, however, ideas of desert, fairness, and proportionality are still resonant in some of the countries that have borrowed problem-solving courts from the United States. In the non-U.S. countries, there is less evidence of a crusade to change the basic nature of the courts. Rather, systems with legal accents characterized by deliberation, moderation, and restraint are less inclined toward the bold and enthusiastic reinventions of justice proposed in the United States, and they are more disposed to sustain justice's classical tenets.

Lady Justice's Blindfold

Consider, in this regard, a 2004 exchange between American and British officials on the topic of community courts and community justice. The exchange, set up in London by the CCI, addressed, among other issues, the establishment of England's first community court in Liverpool. Judge David Fletcher was among those who participated in the forum. In the course of the day's discussion, one participant defined community justice as "removing the blindfolds from Lady Justice."[63] The image of Lady Justice—situated as she is above many courtrooms throughout the United States and Europe—represents several themes central to classical under-standings of justice. Her scales convey notions of fairness and proportion-ality; her sword, the power of the court to impose a punishment and act decisively; and her blindfold, the ideas of neutrality and impartiality and the absence of prejudice and bias. In community courts, as we have seen, the judge is actively engaged with—and directly receives input from—the community. The judge (in the United States anyway) also meets regularly with team members in pre-court sessions to discuss in detail the lives of defendants participating in the court program. In this sense, the commu-nity court judge is decidedly not blind to a considerable amount of infor-mation—information he or she would not normally be privy to in a con-ventional criminal court. Lady Justice without her blindfold, therefore, is a fitting iconic representation of community courts (and other problem-solving courts).

During the 2004 meeting in London, not all British officials agreed with this revised image of justice: "Several participants stated concerns that offering community input in sentencing could ultimately erode the tradi-tional British legal protection of due process and encourage community 'vengeance.'"[64] Such resistance is not surprising. Recall from chapter 6 that restraint is one feature of problem-solving courts in the five non-U.S. countries that distinguishes them from those in the United States. Robert Cover, in fact, sees in Lady Justice's blindfold an act of self-restraint. "The blindfold (as opposed to blindness) suggests an act of self-restraint," he posits. "She could act otherwise and there is, thus, an everpresent element of choice in assuming this posture."[65] As we have seen, even when the structure of specialty courts allows for increased judicial activism, judges and magistrates outside of the United States still restrain themselves in a manner consistent with this understanding of the blindfold's import. Judge Fletcher, for example, unlike his American counterparts, does not attend pre-court meetings in the Liverpool community court.

In chapter 6, the American proclivity for increased judicial boldness was briefly compared to new managerial practices in civil litigation, where judges are likewise given increased knowledge of defendants' lives and greater scope for judicial involvement in cases. According to Judith Resnick, the expanded authority afforded judges in new case management practices may challenge the ideal of judicial impartiality, even while it gives the judge greater power. Invoking the image of Lady Justice, Resnick observes of these developments: "Although the sword remains in place, the blindfold and scales have all but disappeared."[66] With related concerns about certain features of American problem-solving courts, officials in receiving countries are not as convinced that the metaphorical blindfold should be removed.

Importing countries often speak of adaptation and are openly critical of elements of American culture found in U.S. problem-solving courts. Yet it is not always clear that these countries are successful either in identifying the disagreeable elements of American culture or in jettisoning those features that they view as problematic. The importation of the "building confidence" justificatory strategy is a useful example of just how difficult it is to separate law from its cultural roots. In this instance, a specific defense of problem-solving courts was included in the transplantation process (even when the strategy appeared less applicable to the importing legal cultures). Not only does this particular transfer illustrate how difficult it is to disentangle law from its cultural roots, it also shows how cultural attachments, in turn, affect the importing legal culture. In this case, one finds public acceptance of a purported condition that may not, in fact, comport with the local realities of the receiving legal cultures.

A deeper understanding of the relationship between law and culture may prove instructive to importing countries. If citizens in countries around the world loathe America as much as they say, then understanding the law/culture dynamic will aid them in avoiding the importation of the very things they say they do not like. Importers in all five non-U.S. countries speak of careful selection and adaptation. As we have seen, the nature and extent of their selectivity have varied. Just how successful importing countries will ultimately be in rejecting those elements of the American programs that do not fit their local cultures remains to be seen. Much of the data considered in this book suggest that more of American culture has penetrated foreign legal systems than the receiving countries realize. Even in the cases of more careful selectivity, there are signs that overtly American features of problem-solving courts—once openly denigrated by early importers—have crept into the receiving legal cultures.

Only time will tell whether and to what extent these cultural infiltrations—be they welcomed or regretted—will result in further homogenization or some kind of subtle yet transformative legal irritation. While there are certainly examples of at least limited and initial resistance, there are other signs of emergent legal irritation and of fuller Americanization in the receiving legal systems. In any respect, importing countries wishing to maintain such qualities as deliberation, moderation, and restraint in their local legal cultures do well to recognize the difficulty of disentangling law from its cultural roots. Embedded in problem-solving courts (even in the nomenclature used to label them) are the very features of American culture that many say they do not like. To import problem-solving courts is to import elements of the particular culture out of which the programs first emerged—and from which they are not easily extricated. A fuller appreciation of the culturally embedded nature of law, as such, might prevent borrowers from losing the valued and defining features of their local legal accent.

As for Lady Justice's metaphorical accoutrements, such an understanding may lead importing countries to more firmly affix her blindfold. Americans, on the other hand, as long as they have the blindfold removed, may wish to look more carefully at the criminal justice practices of other countries. In so doing, they might not only learn something about the values that animate other legal cultures but also gain some insights into why people around the world perceive the United States as they do.

NOTES

NOTES TO INTRODUCTION

1. George Howe Colt, "Crack: Downfall of a Neighborhood," *Life* 11, no. 8 (July 1988): 92.

2. This is a pseudonym, as are all names of clients/participants identified in the book.

3. Whether Scotland and England should be referred to as separate countries is a somewhat complicated issue, particularly in light of the ongoing devolution process. One could argue that technically England, Scotland, Wales, and Northern Ireland are the four main parts of the country that is called the United Kingdom. Yet, since the 1707 union—which established the United Kingdom—Scotland has in many respects retained its identity as a separate country. The distinction has only become more pronounced in recent years with the 1999 establishment of the Scottish Parliament. The official website of the Scottish Parliament, though acknowledging that "The United Kingdom of Great Britain and Northern Ireland is the full name of the country," also posits that "it is common usage nowadays to describe the four constituent parts of the UK (Scotland, England, Wales, and Northern Ireland) as 'countries'" (available at http://www .scottish.parliament.uk/vli/publicInfo/faq/category2.htm). Thus, Scotland and England are countries within a country. The official website of the Office of the Prime Minister of the United Kingdom, similarly states: "The United Kingdom is made up of four countries: England, Scotland, Wales and Northern Ireland" (available at *http://www.number-10.gov.uk/output/Page823.asp*). In any respect, though the nomenclature is a bit ambiguous and open to some dispute, in this book I have chosen to follow the "common usage" and refer to both England and Scotland as countries.

4. For my previous book, *Reinventing Justice*, I visited an additional twenty-one American drug courts between 1994 and 1998. In this book, I occasionally draw from data collected during this period as well. The overall sample of courts for this project, then, actually exceeds seventy local courts in total—though the vast majority of material presented and analyzed in this book is taken from the more recent research.

5. Quotes without note numbers in this book were taken from statements made at local problem-solving court sites (i.e., either in interviews with the author or in statements made during court sessions, community meetings, court launchings, pre-court meetings, or treatment sessions) or at regional, national, or international conferences (i.e., either in interviews with the author or in statements made during speeches or panel discussions).

6. Richard Schneider, Hy Bloom, and Mark Heerema, *Mental Health Courts: Decriminalizing the Mentally Ill* (Toronto: Irwin Law, 2007), 82.

NOTES TO CHAPTER ONE:
PROBLEM SOLVING AND COURTS OF LAW

1. Peter Berger, Brigitte Berger, and Hansfried Kellner, *The Homeless Mind: Modernization and Consciousness* (New York: Random House, 1973), 30.

2. John Feinblatt, Greg Berman, and Derek Denckla, "Judicial Innovation at the Crossroads: The Future of Problem-Solving Courts," *Court Manager* 15, no. 3 (2000): 28.

3. Bruce J. Winick and David B. Wexler, eds., *Judging in a Therapeutic Key: Therapeutic Jurisprudence and the Courts* (Durham, NC: Carolina Academic Press, 2003), 3.

4. See Mary Ann Glendon, *A Nation Under Lawyers: How the Crisis in the Legal Profession Is Transforming American Society* (New York: Farrar, Straus, and Giroux, 1994); William Pizzi, *Trials Without Truth: Why Our System of Criminal Trials Has Become an Expensive Failure and What We Need to Do to Rebuild It* (New York: New York University Press, 1999); Susan Daicoff, "The Role of Therapeutic Jurisprudence within the Comprehensive Law Movement," in *Practicing Therapeutic Jurisprudence: Law as Helping Profession*, ed. Dennis P. Stolle, David B. Wexler, and Bruce Winick (Durham, NC: Carolina Academic Press, 2000); Arie Freiberg, "Problem Solving Courts: Innovative Solutions to Intractable Problem?" *Journal of Judicial Administration* 11, no. 1 (August 2001): 8–27.

5. Peggy Fulton Hora and Deborah J. Chase, "Judicial Satisfaction When Judging in a Therapeutic Key," *Contemporary Issues in Law* 7, no. 1 (2003–2004): 18.

6. Ibid., 17.

7. Ibid., 30–33.

8. Philip Bean, "Drug Courts, the Judge, and the Rehabilitative Ideal," in *Drug Courts: In Theory and in Practice*, ed. James L. Nolan Jr. (Hawthorne, NY: Aldine de Gruyer, 2002), 244.

9. Hora and Chase, "Judicial Satisfaction when Judging in a Therapeutic Key," 37.

10. Fagan and Malkin, for example, in explaining the origins of the Red Hook community courts, observe: "One of the recurring crises in Red Hook, and many socially and economically disadvantaged neighborhoods, is the low rating by citizens of the legitimacy of law and legal institutions. . . . The dissatisfaction of individuals who suffer the consequences of rising crime levels and/or social disorder, which makes their everyday lives unsafe, created a crisis of legitimacy for legal institutions." Jeffrey Fagan and Victoria Malkin, "Problem-Solving Courts and Therapeutic Jurisprudence: Theorizing Community Justice through Community Courts," *Fordham Urban Law Journal* 20 (2003): 899, 901.

11. David Rottman and Pamela Casey, "Therapeutic Jurisprudence and the Emergence of Problem-Solving Courts," *National Institute of Justice Journal* 12 (July 1999): 13.

12. Greg Berman and John Feinblatt, *Good Courts: The Case for Problem-Solving Justice* (New York: New Press, 2005), 3.

13. Berman and Feinblatt, *Good Courts*, 3.

14. Michael Schrunk, in "What Is a Traditional Judge Anyway? Problem-Solving in the State Courts," ed. Greg Berman, *Judicature* 84, no. 2 (September–October 2000): 80.

15. Judith S. Kaye, "State of the Judiciary," January 10, 2000, available at *http://www.courts.state.ny.us/admin/stateofjudiciary/soj2000.html*.

16. Judith S. Kaye, "Delivering Justice Today: A Problem-Solving Approach," *Yale Law and Policy Review* 22 (Winter 2004): 146. It is a view shared by other supporters of problem-solving courts. Greg Berman, for example, observes, "Advocates of problem-solving courts hail . . . enhanced public confidence in justice" (in "What Is a Traditional Judge Anyway?" *Judicature* 84, no. 2 [September–October 2000]: 78). Indeed, problem-solving courts are often justified on the grounds that they will re-engender public confidence in the American judicial system. It sometimes seems their very raison d'être is to "re-legitimate legal institutions at the local level" (Jeffrey Fagan and Victoria Malkin, "Theorizing Community Justice Through Community Courts," *Fordham Urban Law Journal* 30 [March 2003]: 950).

17. Kaye, "Delivering Justice Today: A Problem-Solving Approach," 129.

18. Daicoff, "The Role of Therapeutic Jurisprudence within the Comprehensive Law Movement," 466. Arie Freiberg similarly observes that the need for new legal approaches has resulted in part from "a breakdown in traditional social and community institutions which have supported individuals in the past," in "Problem-Oriented Courts: Innovative Solutions to Intractable Problems?" *Journal of Judicial Adminstration* 11, no. 1 (August 2001): 9.

19. Rottman and Casey, "Therapeutic Jurisprudence and the Emergence of Problem-Solving Courts," 13. Judge Judith Kaye makes a similar argument: "We've witnessed the breakdown of the family and of other traditional safety nets. So what we're seeing in the courts is many, many more substance abuse cases. We have a huge number of domestic violence cases. We have many, many more quality-of-life crimes. And it's not just the subject of the cases that's different. We get a lot of repeat business. We're recycling the same people through the system. And things get worse. We know from experience that a drug possession or an assault today could be something considerably worse tomorrow," as stated in "What Is a Traditional Judge Anyway? Problem Solving in the State Courts," ed. Greg Berman, *Judicature* 84, no. 2 (September–October 2000): 80.

20. Timothy Casey, "When Good Intentions Are Not Enough: Problem-Solving Courts and the Impending Crisis of Legitimacy," *Southern Methodist University Law Review* 57 (Fall 2004): 1516.

21. Judge Truman Morrison, as quoted in "What Is a Traditional Judge Anyway? Problem Solving in the State Courts," ed. Greg Berman, *Judicature* 84, no. 2 (September–October 2000): 80.

22. In her thoughtful assessment of the Red Hook community court, Victoria Malkin asks whether "the court is the proper arena to develop these [community] programs." She notes further that "the need for new services and programs plagues many communities. Community groups and local organizations which focus on community programs compete for declining public and private resources." When courts enter into this competition, "they have advantages over

smaller grassroots organizations in terms of their political and cultural capital" (Victoria Malkin, "Community Courts and the Process of Accountability: Consensus and Conflict at the Red Hook Community Justice Center," *American Criminal Law Review*, 40, no. 4 [Fall 2003]: 1590). As it specifically concerns domestic violence courts, Betsy Tsai notes concerns about the diversion of resources to offer therapy for perpetrators rather than services for battered women. Tsai notes objections to "the use of valuable domestic violence resources on services for perpetrators. Many battered women's advocates object to spending money on long-term interventions for batterers when doing so diverts limited funds away from services for battered women" (Betsy Tsai, "The Trend Toward Specialized Domestic Violence Courts: Improvements of an Effective Innovation," *Fordham Law Review* 68 [2000]: 1314). Consider also observations by Hal Jackson in a paper presented at a conference in Perth, Australia: "The late twentieth century and the first few years of the twenty-first century are often seen as involving the withdrawal of, and loss of faith in, the welfare state. Is this either the cause of, or at least related to the growth in, alternative forms of criminal justice systems, in the sense that courts have seen the need which governments have abdicated?" Jackson asks whether "it is appropriate that resources be allocated to such [problem-solving] courts."

23. Greg Berman, "What Is a Traditional Judge Anyway? Problem Solving in the State Courts," *Judicature* 84, no. 2 (September–October 2000): 78.

24. Greg Berman and John Feinblatt, "Problem-Solving Courts: A Brief Primer," *Law and Policy* 23, no. 2 (April 2001): 126. Freiberg similarly notes, "The genesis of modern problem-solving courts can be found in the first drug court experiment in Dade County Florida in 1989" ("Problem Solving Courts: Innovative Solutions to Intractable Problem?" 12). See also Jeffrey A. Butts, "Introduction: Problem-Solving Courts," *Law and Policy* 23, no. 2 (April 2002): 21. Butts writes, "Drug courts are the most visible of problem-solving court." Similarly, Bruce Winick and David Wexler note, "The 'modern' antecedents of the problem-solving court movement can be traced to drug treatment court, founded in Miami in 1989" (Winick and Wexler, eds., *Judging in a Therapeutic Key*, 4).

25. Eric J. Miller, "Embracing Addiction: Drug Court and the False Promise of Judicial Interventionism," *Ohio State Law Journal* 65 (2004): 1481.

26. James Q. Wilson and George L. Kelling, "Broken Windows," *Atlantic Monthly* (March 1982): 34.

27. Quintin Johnstone, "The Hartford Community Court: An Experiment that Has Succeeded," *Connecticut Law Review* 34, no. 1 (Fall 2001): 124, 135.

28. Robert Weidner, "Hartford Community Court: Origins, Expectations and Implementation," Center for Court Innovation, Bureau of Justice Administration, U.S. Department of Justice (1999): 9.

29. Victoria Malkin, "Community Courts and the Process of Accountability: Consensus and Conflict at the Red Hook Community Justice Center," *American Criminal Law Review* 40, no. 4 (Fall 2003): 1579.

30. Berman and Feinblatt, *Good Courts*, 74.

31. Johnstone, "The Harford Community Court," 137.

32. Ibid.

33. James L. Nolan Jr., *Reinventing Justice: The American Drug Court Movement* (Princeton, NJ: Princeton University Press, 2001), 178–84.

34. Berman and Feinblatt, "Problem-Solving Courts: A Brief Primer," 22. See also Robert Weidner, "Hartford Community Court: Origins, Expectations and Implementation," 11.

35. Fagan and Malkin, "Problem-Solving Courts and Therapeutic Jurisprudence: Theorizing Community Justice through Community Courts," 898.

36. Berman and Feinblatt, *Good Courts*, 74.

37. *Red Hook Community Justice Center*, prod. Meema Spadola, 10 min., A Sugar Pictures Production, a product of the Center for Court Innovation, 2005, DVD.

38. Arthur Santana, "D.C. Court Tries Problem-Solving," *Washington Post* (September 2, 2002): A1.

39. Johnstone, "The Hartford Community Court," 124.

40. Judge Lester Langer, "Dade County Domestic Violence Court," paper presented at the Second Annual NADCP Training Conference (July 10, 1995), 1.

41. Freiberg, "Problem Solving Courts: Innovative Solutions to Intractable Problem?" 18.

42. Carrie J. Petrucci, "Respect as a Component in the Judge-Defendant Interaction in a Specialized Domestic Violence Court that Utilizes Therapeutic Jurisprudence," *Criminal Law Bulletin* 38, no. 2 (March–April 2002): 268.

43. Center for Court Innovation, Problem-Solving Courts: Chronology, available at http://www.problem-solvingcourts.org (last visited November 20, 2003).

44. Petrucci, "Respect as a Component in the Judge-Defendant Interaction," 288.

45. Lisa Newmark, Mike Rempel, Kelly Diffily, and Kamala Mallik Kane, "Specialized Felony Domestic Violence Courts: Lessons on Implementation and Impacts from the King County Experience," Report Submitted to the Center for Court Innovation and the National Institute for Justice, Urban Institute (October 2001): 13.

46. Even Judge Levanthal, though he may not assume a conspicuously therapeutic style in his courtroom, plays a very active role in monitoring the behavior of offenders. As he puts it, "They need to know they're being watched." Moreover, he regularly assigns offenders to such counseling venues as batterer's intervention programs and drug and alcohol treatment, though he claims these are "for monitoring purposes." The monitoring, however, extends beyond assignment to court-mandated treatment. A Brooklyn public defender reports that Judge Levanthal actually checks up on one of her clients by calling him "at home every weekend" (Amy Waldman, "Striking Back," *New York Times* [June 28, 1998]: 10.). Defendants assigned to batterers' intervention programs also come back to court for regular review sessions. During these sessions, Levanthal can be as interactive and demonstrative as any American drug court judge, where he reportedly "hectors, lectures, harangues and occasionally threatens defendants who appear before him" (Waldman, "Striking Back," 10).

47. Betsy Tsai, "The Trend Toward Specialized Domestic Violence Courts: Improvements of an Effective Innovation," *Fordham Law Review* 68 (2000): 1303.

48. Ibid., 1306.

49. Randal B. Fritzler and Leonore M. J. Simon, "The Development of a Specialized Domestic Violence Court in Vancouver, Washington Utilizing Innovative Judicial Paradigms," *UMKC Law Review* 69 (2000): 148.

50. Ibid., 159.

51. Randall Kleinhesselink and Clayton Mosher, "Process Evaluation of the Clark County Domestic Violence Court" (March 2003): 46–47 (from material attached to paper presented in note 52).

52. Randal Fritzler, "Therapeutic Jurisprudence in a Domestic Violence Court: Reflections on Five Years of Judicial Experimentation," paper presented at conference in Edinburgh (Summer 2003), 13.

53. Fritzler and Simon, "The Development of a Specialized Domestic Violence Court in Vancouver," 171.

54. See Nolan, *Reinventing Justice*, 51–57.

55. Petrucci, "Respect as a Component in the Judge-Defendant Interaction," 272, 282.

56. Ibid., 290.

57. Ibid., 267.

58. Richard Schneider, Hy Bloom, and Mark Heerema, *Mental Health Courts: Decriminalizing the Mentally Ill* (Toronto: Irwin Law, 2007): 103.

59. Wendy N. Davis, "Special Problems for Specialty Courts," *ABA Journal* (February 2003): 37; Wexler and Winick, eds., *Judging in a Therapeutic Key*, 59.

60. John S. Goldkamp and Cheryl Irons-Guynn, "Emerging Judicial Strategies for the Mentally Ill in the Criminal Caseload: Mental Health Courts in Fort Lauderdale, Seattle, San Bernardino, and Anchorage," Bureau of Justice Assistance, Office of Justice Programs, U.S. Department of Justice (April 2000): viii.

61. Goldkamp and Irons-Guynn, "Emerging Judicial Strategies for the Mentally Ill in the Criminal Caseload," 10.

62. Richard Marini observes of the Broward County mental health court, for example, that "while a judge, defense attorney and prosecuting attorneys are usually present, there also may be social workers and mental health case workers on hand to evaluate patients and offer their expertise" (Richard A. Marini in Winick and Wexler, eds., *Judging in a Therapeutic Key*, 61).

63. Michael D. Jones and Louraine C. Arkfeld, "The Judge's Role in the Mental Health Court," paper distributed at conference in Edinburgh, Scotland (Summer 2003), 7.

64. See, for example, Winick and Wexler, eds., *Judging in a Therapeutic Key*, 63–66.

65. Goldkamp and Irons-Guynn, "Emerging Judicial Strategies for the Mentally Ill in the Criminal Caseload," viii.

66. Ibid., 42–43.

67. Schneider, Bloom, and Heerema, for example, observe, "American diversion programs and mental health courts will frequently impose penalties for non-compliance, and the use of jail as a penalty for non-compliance has been increasing" (Richard Schneider, Hy Bloom, and Mark Heerema, *Mental Health Courts: Decriminalizing the Mentally Ill* [Toronto: Irwin Law, 2007]: 90).

68. Richard A. Marini in Winick and Wexler, eds., *Judging in a Therapeutic Key*, 61.

69. Goldkamp and Irons-Guynn, "Emerging Judicial Strategies for the Mentally Ill in the Criminal Caseload," 57.

70. *Mental Health Court: A Better Way to Manage Mental Health Issues*, promotional video supplied by Hennepin County Mental Health Court (January 2005).

71. Ibid., 66.

72. Ibid., 57.

73. Arie Freiberg, "Specialized Courts and Sentencing," paper presented at the Probation and Community Corrections: Making the Community Safer Conference in Perth, Australia (September 23–24, 2002), 4.

74. Goldkamp and Irons-Guynn, "Emerging Judicial Strategies for the Mentally Ill in the Criminal Caseload," xiv. Similarly, Richard Marini argues: "The flood of mentally ill inmates began about 40 years ago when many huge, state-run mental hospitals—criticized for warehousing and, at times, abusing patients—were closed in a process that came to be known as deinstitutionalization. Smaller, community-based facilities were supposed to be opened to care for these just-released patients, but the money for these clinics never materialized. As a result, thousands upon thousands of the mentally ill, many suffering from psychoses, were essentially left on their own, often to the streets, increasingly to jails and prisons" (Richard A. Marini, in Winick and Wexler, eds., *Judging in a Therapeutic Key*, 60).

75. Goldkamp and Irons-Guynn, "Emerging Judicial Strategies for the Mentally Ill in the Criminal Caseload," 21.

76. Ibid., xv.

77. C. West Huddleston, Karen Freeman-Wilson, and Donna L. Boone, "Painting the Current Picture: A National Report on Drug Courts and Other Problem Solving Court Programs in the United States," National Drug Court Institute, Bureau of Justice Assistance, vol. 1, no. 1 (May 2004). See also C. West Huddleston, Karen Freeman-Wilson, Douglas B. Marlowe, and Aaron Roussell, "Painting the Current Picture: A National Report on Drug Courts and Other Problem-Solving Court Programs in the United States," National Drug Court Institute, Bureau of Justice Assistance, vol. 1, no. 2 (May 2005).

78. Integrated domestic violence courts will handle not only domestic violence, but issues normally handled in civil courts, such as the status of spousal relations, civil protection orders, visitation rights, and custody issues. For a discussion of problem-solving processes in unified family courts see Barbara Babb and Jeff Kuhn, "Maryland's Family Divisions Performance Standard 5.1: A Therapeutic, Holistic, Ecological Approach to Family Law Decision Making," in Winick and Wexler, eds., *Judging in a Therapeutic Key*, 125–27. See also Richard Boldt and Jana Singer, "Problem-Solving Judges and Therapeutic Jurisprudence in Drug Treatment Courts and Unified Family Courts," *Maryland Law Review* 65 (2002): 82–99.

79. John Feinblatt and Derek Denckla, eds., "Prosecutors, Defenders, and Problem-Solving Courts," *Judicature* 84, no. 4 (January–February 2001): 214.

80. Berman and Feinblatt, *Good Courts*, 196.

81. Winick and Wexler, eds., *Judging in a Therapeutic Key*, 87.

82. Berman and Feinblatt, *Good Courts*, 190.

83. John Feinblatt and Derek Denckla, eds., "Prosecutors, Defenders, and Problem-Solving Courts," *Judicature* 84, no. 4 (January–February 2001): 214.

NOTES TO CHAPTER TWO:
LAW AND CULTURE IN COMPARATIVE PERSPECTIVE

1. Roland Robertson, "Glocalization: Time-Space and Homogeneity-Heterogeneity," in *Global Modernities*, ed. Mike Featherstone, Scott Lash, and Roland Robertson (London: Sage, 1995), 38.

2. Peter L. Berger, "Introduction: The Cultural Dynamics of Globalization," in *Many Globalizations: Cultural Diversity in the Contemporary World*, ed. Peter L. Berger and Samuel P. Huntington (Oxford: Oxford University Press, 2002), 2.

3. Hsin-Huang Michael Hsiao, "Coexistence and Synthesis: Cultural Globalization and Localization in Contemporary Taiwan," in *Many Globalizations*, ed. Peter L. Berger and Samuel P. Huntington, 49.

4. Benjamin Barber, *Jihad vs. McWorld: Terrorism's Challenge to Democracy* (London: Random House, 1995), 157.

5. Ibid., 19.

6. Robertson, "Glocalization," 30.

7. Berger, "Introduction: The Cultural Dynamics of Globalization," 9.

8. Robertson, "Glocalization: Time-Space and Homogeneity-Heterogeneity," 462.

9. Ritzer introduces the notion of "grobalization" to capture an understanding of globalization that is more sensitive to homogenizing processes, while he characterizes Roland's preference for "glocalization" as more akin to heterogenization. See George Ritzer, *The McDonaldization of Society: Revised New Century Edition* (Thousand Oaks, CA: Pine Forge Press, 2004), 162–65.

10. As David Nelken observes, each type of metaphor "reflects and advances a different approach to the relationship between law and society" (David Nelken, "Toward a Sociology of Legal Adaptation," in *Adapting Legal Cultures*, ed. David Nelken [Oxford: Hart, 2001], 16).

11. Otto Kahn-Freund, "On the Uses and Misuses of Comparative Law," *Modern Law Review* 37, no. 1 (1974): 6.

12. David Nelken, "Beyond the Metaphor of Legal Transplants? Consequences of Autopoietic Theory for the Study of Cross-Cultural Legal Adaptation," in *The New Boundaries of Law: The Debate over Legal Autopoiesis*, ed. Jiri Priban and David Nelken (Aldershot: Ashgate, 2001), 265–302.

13. William Ewald defines the mirror theory of law as "the theory that law is the mirror of some set of forces (social, political, economic, whatever) external to the law" (William Ewald, "Comparative Jurisprudence II: The Logic of Legal Transplants," in *American Journal of Comparative Law* 43, no. 4 [Autumn 1995]).

14. David Nelken, "Legal Transplants and Beyond: Of Disciplines and Metaphors," in *Comparative Law in the 21ˢᵗ Century*, ed. Andrew Harding and Esin Orucu (The Hague: Kluwer Law International, 2002), 19–34.

15. Donald Joralemon, "Organ Wars: The Battle for Body Parts," *Medical Anthropology Quarterly* 9, no. 3 (1995): 337.

16. Nelken, "Legal Transplants and Beyond," 26.

17. Alan Watson, *Legal Transplants: An Approach to Comparative Law*, 2ⁿᵈ ed. (Athens: University of Georgia Press), 51.

18. Ibid., 97.

19. Ibid.

20. Lawrence Freidman, "Some Comments on Cotterell and Legal Transplants," in *Adapting Legal Cultures*, ed. David Nelken (Oxford: Hart, 2001), 93.

21. Lawrence Friedman, "Borders: On the Emerging Sociology of Transnational Law," *Stanford Journal of International Law* 32 (Winter 1996): 71.

22. Nelken, "Toward a Sociology of Legal Adaptation," 13.

23. Friedman, "Borders: On the Emerging Sociology of Transnational Law," 75.

24. Kahn-Freund, "On the Uses and Misuses of Comparative Law," 6.

25. Charles de Secondat, Baron de Montesquieu, "Of Positive Laws," book I, chap. 3 of *The Spirit of Law* (1748), trans. Thomas Nugent in 1752 (Kitchener, Ontario: Batoche Books, 2001), 23.

26. Bernhard Grossfield, *The Strengths and Weakness of Comparative Law*, trans. Tony Weir (Oxford: Clarendon Press, 1990), 41.

27. Pierre Legrand, "What 'Legal Transplants'?" in *Adapting Legal Cultures*, ed. David Nelken (Oxford: Hart, 2001), 68.

28. Mary Ann Glendon, Michael W. Gordon, and Christopher Osakwe, *Comparative Legal Traditions* (St. Paul: West Publishing, 1982), 10.

29. Clifford Geertz, *Local Knowledge: Further Essays in Interpretive Anthropology* (New York: Basic Books, 1983), 123.

30. Ibid., 215.

31. David Garland, *Punishment and Modern Society: A Study in Social Theory* (Chicago: University of Chicago Press, 1990), 21.

32. Ibid., 210.

33. Susan Daicoff, "The Role of Therapeutic Jurisprudence within the Comprehensive Law Movement," in *Practicing Therapeutic Jurisprudence: Law as Helping Profession*, ed. Dennis P. Stolle, David B. Wexler, and Bruce Winick (Durham, NC: Carolina Academic Press, 2000), 465.

34. Bruce Winick, "The Jurisprudence of Therapeutic Jurisprudence," in *Law in a Therapeutic Key: Developments in Therapeutic Jurisprudence*, ed. David B. Wexler and Bruce J. Winick (Durham, NC: Carolina Academic Press, 1996), 646.

35. Richard Young and Carolyn Hoyle, "Restorative Justice and Punishment," *The Use of Punishment*, ed. S. McConville (Collompton: Willan, 2003), 200.

36. Andrew von Hirsch, Andrew Ashworth, and Clifford Shearing, "Specifying Aims and Limits for Restorative Justice: A 'Making Amends' Model?" in *Restorative Justice and Criminal Justice: Competing or Reconcilable Paradigms?* (Oxford: Hart Publishing, 2003), 22.

37. John Braithwaite, "Restorative Justice and Therapeutic Jurisprudence," *Criminal Law Bulletin*, 38, no. 2 (March–April 2002): 244.

38. Ibid., 246.

39. Ibid., 247. See also John Braithwaite, *Restorative Justice and Responsive Regulation* (Oxford: Oxford University Press, 2002), 12. Here Braithwaite asserts, "It should be forbidden for a restorative justice process to impose a punishment beyond that which would be imposed by the courts for that kind of wrongdoing. . . . Restorative justice processes should be constrained by all the rights that are foundational to liberal legalism."

40. John Braithwaite and Philip Pettit, *Not Just Deserts* (Oxford: Oxford University Press, 1990), 101–2.

41. Andrew von Hirsch and Andrew Ashworth, "Not Not Just Deserts: A Response to Braithwaite and Pettit," *Oxford Journal of Legal Studies* 12, no. 1 (Spring 1992): 88.

42. Richard Young and Carolyn Hoyle, "Restorative Justice and Punishment," 224. See also Kathleen Daly and Russ Immarigeon, "The Past, Present, and Future of Restorative Justice: Some Critical Reflections," *Contemporary Justice Review* 1, no. 1 (1998): 21–45, and Kathleen Daly, "Restorative Justice, The Real Story," in *A Restorative Justice Reader*, ed. Gerry Johnstone (Cullompton: Willan, 2003), 363–81.

43. Young and Hoyle, "Restorative Justice and Punishment," 224.

44. Antony Duff, "Restoration and Retribution," in *Restorative Justice and Criminal Justice: Competing or Reconcilable Paradigms?* ed. Andrew von Hirsch, Julian Roberts, Anthony E. Bottoms, Kent Roach, and Mara Schiff (Oxford: Hart Publishing, 2003), 43.

45. Braithwaite, "Restorative Justice and Therapeutic Jurisprudence," 254.

46. Ibid., 253.

47. Bruce Winick, "The Jurisprudence of Therapeutic Jurisprudence," in *Law in a Therapeutic Key: Developments in Therapeutic Jurisprudence,* ed. David B. Wexler and Bruce Winick (Durham, NC: Carolina Academic Press, 1996), 665.

48. According to Braithwaite, "Reintegrative shaming communicates disapproval within a continuum of respect for the offender; the offender is treated as a good person who has done a bad deed." He distinguishes reintegrative shaming from stigmatization and sees the former as clearly preferable. An "apology" from an offender to a victim, for example, "is a kind of shaming that is morally preferable to stigmatization" (Braithwaite, "Restorative Justice and Therapeutic Jurisprudence," 257–58).

49. Ibid., 247.

50. Ibid.

51. As Mae Quinn, for example, observes, "Indeed, despite TJ's desire not to 'suboridinat[e] due process or other justice values,' even in theory the new model seems to run the risk of doing just that"; "Thus, both in theory and practice, TJ defense lawyering seems to subordinate zeal to therapeutic considerations"; and "What is more, despite its claims to the contrary, TJ runs the risk of gutting worthwhile core values of our current criminal justice system" (Mae Quinn, "An RSVP to Professor Wexler's Warm Invitation to the Criminal Defense Bar: Unable to

Join You, Already (Somewhat Similarly) Engaged," *Boston College Law Review* 48 [2007]: 568, 578, 591).

52. See James L. Nolan Jr., *Reinventing Justice: The American Drug Court Movement* (Princeton, NJ: Princeton University Press, 2001).

53. Young and Hoyle, "Restorative Justice and Punishment," 202; Braithwaite, *Restorative Justice and Responsive Regulation*, 8.

54. Because of its widespread use of family group conferencing, New Zealand has been described as "the country with the most developed programmatic commitment to restorative justice" (Braithwaite, *Restorative Justice and Responsive Regulation*, 10).

55. Freiberg, "Three Strikes and You're Out—It's Not Cricket: Colonization and Resistance in Australian Sentencing" *Sentencing and Sanctions in Western Countries,* ed. Michael Tonry and Richard S. Frase (Oxford: Oxford University Press, 2001), 54; Daly and Immarigeon, "The Past, Present, and Future of Restorative Justice," 28.

56. Susan Daicoff observes the same, noting that restorative justice "appears to have been most enthusiastically employed in Australia, Canada, and the United Kingdom" (Daicoff, "The Role of Therapeutic Jurisprudence within the Comprehensive Law Movement," 477).

57. In Atlanta, for example, an entity called the Restorative Justice Center works directly alongside the Atlanta community court. The center's stated mission is to "raise awareness, develop resources, and provide advocacy to enhance and expand court programs that improve outcomes and restorative solutions for offenders, victims, and the larger community."

58. Wexler and Winick, eds., *Judging in a Therapeutic Key*, 6.

59. Richard A. Posner, *Law, Pragmatism, and Democracy* (Cambridge: Harvard University Press, 2003): 76–77. Not all pragmatists, however, would agree with Posner on this point.

60. See, for example, Alfonso Morales, ed., *Renascent Pragmatism* (Aldershot: Ashgate, 2003); and Morris Dickstein, ed., *The Revival of Pragmatism: New Essays on Social Thought, Law, and Culture* (Durham, NC: Duke University Press, 1998).

61. David Luban notes that legal pragmatism "is, first of all eclecticism" (David Lubin, "What's Pragmatic about Legal Pragmatism?" in *The Revival of Pragmatism*, ed. Morris Dickstein, 275). Legal pragmatist Daniel Farber observes that "legal pragmatism is not easy to define. It is part of a loosely connected collection of antifoundationalist views, a category that includes believers in Aristotelian practical reason, some feminist theorists, adherents to literary theories such as hermeneutics and deconstruction, and students of the philosophy of language" (Daniel Farber, "Reinventing Brandeis: Legal Pragmatism for the Twenty-First Century," *University of Illinois Law Review* [1995]: 167). Likewise, Richard Posner speaks of the "new pragmatism" as an umbrella term for diverse tendencies in philosophical thought"(Richard Posner, "What Has Pragmatism to Offer the Law?" *Southern California Law Review* 63 [1990]: 1653).

62. Thomas Grey, for example, sees as among the common strains of philosophical and legal pragmatism "an account of inquiry that is at the same time contextualist and instrumentalist" (Thomas C. Grey, "Freestanding Legal Prag-

matism," in *The Revival of Pragmatism*, ed. Dickstein, 255). Posner says of the pragmatic disposition that it is an "outlook that is progressive (in the sense of forward-looking), secular, and experimental, and that is commonsensical without making a fetish of common sense" (Posner, "What Has Pragmatism to Offer Law?" 1660.

63. Though antifoundationalist in orientation, legal pragmatists, like TJ theorists, may still make deferential statements about the importance of due process and so on, not because of any philosophical commitment to such principles, but because it may be pragmatically useful to reference a system's traditions and history in order to achieve a particular end determined to best serve the social needs of a particular society.

64. Susan Daicoff, "The Role of Therapeutic Jurisprudence within the Comprehensive Law Movement," 468.

65. Philip Rieff, *The Triumph of the Therapeutic* (Chicago: University of Chicago Press, 1966). For a more recent discussion of the therapeutic culture, see Jonathan B. Imber, ed., *Therapeutic Culture: Triumph and Defeat* (New Brunswick, NJ: Transaction, 2004).

66. For a discussion of the impact of the therapeutic ethos on the American drug court movement, see James L. Nolan Jr, *Reinventing Justice: The American Drug Court Movement* (Princeton, NJ: Princeton University Press, 2001). Here, I offer a summary overview of the therapeutic culture as one that is typified by "an elevated concern with the self, by a conspicuously emotivist form of discourse and self-understanding, by a proclivity to invoke the language of victimhood and to view behaviors in pathological rather than moral/religious terms, and by the elevated social status of psychologists and other therapeutic practitioners," 47. For a fuller discussion of the defining features of the therapeutic culture, see James L. Nolan Jr., *The Therapeutic State: Justifying Government at Century's End* (New York: New York University Press, 1998), especially chapter 1; and for a more recent discussion of the therapeutic culture, see Eva Illouz, *Saving the Modern Soul: Therapy, Emotions, and the Culture of Self-Help* (Berkeley: University of California Press, 2008).

67. William Nelson, "What Is a Traditional Judge Anyway? Problem Solving in State Courts," *Judicature* (September–October 2000): 83.

68. Wexler and Winick, eds., *Judging in a Therapeutic Key*, 249.

69. Mary Ann Glendon, *Abortion and Divorce in Western Law: American Failures, European Challenges* (Cambridge: Harvard University Press, 1990), 59.

70. Gary Jeffrey Jacobsohn, "The Permeability of Constitutional Borders," *Texas Law Review* 82, no. 7 (June 2004): 1771, 1812.

71. Teubner, "Legal Irritants: How Unifying Law Ends up in New Divergences," in *Varieties of Capitalism*, ed. Peter A. Hall and David Soskice (Oxford: Oxford University Press, 2001), 418.

72. Ibid.

73. Ibid.

74. Jack A. Hiller, "Language, Law, Sports and Culture: The Transferability or Non-Transferability of Words, Lifestyles, and Attitudes Through Law," *Valparaiso University Law Review* 12, no. 3 (1978): 434.

75. Ibid., 439.

76. Ibid., 443.

77. Ibid., 439.

78. Ibid., 440.

79. Ibid., 461.

80. Berger, "Four Faces of Global Culture," *National Interest* (Fall 1997): 26–27.

81. Ritzer, *The McDonaldization of Society*, 179, 182.

82. Arie Freiberg, "Three Strikes and You're Out—It's Not Cricket: Colonization and Resistance in Australian Sentencing," in *Sentencing and Sanctions in Western Countries*, ed. Michael Tonry and Richard S. Frase (Oxford: Oxford University Press, 2001), 30.

83. Ibid., 32.

84. Philip Bean, "American Influence on British Drug Policy," in *Drug War, American Style: The Internationalization of Failed Policy and its Alternatives*, ed. Jurg Gerber and Eric L. Jensen (New York: Garland, 2001), 94.

NOTES TO CHAPTER THREE:
ANGLO-AMERICAN ALTERNATIVES: ENGLAND AND THE UNITED STATES

1. As with Scotland—though in slightly different ways—the relationship between England and Wales is not entirely clear. Wales, like Scotland, has been affected by devolution. Though Wales voted by a slim majority to establish its own Assembly in 1997, it remains less devolved from England than does Scotland. And the development of problem-solving courts has been generated from London, not from Cardiff. In fact, the vast majority of the new problem-solving courts in this region of the world have been developed in England. Thus, as reflected in the title, this chapter is primarily focused on England. That said, one of the first UK domestic violence courts was established in Cardiff, Wales, and some of the national schemes (e.g., DTTOs) were rolled out across England and Wales. Therefore, on occasion I refer to both England and Wales, a descriptive strategy that reflects both the ambiguity of the current political/legal situation in the United Kingdom, and the reality of where most of the problem-solving courts are actually concentrated.

2. For some reason, the British have always preferred the plural version of "drugs" when referring to "drugs courts," which is arguably more technically accurate than the U.S. nomenclature ("drug courts"), given that these courts invariably deal with the use of a variety of drugs. For the sake of consistency, however, I will use the singular version throughout the book, even if the plural "drugs court" is the favored term in places like the United Kingdom.

3. Philip Bean, for example, observes that "clearly, the model for the DTTO is that of the U.S. drug treatment court," though both Bean and Paul Hayes acknowledge some reluctance among policy makers to acknowledge this publicly. See Bean, "Drug Courts, British Style: The Drug Treatment Court Movement in Britain," *Substance Use and Misuse* 37, nos. 12 & 13 (2002): 1612.

4. Sir Robin Auld concludes the same in his comprehensive *Review of the Criminal Courts of England and Wales*, released in 2001. Here Auld observes that

DTTOs "incorporate some of their [U.S. drug courts] procedures and options for disposal." See Sir Robin Auld, *Review of the Criminal Courts of England and Wales*, Home Office, September 2001.

5. According to Judge Justin Philips, the Leeds court was actually started several years earlier, but was named a pilot program at the same time as the start of the West London drug court.

6. Mary Ann Glendon, Michael W. Gordon, and Christopher Osakwe, *Comparative Legal Traditions* (St. Paul: West Publishing, 1982), 177.

7. Auld, *Review of the Criminal Courts in England and Wales*, 94.

8. The title for a "stipendiary magistrate" became "district judge" on August 31, 2000.

9. Robin Auld, *Review of the Criminal Courts in England and Wales*, 94.

10. Lord Falconer of Thoroton, Bench Chair Conference, London, England, February 27, 2004.

11. Glendon, Gordon, and Osakwe, *Comparative Legal Traditions*, 174.

12. As Andrew Wells, the United Nations official responsible for international drug control programs, stated at a 2000 international conference on drug courts in Scotland, "Clearly the U.S. drug courts do have a wider range of intermediate sanctions that are not currently available under DTTO regimes."

13. Auld, *Review of the Criminal Courts of England and Wales*, 100.

14. The probation officer explained further, "They [the magistrates] may not have done a DTTO court before. They may not know the difference between a review and a normal session. . . . I mean, they'll know it's not a sentencing exercise, but they may not have any particular knowledge about cocaine use. They may be reading for the first time about someone and not know the client's history—it could be someone's fifth or sixth review."

15. Todd R. Clear and Judith Rumgay, "Divided by a Common Language: British and American Probation Cultures," *Federal Probation* (September 1992): 9.

16. Philip Bean, "Drug Treatment Courts, British Style: The Drug User Treatment Court Movement in Britain," in *Drug Courts: Current Issues and Future Perspectives*, ed. Lana D. Harrison, Frank R. Scarpitti, Menachem Amir, and Stanley Einstein (Office of International Criminal Justice, 2002), 149.

17. Ibid., 151.

18. Laurie Robinson, "Commentary on Candace McCoy," *American Criminal Law Review* 40, no. 4 (Fall 2003): 1536.

19. Candace McCoy, "The Politics of Problem-Solving: An Overview of the Origins and Development of Therapeutic Courts," *American Criminal Law Review* 40, no. 4 (Fall 2003): 1527.

20. Robinson, "Commentary on Candace McCoy," 1536.

21. Ibid.

22. Jonathan Freedland, *Bring Home the Revolution* (London: Fourth Estate, 1998), 19, 22.

23. "Delivering Justice, Rights and Democracy, DCA Strategy 2004–09," Department of Constitutional Affairs (December 2004): 39.

24. As early as the mid-1970s, sociologist Edwin Schur observed that in America, "every emotion has value. . . . We must recognize all feelings, express

them, open them up to the people around us." See Edwin M. Schur, *The Aware-ness Trap: Self-Absorption Instead of Social Change* (New York: Quadrangle/New York Times Book, 1976), 17. Identification of this peculiarly American predi-lection continued in the 1980s, when Alasdair MacIntyre identified emotivism as a distinguishing cultural ethic. Several years later, sociologist Robert Bellah and his colleagues recognized "expressive individualism" as a dominant language in American society, and political philosopher Jean Bethke Elshtain observed that "all points seem to revolve around the individual's subjective feelings." See Robert Bellah, Richard Madsen, Williams M. Sullivan, Ann Swidler, and Steven M. Tip-ton, *Habits of the Heart: Individualism and Commitment in American Life* (Berkeley: University of California Press, 1985); Jean Bethke Elshtain, *Medita-tions on Modern Political Thought* (New York: Praeger, 1986). For more recent analyses, see James L. Nolan Jr., *The Therapeutic State: Justifying Government at Century's End* (New York: New York University Press, 1998); and John Hewitt's description of the "ascendancy of feelings and emotional well-being in the culture as a whole," in John P. Hewitt, *The Myth of Self-Esteem: Finding Happiness and Solving Problems in America* (New York: St. Martin's Press, 1998), 96.

25. Alasdair MacIntyre, *After Virtue: A Study in Moral Theory* (Notre Dame, IN: University of Notre Dame Press, 1984), 22.

26. Sally Satel, "Observational Study of Courtroom Dynamics in Selected Drug Courts," *National Drug Court Institute Review* 1, no. 1 (Summer 1998): 51.

27. Ibid., 62–64.

28. George Howarth, MP, in a speech given at Loughborough University, July 6, 1998.

29. The quote to which Judge Philips refers in this interview was cited in the following article: Ben Leapman, "In Session: London's First Drugs-Only Court," *Evening Standard* (December 23, 2005). Judge Philips was speaking to Rodney, "a van driver who lost his job due to crack addiction." Leapman quotes Judge Philips as having said to Rodney, "If I see any positive test results next time you come here, I'm going to kick your arse."

30. James L. Nolan Jr., *Reinventing Justice: The American Drug Court Move-ment* (Princeton, NJ: Princeton University Press, 2001): 61–89.

31. Caroline S. Cooper, Shanie R. Bartlett, Michelle A. Shaw, and Kayla K. Yang, "Drug Courts: 1997 Overview of Operational Characteristics and Imple-mentation Issues, Part Six: Drug Treatment Services," Drug Court Clearinghouse and Technical Assistance Project, Office of Justice Programs, U.S. Department of Justice (1997): 83.

32. See James L. Nolan Jr., "Separated by an Uncommon Law: Drug Courts in Great Britain and America," in *Drug Courts: In Theory and in Practice*, ed. James L. Nolan Jr. (New York: Aldine de Gruyter, 2002), 93–98.

33. Joel Best, *Random Violence: How We Talk About New Crimes and New Victims* (Berkeley: University of California Press, 1999), 124.

34. Charlotte Walsh, "The Trend Toward Specialisation: West Yorkshire Inno-vations in Drugs and Domestic Violence Courts," *Howard Journal* 40, no. 1 (Feb-ruary 2001): 30. A one-year overview of the Leeds program, likewise, makes refer-ence to "successful and comparable systems overseas" and specifically identifies

domestic violence courts in Brooklyn, New York, and Memphis, Tennessee. See "Leeds Domestic Violence Court Overview Report, June 1999–June 2000," produced by the Leeds Interagency Project (2001): 15. A comprehensive review of the five programs, likewise, referenced the "growing literature on specialist courts in other jurisdictions, most notably from the United States of America" to highlight lessons learned from "domestic violence courts in other jurisdictions." See Dee Cook, Mandy Burton, Amanda Robinson, and Christine Vallely, "Evaluation of Specialist Domestic Violence Courts/Fast Track Systems" (March 2004): 29.

35. Dee Cook, Mandy Burton, Amanda Robinson, Jasmin Tregidga, and Christine Vallely, "Evaluation of Domestic Violence Pilot Sites at Gwent and Croydon 2004/05, Interim Report," Crown Prosecution Service (September 2004): 6.

36. "One Year On: The First Annual Review of the Specialist Domestic Violence Court at West London Magistrates Court," produced by Standing Together Against Domestic Violence, London, England (November 24, 2003): 28.

37. "Specialist Domestic Violence Programme: Guidance," produced by Her Majesty's Court Service, Crown Prosecution, and the Home Office (October 2005): 9–10.

38. Cook et al., "Evaluation of Specialist Domestic Violence Courts/Fast Track Systems," 42.

39. Ibid., 40.

40. As Walsh puts it, "A rehabilitative response will only be appropriate where the abuse in question is relatively 'minor.' The emphasis should predominantly be on addressing offenders' violent tendencies, not on the maintenance of family units." She notes further, "Commendably, this is the case in West Yorkshire." See Walsh, "The Trend Toward Specialisation," 30.

41. Mandy Burton, "Judicial Monitoring of Compliance: Introducing 'Problem Solving' Approaches to Domestic Violence in England and Wales," *International Journal of Law, Policy and the Family* 20 (2006): 366.

42. Burton, "Judicial Monitoring of Compliance," 377.

43. "Specialist Domestic Violence Court Progamme: Guidance," HM Court Service, Crown Prosecution Service and the Home Office (2005): 19.

44. Audrey Mullender and Sheila Burton, "Reducing Domestic Violence . . . What Works? Perpetrator Programmes," Policing and Reducing Crime Unit, Home Office (January 2000): 1.

45. "Leeds Domestic Violence Court Overview Report," 27.

46. Ibid., 28.

47. As quoted in Adam Mansky, "Straight Out of Red Hook: A Community Justice Centre Grows in Liverpool," *Judicature* 87, no. 5 (March–April 2004): 255.

48. Ibid., 255, 257.

49. David Blunkett, "Civil Renewal: A New Agenda," CSV Edith Kahn Memorial Lecture (June 11, 2002): 40.

50. Press release 193/2003, "Serving the Community—Major Internation Criminal Justice Conference," issued by the Community Justice Programme (July 8, 2003).

51. Susan Saulny, "Chief of British Courts Takes a Cue from New York," *New York Times* (December 16, 2003): sec. B3.

52. Ibid.

53. Lord Falconer of Thoronton, Lord Chancellor and Secretary of Constitutional Affairs, "Issues in Criminal Justice: A Criminal Justice System for the 21st Century," lecture given at the University of Birmingham School of Law on January 29, 2004.

54. Lord Falconer of Thoronton, Lord Chancellor and Secretary of Constitutional Affairs, speech given at the Bench Chairs Conference in London on February 27, 2004.

55. Charlotte Day, "Key Principles of Community Justice Projects," Community Justice National Programme, 2:2 (August 17, 2006): 6.

56. Ibid., 4.

57. Lord Falconer, speech at a Community Justice Conference at the Jolly St. Ermin's Hotel in London on November 27, 2006, available at http://www.dca .gov.uk/speeches/2006/sp061127.htm. An evaluation of the Salford community court identified the initiation of a total of eleven new community courts, with three (as opposed to two, as noted by Lord Falconer) to be launched in London: Haringey, Newham, and Wandsworth. All eleven were to be "up and running by January 2008." See Rick Brown and Sian Payne, "Process Evaluation of the Salford Community Justice Initiative," Ministry of Justice Research Series 14/07, Ministry of Justice (October 2007): 3.

58. Ibid.

59. "North Liverpool Residents Support New Community Justice Initiative," press release issued by the Community Justice Programme on November 29, 2004.

60. Katharine McKenna, "Evaluation of the North Liverpool Community Justice Centre," Ministry of Justice Research Series 12/07, Ministry of Justice (October 2007): 56.

61. Frances Gibb, "When Crime Is a Community Affair," *Times Online* (September 12, 2006), available at http://www.timesonline.co.uk/article/0,,27969 -2349133,00.html.

62. McKenna, "Evaluation of the North Liverpool Community Justice Centre," 20.

63. Charlotte Day, "Key Principles for Community Justice Projects," Community Justice National Programme, Department of Constitutional Affairs, London, United Kingdom, version 2.2 (August 17, 2006): 5.

64. McKenna, "Evaluation of the North Liverpool Community Justice Centre," 44.

65. Ibid., 44–45.

66. Rick Brown and Sian Payne, "Process Evaluation of the Salford Community Justice Initiative," Ministry of Justice Research Series 14/07, Ministry of Justice (October 2007): 37–40.

67. Lord Falconer, lecture given at the University of Birmingham School of Law, January 29, 2004.

68. Lord Falconer of Thoroton, speech given at Community Justice Conference, Jolly St. Ermin's Hotel, London, United Kingdom, on November 27, 2006,

available at http://www.dca.gov.uk/speeches/2006/sp061127.htm. The Community Justice Programme likewise puts forth as one of its main goals for community courts an increase in "public confidence in the courts and criminal justice agencies." By "strengthening the connections between the court and local people," community courts will "raise public confidence in the work of the courts and wider criminal justice agencies." See Day, "Key Principles of Community Justice Projects," 4, 6.

69. "Specialist Domestic Violence Court Programme: Guidance," 8. An evaluation of the first five British domestic violence courts, likewise, found that with the improved "victim participation and satisfaction" fostered in domestic violence courts, "public confidence in the Criminal Justice System is increased." See Cook et al., "Evaluation of Domestic Violence Pilot Sites at Gwent and Croydon," 6. Catherine Elkington sees domestic violence courts engendering confidence on two levels: the courts build confidence on the individual level of the victim, whose claims and injuries are taken seriously by the system, and the courts "build confidence in the community."

70. "Delivering Justice, Rights and Democracy, DCA Strategy 2004–09," Department of Constitutional Affairs, London, United Kingdom (December 2004). Jocelyn Green, at the Ministry of Justice, similarly sees drug courts as improving "confidence in the criminal justice system" by "getting more offenders through treatment," thus "reducing or putting a stop to their drug habits, thereby reducing offending." An evaluation of British drug court pilots likewise states: "MOJ [Ministry of Justice] identified that a successful drug court model for England could . . . build public confidence in the criminal justice system" ("Dedicated Drug Court Pilots: A Process Report," Ministry of Justice Research Series 7/08, Ministry of Justice [April 2008], 1).

71. Joyce Plotnikoff and Richard Woolfson, "Review of the Effectiveness of Specialist Courts in Other Jurisdictions," Department of Constitutional Affairs (May 2005): 3.

72. Charlotte Day, "Key Principles of Community Justice Projects," 4.

73. Plotnikoff and Woolfson, "Review of the Effectiveness of Specialist Courts in Other Jurisdictions," 4.

74. Ibid., 63.

75. Humphrey Malins, MP, "Crackpot: A Fresh Approach to Drugs Policy," *Policy Brief* 27 (December 2006): 14.

76. As stated in an evaluation of the North Liverpool community court: "The layout of the NLCJC [North Liverpool Community Justice Centre] court is also more amenable to engagement with the defendant. While the NLCJC court retains the raised bench to maintain the distance and formality of traditional courts, the overall size and layout of the court place the defendant physically closer to the judge. By contrast, in many courts the defendant's stand is located at the back of the courtroom, inhibiting the potential for the judge to interact directly with the defendant." See McKenna, "Evaluation of the North Liverpool Community Justice Centre," 18.

77. Furedi adds that therapy is no longer just "an American eccentricity." The "impact of therapeutic intervention on British society is no less significant." See

Frank Furedi, *Therapy Culture: Cultivating Vulnerability in an Uncertain Age* (New York: Routledge, 2004), 18.

78. As cited in Mandy Merk, ed., *After Diana: Irreverent Elegies* (London: Verso, 1998), 2; Freedland, *Bring Home the Revolution*, 189.

79. Richard Davenport-Hines, review of *Our Culture, What's Left of It: The Mandarins and the Masses* by Theodore Dalrymple, in *The Times Literary Supplement* (November 13, 2005), available at http://www.powells.com/review/ 2005.11.13.html. In the book, Dalrymple decries in rather polemical terms the "orgy of sentimentality into which much of the country sank after Diana's death." In a society where everyone must "wear his emotion or pseudo-emotion on his sleeve," the British have lost "their only admirable qualities—stoicism, self-deprecation, and a sense of irony." See Theodore Dalrymple, *Our Culture, What's Left of It: The Mandarins and the Masses* (Chicago: Ivan R. Dee, 2005), 206. In the *TLS* review of Dalrymple's book, Davenport-Hines agrees with Dalrymple's assessment of British culture but scolds him for not properly identifying its source, namely, American culture. "If the British pride in understatement has been largely destroyed, if the public-school values of emotional reticence and self-mastery are widely regarded now as obsolete or as emotional disorders, surely the aggressive, degrading spectacle of shrieking pseudo-emotion of American television is most to blame."

NOTES TO CHAPTER FOUR:
COMMONWEALTH CONTRASTS: CANADA AND AUSTRALIA

1. Michael S. King, "Therapeutic Jurisprudence in Australia: New Direction in Courts, Legal Practice, Research and Legal Education," *Journal of Judicial Administration* 15, no. 3 (February 2006): 132, 141.

2. Arie Freiberg, "Innovations in the Court System," paper given at the Australian Institute of Criminology, Melbourne, Australia, November 30, 2004.

3. In preparation for their new roles, staff at the Vancouver drug court—including the judge, defense counsel, and prosecution—traveled to the United States to attend special training sessions put on by the NADCP.

4. Sherry L. Van de Veen, "Some Canadian Problem Solving Court Processes," *Canadian Bar Review* 83 (2004): 110. This feature of Canadian mental health courts is common enough that Van de Veen can conclude, "In the mental health courts mental health offenders are also monitored in order to establish a structure within which the accused can progress on the treatment plan" (97).

5. Richard Schneider, Hy Bloom, and Mark Heerema, *Mental Health Courts: Decriminalizing the Mentally Ill* (Toronto: Irwin Law, 2007), 103.

6. Van de Veen, "Some Canadian Problem Solving Court Processes," 136–37.

7. "First National Drug Treatment Court Workshop," in section on "Home-Front, Domestic Violence Court, Calgary, Alberta," Toronto, Ontario, Canada (September 23–26, 2001): 27.

8. Van de Veen, "Some Canadian Problem Solving Court Processes," 132.

9. In one session where this was emphasized, several participants struggled with the analysis. As is their common practice, the group was co-facilitated by a

male and a female. The female facilitator was discussing the continued gender inequalities in Canadian society with respect to salary levels, the persistence of traditional gender roles, and the extent to which females still "defer to men for important decisions." One client objected, asserting that "women do it too. They will say, 'You mow the lawn, that's what men do.'" The female facilitator reasserted, "Historically, men have had more power." Another participant then observed, "Women are often the silent authorities." The female facilitator agreed in part and then explained that "it just shows that men have power and are supposed to have power. Therefore, women have to invent other ways, invisible ways, to get power."

10. Joseph P. Hornick, Michael Boyes, Leslie Tutty, and Leah White, "The Domestic Violent Treatment Option (DVTO) Whitehorse, Yukon: Final Evaluation Report," Canadian Research Institute for Law and the Family, October 2005.

11. See, for example, Van de Veen, "Some Canadian Problem Solving Court Processes"; Natasha Bakht, "Problem Solving Courts as Agents of Change," National Judicial Institute, 2004; and Susan Goldberg, "Judging for the 21st Century: A Problem-Solving Approach," National Judicial Institute, Ottawa, Canada, 2005.

12. The Yukon court, for example, provides a program in which "treatment personnel, probation services and the Court closely monitor the performance of the offender for a minimum of 16 months." See "First National Drug Treatment Court Workshop," in section on "HomeFront, Domestic Violence Court, Calgary, Alberta," Toronto, Ontario, Canada (September 23–26, 2001): 27.

13. Susan Eley, "Changing Practices: The Specialised Domestic Violence Court Process," *Howard Journal* 44, no. 2 (May 2005): 116.

14. "Partner Assault Response (PAR) Program Standards," Victim Services Division, Ministry of the Attorney General, Ontario (June 2003).

15. "Beyond the Revolving Door: A New Response to Chronic Offenders," report of the Street Crime Working Group to the Justice Review Task Force, British Columbia Justice Review Task Force, Vancouver, British Columbia, Canada (March 31, 2005).

16. "Mayor Sullivan calls for Community Court pilot project," news release, City of Vancouver, Mayor's Office, June 21, 2006, available at http://www.city .vancouver.bc.ca/ctyclerk/councillors/mayor/announcements/2006/062106.htm.

17. Van de Veen, "Some Canadian Problem Solving Court Processes," 121.

18. Ibid., 122.

19. Criminal Code of Canada, section 718(2)e.

20. *R. v. Gladue* (1999) 1 S.C.R. 688, para. 64.

21. Ibid.

22. In recent years, even Tasmania has shown some interest in starting a drug court. See, for example, a 2006 report on drug courts issued by the Tasmania Law Reform Institute. Available at http://www.law.utas.edu.au/reform/.

23. Samantha Jeffries, "Scoping Paper: Transforming the Criminal Courts: Politics, Managerialism, Consumerism, Therapeutic Jurisprudence and Change," Criminal Research Council (2002): 19.

24. The "scaled-down" family violence programs lack the range of resources available in the Heidelberg and Ballarat courts. Importantly, they do not have

"defendant workers" in these programs, who provide counsel and services to the accused.

25. Robert V. Wolf, "Community Justice Around the Globe: An International Overview," *Crime and Justice International* 22, no. 93 (July/August 2006): 17–18.

26. Michael S. King and Kate Auty, "Therapeutic Jurisprudence: An Emerging Trend in Courts of Summary Jurisdiction," *Alternative Law Journal* 30, no. 2 (April 2005): 72.

27. "Service Delivery Model for the Court Integrated Services Program," Courts Program Development Unit, Department of Justice, Victoria (April 2006): 2.

28. "Court Integrated Services Program—Overview," Department of Justice, Victoria: 3.

29. Kate Auty, "We Teach All Hearts to Break—But Can We Mend Them? Therapeutic Jurisprudence and Aboriginal Sentencing Courts," *eLaw Journal*, Special Series 1 (2006): 104.

30. Ibid.

31. Ibid., 101.

32. Mark Harris, "The Koori Court and the Promise of Therapeutic Jurisprudence," *eLaw Journal*, Special Series 1 (2006): 131.

33. Gay Murrell, "Breaking the Cycle: NSW Drug Court," *Reform* 77 (Spring 2000): 21–22.

34. Julie Wager, "The Perth Drug Court Experience," paper presented at conference, At the Cutting Edge: Therapeutic Jurisprudence in Magistrates' Courts, Perth, Western Australia, May 6, 2005.

35. Tina Previtera, "The Queensland Drug Court: Therapeutic Jurisprudence in Practice," paper given at the State Legal Educators and Young Lawyers Conference, Brisbane, Queensland, June 9, 2006.

36. King, "Therapeutic Jurisprudence in Australia," 139.

37. David K. Malcolm, Chief Justice of Western Australia, "Perth Drug Court and Geraldton Magistrates Court," paper presented at conference, At the Cutting Edge: Therapeutic Jurisprudence in Magistrates' Courts, Perth, Western Australia, May 6, 2005.

38. Lynne A. Barnes and Patrizia Poletti, *MERIT: A Survey of Magistrates* (Judicial Commission of New South Wales, 2004): available at http://www .judcom.nsw.gov.au/monograph24/screenmerit.pdf. The survey asked magistrates the following question: "To what extent do you support the concept of therapeutic jurisprudence, where a sentencing court uses its authority to forge new responses to chronic social, human and legal problems, which have proven resistant to conventional solutions?" Respondents were asked to indicate on a scale from 1 ("no support") to 5 ("fully support") whether they supported therapeutic jurisprudence. A full 88.6 percent chose either 4 or 5, with a majority (52.8 percent) choosing 5.

39. King, "Therapeutic Jurisprudence in Australia," 133.

40. King and Auty, "Therapeutic Jurisprudence: An Emerging Trend in Courts of Summary Jurisdiction," 69.

41. Attorney General's Justice Statement, *New Directions for the Victorian Justice System 2004–2014*, Department of Justice, Melbourne, Victoria (2004): 61, 63.

42. Susan Goldberg, "Judging for the 21ˢᵗ Century: A Problem-Solving Approach," 6.

43. Ibid., 7.

44. Natasha Bakht and Paul Bentley, "Problem Solving Courts as Agents of Change," National Judicial Institute with funding provided by the National Crime Prevention Centre and the Department of Justice (2004): 2, 35.

45. Paul Bentley, "Canada's First Drug Treatment Court," *Criminal Reports* 31, no. 5 (2000): 258.

46. Van de Veen, "Some Canadian Problem Solving Court Processes," 94.

47. Sherry L. Van de Veen and David B. Wexler, "Therapeutic Jurisprudence: Sentencing Principles in a Canadian Context," unpublished paper, 2006.

48. Ibid., 2.

49. Richard D. Schneider, Hy Bloom, and Mark Heerema, *Mental Health Courts: Decriminalizing the Mentally Ill* (Toronto: Irwin Law, 2007), 39.

50. Ibid., 58.

51. Ibid., 7.

52. Mark Harris, "The Koori Court and the Promise of Therapeutic Jurisprudence," *eLaw Journal*, Special Series 1 (2006): 130.

53. Jelena Popovic, "Court Process and Therapeutic Jurisprudence: Have We Thrown the Baby Out with the Bathwater?" *eLaw Journal*, Special Series 1 (2006): 61.

54. Ibid.

55. Ibid., 61–65, 76.

56. Ibid., 61, 66.

57. Gay Murrell, "Breaking the Cycle: NSW Drug Court," *Reform* 77 (Spring 2000): 22.

58. Ibid., 23–24.

59. Jeffrey S. Tauber, "A Judicial Primer on Drug Courts and Court-Ordered Drug Rehabilitation Programs," paper presented at the California Continuing Judicial Studies Program, Dana Point, California (August 20, 1993): 4.

60. Tina Previtera, "The Queensland Drug Court: Therapeutic Jurisprudence in Practice," paper given at the State Legal Educator's and Young Lawyers Conference, Brisbane, Queensland, June 9, 2006.

61. Joyce Plotnikoff and Richard Woolfson, "Review of the Effectiveness of Specialist Courts in Other Jurisdictions," Department of Constitutional Affairs (May 2005): 43.

62. "First National Drug Treatment Court Workshop," Toronto, Ontario, Canada (September 23–26, 2001): 8.

63. Dawn Moore, "Translating Justice and Therapy: The Drug Treatment Court Networks," *British Journal of Criminology* 47 (2007): 44.

64. Ibid., 50.

65. Bentley, "Canada's First Drug Treatment Court," 266.

66. Moore, "Translating Justice and Therapy: The Drug Treatment Court Networks," 48.

67. Bakht and Bentley, "Problem Solving Courts as Agents of Change," 10–11.

68. David Indermaur, Lynne Roberts, Neil Morgan, and Giulietta Valuri, "Evaluation of the Perth Drug Court Pilot Project, Final Report," prepared by the Crime Research Centre for the Western Australia Department of Justice (May 2003): 22.

69. Arie Freiberg and Neil Morgan, "Between Bail and Sentence: The Conflation of Dispositional Options," *Journal of the Institute of Criminology* 15, no. 3 (March 2004): 227–28.

70. Julie Wager, "The Perth Drug Court Experience," paper presented at conference, At the Cutting Edge: Therapeutic Jurisprudence in Magistrates' Courts, Perth, Western Australia, May 6, 2005.

71. Indermaur et al., "Evaluation of the Perth Drug Court Pilot Project, Final Report," vi.

72. Arie Freiberg and Neil Morgan, "Between Bail and Sentence: The Conflation of Dispositional Options," *Journal of the Institute of Criminology* 15, no. 3 (March 2004): 222.

73. Ibid., 228.

74. Ibid., 221.

75. Wager, "The Perth Drug Court Experience."

76. Freiberg and Morgan, "Between Bail and Sentence: The Conflation of Dispositional Options," 227.

77. Van de Veen, Bakht and Bentley, Van de Veen and Wexler, and Goldberg all cite the legislation.

78. Goldberg, "Judging for the 21st Century: A Problem-Solving Approach," 32.

79. Criminal Code of Canada, R.S.C. 1985, c. C-46, s. 742.1(b).

80. Criminal Code of Canada, R.S.C. 1985, c. C-46, ss. 718.2(d)(e).

81. Brent Knazan, "The Toronto Gladue (Aboriginal Persons) Court: An Update," paper presented at the National Judicial Institute Aboriginal Law Seminar (April 2005).

82. Criminal Code of Canada, R.S.C. 1985, c. C-46, ss. 718.1.

83. Van de Veen and Wexler, "Therapeutic Jurisprudence: Sentencing Principles in a Canadian Context," 5.

84. "First National Drug Treatment Court Workshop," Toronto, Ontario, Canada (September 23–26, 2001): 17.

85. Arie Freiberg, "Problem-Oriented Courts: Innovative Solutions to Intractable Problems?" *Journal of Judicial Adminstration* 11, no. 1 (August 2001): 9.

86. Ibid., 25, fn. 5.

87. Eley, "Changing Practices: The Specialised Domestic Violence Court Process," 113.

88. Dawn Moore, "Translating Justice and Therapy: The Drug Treatment Court Networks," 47. The "supervised injection site," in Vancouver, which is called Insite, has on average between eight hundred and one thousand visits every day.

89. This program, called North American Opiate Medication Initiative (NAOMI), began in Vancouver in February 2005 and in Montreal in June 2005.

90. Bakht and Bentley, "Problem Solving Courts as Agents of Change," 11.

91. Ibid., 10.

92. Selma Milovanovic, "Journalist Defends Article," *Age* (April 17, 2002), available at http://www.theage.com.au/articles/2002/04/16/1018333501199.html.

93. Selma Milovanovic, "Magistrate 'Hugged' Drug Pair," *Age* (April 19, 2002), available at http://www.theage.com.au/articles/2002/04/1810190206855 12.html.

94. Milovanovic, "Journalist Defends Article."

95. Matthew Ricketson, "Columnist v. Magistrate: The Lessons," *Age* (June 7, 2002), available at http://www.theage.com.au/articles/2002/06/06/1022982 744612.html.

96. Mark Harris, "'A Sentencing Conversation': Evaluation of the Koori Courts Pilot Program, October 2002–October 2004," Courts and Program Development Unit, Department of Justice, Melbourne, Victoria (March 2006): 74.

97. Ibid., 71.

NOTES TO CHAPTER FIVE:
DEVOLUTION AND DIFFERENCE: SCOTLAND AND IRELAND

1. Working Group on Courts Commission, *Fifth Report: Drug Courts* (Dublin, 1998): 99.

2. Ibid.

3. Ibid., 100.

4. Ibid., 101.

5. Judge Gerard Haughton, "The Irish Experience of Drug Courts," paper presented at the European Perspectives on Drug Courts Conference, Strasbourg, France, March 27, 2003.

6. Carol Coulter, *Irish Times* (February 2, 2006): 4. As reported in this article, "The drug court, which has been operating on a part-time and pilot basis in Dublin for five years, is to be put on a permanent basis and extended throughout Dublin, the Courts Service announced yesterday. It will be available for use in all courts in the Dublin Metropolitan area on a phased basis."

7. "Problem Solving Justice: The Case for Community Courts in Ireland," National Crime Council (Dublin, 2007): 11.

8. Ibid., 13.

9. Ibid., 52.

10. Report of the Working Group for Piloting a Drug Court in Glasgow (May 1, 2001): 5.

11. Criminal Justice (Scotland) Act 2003, part 5.

12. "Evaluation of the Pilot Domestic Abuse Court," Scottish Executive, Justice Department (Edinburgh, 2007), 9.

13. Ibid. As noted in the evaluation, "There was considerable preparation for the development of the pilot in Glasgow, including examination of literature relating to other court models, and detailed examination of models in England and Wales, prior to identifying the approach to take," 2.

14. Ibid., 2.

15. Ibid., iv, vi–vii.

16. Ibid., iv.

17. Ibid., 40.

18. Ibid., 40; appendix D, table 13.

19. See "CHANGE Men's Programme," available at *http://www.change web.org.uk/CHANGE%20Men's%20Programme.htm.*

20. "Evaluation of the Pilot Domestic Abuse Court," 15.

21. Dr. Richard Simpson, the Deputy Minister of Justice, Scottish Parliament—Official Report, June 13, 2002, col. 12698.

22. Youth Court Feasibility Project Group Report (December 2002): 6.

23. Ibid., 9.

24. For a useful discussion of Scottish children's hearings, see Christine Hallett, "Ahead of the Game or Behind the Times? The Scottish Children's Hearings System in International Context," *International Journal of Law, Policy, and the Family* 14 (2000): 31–44.

25. Youth courts were introduced in part to complement (or correct) the Children's Hearing System. As cited in the feasibility study for youth courts: "The development of a Youth Court would complement and build on the existing Youth Crime Strategy. Persistent offenders cause concern in communities, and have often had a history of unsuccessful interaction with the Children's Hearings. Youth Courts would depend on a multi-agency approach with access to intensive programmes to tackle repeat offending" (Youth Court Feasibility Project Group Report [December 2002]: 6).

26. "Youth Courts to be Expanded," *BBC News* (24 November 2006), available at http://news.bbc.co.uk/2/hi/uk_news/scotland/glasgow_and_west/6180126.stm.

27. "First Community Justice Centre," News Release, Scottish Executive (March 26, 2007), available at http://www.scotland.gov.uk/News/Releases/2007/03/26101403.

28. Ibid.

29. Philip Bean observes the same mentality among the Irish in his discussion of drug courts in the British Isles: "The thinking behind the Irish drug treatment court was that whilst it had to be based on the American system it recognized there are many different models or paths to the 'truth.' Therefore, as long as the final proposal remained within the framework of a program of judicially supervised and enforced treatment, it was best to 'do what suits your particular siuation.'" See Philip Bean, "Drug Treatment Courts, British Style: The Drug Treatment Court Movement in Britain," ed. Lana Harrison and Frank Scarpitti, *Substance Use and Misuse* 37, nos. 12–13 (2002): 1608.

30. SNP Manifesto for the Scottish Parliament Elections 1999, 8.

31. Scottish Parliament Official Report, vol. 2, no. 8, col. 708, Thursday, September 23, 1999.

32. Scottish Parliament Official Report, vol. 11, no. 4, col. 389, Thursday, January 20, 2000.

33. Scottish Parliament Official Report, vol. 6, no. 6, col. 520–1, Thursday, May 11, 2000.

34. Scottish Parliament Official Report, vol. 6, no. 6, col. 520, Thursday, May 11, 2000.

35. Scottish Parliament Official Report, vol. 8, no. 15, col. 1268, Thursday, November 30, 2000.

36. Scottish Parliament Official Report, vol. 8, no. 15, col. 1269, Thursday, November 30, 2000.

37. Hugh Matthews, "The Glasgow Drug Court: Reducing Drug-Related Offending," *Journal of the Law Society of Scotland* 46, no. 12 (December 2001): 26, emphasis added.

38. Gill McIvor, Lee Barnsdale, Susan Eley, Margaret Malloch, Rowdy Yates, and Alison Brown, "The Operation and Effectiveness of the Scottish Drug Court Pilots," Scottish Executive Social Research (Edinburgh, 2006): 64.

39. Ibid., 63.

40. Ibid.

41. Criminal Justice (Scotland) Act 2003, part 5.

42. "Evaluation of the Airdrie and Hamilton Youth Court Pilots," Scottish Executive (April 2006): 55.

43. Working Group on Courts Commission, Fifth Report: Drug Courts, 64.

44. Bean, "Drug Treatment Courts, British Style," 1609.

45. Haughton, "The Irish Experience of Drug Courts."

46. Ibid.

47. *Fife Drug Court Reference Manual* (July 2002), 9. The manual also states, "An offender will have the right to legal representation by a solicitor of his or her choice for all appearances before the drug court, including at reviews. Legal aid is available for such purposes."

48. McIvor et al., "The Operation and Effectiveness of the Scottish Drug Court Pilots," 59.

49. Matthews, "The Glasgow Drug Court: Reducing Drug-Related Offending," 21.

50. Michael Farrell, "Final Evaluation of the Pilot Drug Court," Courts Service (Dublin, 2002), 79.

51. Matthews, "The Glasgow Drug Court: Reducing Drug-Related Offending," 26.

52. Farrell, "Final Evaluation of Pilot Drug Court," 96.

53. McIvor et al., "The Operation and Effectiveness of the Scottish Drug Court Pilots," 58.

NOTES TO CHAPTER SIX:
AMERICAN EXCEPTIONALISM

1. Arie Freiberg, "Three Strikes and You're Out—It's Not Cricket: Colonization and Resistance in Australian Sentencing," in *Sentencing and Sanctions in Western Countries*, ed. Michael Tonry and Richard S. Frase (Oxford: Oxford University Press, 2001), 53.

2. For example, former drug czar Barry McCaffrey has said of drug courts, in particular: "The establishment of drug courts, coupled with [their] judicial leadership, constitutes one of the most monumental changes in social justice in this country since WWII," as cited in "Taking Drug Courts to Scale," 2007 National

Drug Court Month Field Kit, National Association of Drug Court Professionals (May 2007): 15.

3. Greg Berman, "The Hardest Sell? Problem-Solving Justice and the Challenge of Statewide Implementation," Center for Court Innovation Think Piece (New York: Center for Court Innovation): 5.

4. Greg Berman and John Feinblatt, "Problem-Solving Courts: A Brief Primer," Center for Court Innovation Think Piece (New York: Center for Court Innovation): 15 (Originally published in *Law and Policy* 23, no. 2 [2001]); Greg Berman and John Feinblatt, "Judges and Problem-Solving Courts," Center for Court Innovation Think Piece (New York: Center for Court Innovation, 2002): 22.

5. Bruce J. Winick and David B. Wexler, eds., *Judging in a Therapeutic Key: Therapeutic Jurisprudence and the Courts* (Durham, NC: Carolina Academic Press, 2003), 3.

6. Judith S. Kaye in "What Is a Traditional Judge Anyway?" ed. Greg Berman, *Judicature* 84, no. 2 (September–October 2000): 82.

7. Judith S. Kaye, "Delivering Justice Today: A Problem-Solving Approach," *Yale Law and Policy Review* 22 (Winter 2004): 140.

8. Judith S. Kaye, "Making the Case for Hands-On Court," *Newsweek* (October 11, 1999): 13.

9. Kaye, "Delivering Justice Today: A Problem-Solving Approach," 139–40.

10. Laurie O. Robinson, "Commentary on Candace McCoy," *American Criminal Law Review* 40, no. 4 (Fall 2003): 1539.

11. Mary Ann Glendon, *A Nation Under Lawyers: How the Crisis in the Legal Profession Is Transforming American Society* (New York: Farrar, Straus, and Giroux, 1994), 152.

12. Greg Berman and John Feinblatt, "Problem-Solving Courts: A Brief Primer," 8. See also Berman and Feinblatt, "Judges and Problem-Solving Courts," 5. In a section titled "Using the Power of Judges," they write, "Problem-solving courts make aggressive use of a largely untapped resource: the power of judges to promote compliance with court orders. Instead of passing off cases after rendering a sentence—to other judges, to probation departments, to community-based treatment programs or, in all too many cases, to no one at all—judges at problem-solving courts stay involved with each case over the long haul."

13. Judy Harris Kluger, "Judicial Roundtable: Reflections of Problem-Court Justices," *Journal* (New York State Bar Association) 72, no. 5 (June 2000): 11.

14. Rosalyn Richter, "Judicial Roundtable: Reflections of Problem-Court Justices," *Journal* (New York State Bar Association) 72, no. 5 (June 2000): 11.

15. Cindy Lederman, "What Is a Traditional Judge Anyway? Problem Solving in State Courts," *Judicature* 84, no. 2 (September–October 2000): 80, 82.

16. Richter, "Judicial Roundtable: Reflections of Problem-Court Justices," 11.

17. Aubrey Fox and Robert V. Wolf, "The Future of Drug Courts: How States Are Mainstreaming the Drug Court Model," Center for Court Innovation Think Piece (New York: Center for Court Innovation, 2004): 5–6.

18. Michael Schrunk, as cited in "What Is a Traditional Judge Anyway?" ed. Greg Berman, *Judicature* 84, no. 2 (September–October 2000): 81.

19. In "Judges and Problem Solving Courts," Berman and Feinblatt observe, "Problem-solving courts tend not to confine their reformist energies to the four

walls of the courthouse. In addition to re-examining individual case outcomes, problem-solving courts also seek to achieve broader goals in the community at large, using their prestige to affect [*sic*] change outside the courtroom without compromising the integrity of the judicial process within the courtroom. . . . Outside the courthouse walls, problem-solving courts have asked judges to reach out to communities, to broker relations with government and non-profit agencies and to think through the real-life impacts of judicial decisions. As judges have performed this work, they have called into question the independence and neutrality of the judiciary and even the separation of powers doctrine" (5, 24).

20. Alexis de Tocqueville, *Democracy in America*, vol. 1 (New York: Vintage Books, 1945), 103–4.

21. Alex Calabrese, "The Red Hook Community Justice Center," *Judges' Journal* (Winter 2002): 9.

22. Ibid.

23. James L. Nolan Jr., *Reinventing Justice: The American Drug Court Movement* (Princeton, NJ: Princeton University Press, 2001), 94–99.

24. Fox and Wolf, "The Future of Drug Courts: How States Are Mainstreaming the Drug Court Model," 5–6.

25. Peggy Fulton Hora, in *Drug Courts: Current Issues and Future Perspectives,* ed. Lana D. Harrison, Frank R. Scarpitti, Menachem Amir, and Stanly Einstein (Huntsville, TX: Office of International Criminal Justice, 2002), 278.

26. Glendon, *A Nation Under Lawyers,* 131.

27. See, for example, Judith Resnik, "Managerial Judges," *Harvard Law Review* 96 (December 1982): 376–448; and Arthur Miller, "The Adversary System: Dinosaur or Phoenix," *Minnesota Law Review* 69 (October 1984): 1–37.

28. Maria Rosaria Ferrarese, "An Entrepreneurial Conception of the Law? The American Model through Italian Eyes," in *Comparing Legal Cultures*, ed. David Nelken (Aldershot: Dartmouth, 1997), 168.

29. Oscar G. Chase, *Law, Culture, and Ritual: Disputing Systems in Cross-Cultural Context* (New York: New York University Press, 2005), 84–85.

30. Robinson, "Commentary on Candace McCoy," 1537.

31. Eric Lane, "Due Process and Problem-Solving Courts," *Fordham Urban Law Journal* 30 (March 2003): 956.

32. Kaye, "Lawyering for a New Age," *Fordham Law Review* 68, no. 1 (October 1998): 3. In a more recent article, Kaye again underscores the central focus of efficiency in the problem-solving court model: "Problem-solving courts bring together prosecution and defense, criminal justice agencies, treatment providers and the like, all working with the judge toward a more *effective* outcome than the costly revolving door." See Kaye, "The State of the Judiciary 2002," New York (January 14, 2002): 14.

33. As cited in "Taking Drug Courts to Scale," 2007 National Drug Court Month Field Kit, National Association of Drug Court Professionals (May 2007): 15.

34. Ellen Shall in "What is a Traditional Judge Anyway?" ed. Greg Berman, *Judicature* 84, no. 2 (September–October 2000): 83.

35. Timothy Casey, "When Good Intentions Are Not Enough: Problem-Solving Courts and the Impending Crisis of Legitimacy," *SMU Law Review* 57 (Fall 2004): 1502.

36. Ferrarese, "An Entrepreneurial Conception of the Law? The American Model through Italian Eyes," 162.

37. One specific reference to the work of legal pragmatists was made by Greg Berman, who in an interview noted that he had been reading some of the "Richard Posner pragmatism stuff" and said he thought that "there is a lot there" that is relevant to problem-solving courts.

38. Richard A. Posner, *Law, Pragmatism, and Democracy* (Cambridge: Harvard University Press, 2003): 94.

39. Richard A. Posner, "Pragmatic Adjudication," in *The Revival of Pragmatism: New Essays on Social Thought, Law, and Culture*, ed. Morris Dickstein (Durham, NC: Duke University Press, 1998), 250.

40. Richard Schneider, Hy Bloom, and Mark Heerema, *Mental Health Courts: Decriminalizing the Mentally Ill* (Toronto: Irwin Law, 2007), 8.

41. Scottish Parliament Official Report, vol. 11, no. 4, col. 304, January 20, 2000.

42. Scottish Parliament Official Report, vol. 8, no. 15, col. 1265, November 2, 2000.

43. Scottish Parliament Official Report, vol. 8, no. 15, col. 1285, col. 1277, November 2, 2000.

44. Working Group on Courts Commission, *Fifth Report: Drug Courts* (Dublin, 1998): 13.

45. Gerard Haughton, "The Irish Experience of Drug Courts," paper presented at the European Perspectives on Drug Courts Conference, Strasbourg, France, March 27, 2003.

46. Arie Freiberg, "Problem-Oriented Courts: Innovative Solutions to Intractable Problems?" *Journal of Judicial Adminstration* 11, no. 1 (August 2001): 25, fn. 5.

47. Arie Freiberg, "Specialized Courts and Sentencing," paper presented at the Probation and Community Corrections: Making the Community Safer Conference, Perth, Australia, September 23–24, 2002.

48. It should be noted that over time, a few state legislatures in the United States have adopted statutes to authorize and regulate the operation of problem-solving courts—though court programs in these states were typically initiated at the local level with "no statutes authorizing their development." See Glade F. Roper, "The Legal Basis for Drug Courts," in *Drug Courts: A New Approach to Treatment and Rehabilitation*, ed. James E. Lessenger and Glade F. Roper (New York: Springer, 2007), 301–4.

49. Mary Ann Glendon, *A Nation Under Lawyers: How the Crisis in the Legal Profession Is Transforming American Society* (New York: Farrar, Straus, and Giroux), 118.

50. Gay Murrell, "Breaking the Cycle: NSW Drug Court," *Reform* 77 (Spring 2000): 23–24.

51. Tina Previtera, "The Queensland Drug Court: Therapeutic Jurisprudence in Practice," paper given at the State Legal Educator's and Young Lawyers Conference, Brisbane, Queensland, June 9, 2006.

52. Jelena Popovic, "Court Process and Therapeutic Jurisprudence: Have We Thrown the Baby Out with the Bathwater?" *eLaw Journal*, Special Series 1 (2006): 76.

NOTES TO CHAPTER SEVEN:
AMBIVALENT ANTI-AMERICANISM

1. Pew Global Attitudes Project, *What the World Thinks in 2002* (December 4, 2002): 63.

2. Ibid.

3. Pew Global Attitudes Project, *Global Unease with Major World Powers* (June 27, 2007): 28.

4. Pew Global Attitudes Project, *What the World Thinks in 2002*, 63; *Global Unease with Major World Powers*, 99.

5. Pew Global Attitudes Project, *Global Unease with Major World Powers* (June 27, 2007): 3.

6. Ibid., 98.

7. Ibid., 5, 106.

8. Pew Global Attitudes Project, *What the World Thinks in 2002*, 66, T58.

9. In 2007, 74 percent of Canadians and 74 percent of the British said they admire the United States for its technological and scientific advances, and 73 percent of Canadians and 63 percent of the British said they like American movies, music, and television. See *Global Unease with Major World Powers*, 102, 103.

10. Ibid., 6.

11. David Indermaur and Lynn Roberts also note problems with the "evidence" of efficacy from U.S. courts. In the literature review of the Perth drug court evaluation, they observe the following: "It is also necessary to realize that the rapid spread of drug courts has not been a function of their proved effectiveness, but because they represented 'an idea whose time has come.'" They are specifically critical of some of the summary reviews of evaluation studies: "However these summaries mask substantial differences between evaluation studies and the fact that most of the evaluation studies suffer from major methodological flaws that disallow a simple kind of accumulation of evidence or attempt to ascertain what the 'balance' of the evidence suggests." See David Indermaur and Lynn Roberts, "Evaluation of the Perth Drug Court Pilot Project: Final Report," prepared by the Crime Research Centre for the Department of Justice, Western Australia (May 2003): 10, 36.

12. *Atkins v. Virginia*, 536 U.S. 304, 347–48 (Scalia, dissenting).

13. See, for example, Gary Jacobsohn, "The Permeability of Constitutional Borders," *Texas Law Review* 82, no. 7 (June 2004): 1763–1818. Jacobsohn observes, "Justices in Indian, Israeli, and Irish Supreme Courts all regularly consider judgments and approaches from the courts of other nations. They do this presum-

ably to determine what might profitably be transplanted to native constitutional soil," 1812.

14. Anne-Marie Slaughter, *A New World Order* (Princeton, NJ: Princeton University Press, 2004): 74.

15. Frederick Schauer, "The Politics of Incentives of Legal Transplantation," in *Governance in a Globalizing World*, ed. Joseph S. Nye Jr., and John D. Donahue (Washington, DC: Brookings Institute, 2000), 260.

16. Joyce Plotnikoff and Richard Woolfson, "Review of the Effectiveness of Specialist Courts in Other Jurisdictions," Department of Constitutional Affairs, DCA Research Series 3/05 (May 2005): 1–2.

17. *Report of the Working Group for Piloting a Drug Court in Glasgow* (May 1, 2001): 2.

18. SNP Manifesto for the Scottish Parliament Elections 1999, 8.

19. Anne-Marie Slaughter, *A New World Order*, 76–77.

20. Robert V. Wolf, "Community Justice Around the Globe: An International Overview," *Crime and Justice* 22, no. 93 (July–August 2006): 4.

21. Ibid.

22. Center for Court Innovation, White Paper, "A Decade of Change: The First 10 Years of the Center for Court Innovation" (2006): 10; available at http://www.courtinnovation.org/_uploads/documents/10th_Anniversary1.pdf.

23. Ibid., 16.

24. Ibid., 4.

25. Ibid., 15.

26. See Jeffrey Toobin, "Swing Shift," *New Yorker* (September 12, 2005): 42–48. Justice Anthony Kennedy observes that European judges are "concerned" and "feel demeaned" that American judges do not "cite their decisions with more regularity." Kennedy, moreover, thinks American ideas would be more welcomed overseas if the U.S. posture included "listening as well as lecturing," 47.

27. *Global Unease with Major World Powers* (2007), 97.

28. Ibid.

29. In the 2007 Pew Global Attitudes Survey, 67 percent of Americans said the spread of American ideas and customs was a good thing. Only one other country had a higher percentage on this survey question: the Ivory Coast at 79 percent. See *Global Unease with Major World Powers* (2007), 99.

30. This phrase comes from Indermaur and Roberts ("Evaluation of the Perth Drug Court Pilot Project: Final Report"), who, in their discussion of problem-solving courts in Australia, offer "a number of reasons to be cautious in too quickly and slavishly adopting American models that may not be suited to an Australian environment," (14).

31. Philip Bean observes the same mentality among the Irish in his discussion of drug courts in the British Isles: "The thinking behind the Irish drug treatment court was that whilst it had to be based on the American system it recognized there are many different models or paths to the 'truth.' Therefore, as long as the final proposal remained within the framework of a program of judicially supervised and enforced treatment, it was best to 'do what suits your particular situation.'" See Philip Bean, "Drug Treatment Courts, British Style: The Drug Treat-

ment Court Movement in Britain," ed. Lana Harrison and Frank Scarpitti, *Substance Use and Misuse* 37, no. 12–13 (2002): 1608.

32. Ibid.

33. Indermaur and Roberts, "Evaluation of the Perth Drug Court Pilot Project: Final Report,"14.

34. Philip Bean, "American Influence on British Drug Policy," *Drug War American Style: The Internationalization of Failed Policy and Its Alternatives*, ed. Jurg Gerber and Eric L. Jensen (London: Garland Publishing, 2001), 93.

35. Ibid.

36. Ibid., 94.

37. "Clearly, the model for the DTTO is that of the American 'Drug Court,' although nowhere is there any public acknowledgement that this is so" (Bean, "Drug Treatment Courts, British Style," 150).

38. Bean, "American Influence on British Drug Policy," 94.

39. Ibid.

40. Bean, "Drug Treatment Courts, British Style," 140–46.

41. Jonathan Freedland, *Bring Home the Revolution: The Case for a British Republic* (London: Fourth Estate, 1998), 14.

42. Ibid., 11.

43. Ibid.

44. Ibid.

45. Ibid., 10.

46. Ibid., 12.

47. Ibid., 13.

48. Arie Freiberg, "Problem-Oriented Courts: Innovative Solutions to Intractable Problems?" *Journal of Judicial Administration* 11, no. 1 (August 2001): 20.

49. Ibid., 27.

50. Freiberg, "Three Strikes and You're Out—It's Not Cricket: Colonization and Resistance in Australian Sentencing," in *Sentencing and Sanctions in Western Countries*, ed. Michael Tonry and Richard S. Frase (Oxford: Oxford University Press, 2001), 30.

51. Ibid., 53.

52. Ibid., 55

53. Ibid.

54. Ibid., 56

55. Peter Berger, Brigitte Berger, and Hansfried Kellner, *The Homeless Mind: Modernization and Consciousness* (New York: Random House, 1973), 30.

56. Attorney-General's Justice Statement, *New Directions for the Victorian Justice System 2004–2014*, Department of Justice, Melbourne, Victoria (2004): 61.

57. As stated in an evaluation of the Liverpool community court: "There was also a consensus among staff that the strong personality of Judge Fletcher underlies the effectiveness of much of the Centre's work." See Katharine McKenna, "Evaluation of the North Liverpool Community Justice Centre," Ministry of Justice Research Series 12/07, Ministry of Justice (October 2007): 18.

58. Jack A. Hiller, "Language, Law, Sports and Culture: The Transferability or Non-transferability of Words, Lifestyles, and Attitudes Through Law," *Valparaiso University Law Review* 12, no. 3 (1978): 439.

59. John M. Conley and William M. O'Barr, "Back to the Trobriands: The Enduring Influence of Malinowski's Crime and Custom and Savage Society," *Law and Social Inquiry* 27 (Fall 2002): 871–72.

60. Pierre Legrand, "What 'Legal Transplants'?" in *Adapting Legal Cultures*, ed. David Nelken (Oxford: Hart, 2001), 59. Hiller likewise, in "Language, Law, Sports and Culture," makes reference to the transference of legal rules, saying that "law, too, is a product of culture" (443).

61. Gill McIvor, Lee Barnsdale, Susan Eley, Margaret Malloch, Rowdy Yates, and Alison Brown, *The Operation and Effectiveness of the Scottish Drug Court Pilots*, Scottish Executive Social Research (Edinburgh, 2006), 55.

62. McIvor et al., "Establishing Drug Courts in Scotland: Early Experiences of the Pilot Drug Courts in Glasgow and Fife," Scottish Executive, Crime and Criminal Justice Research Progamme, 4.

63. McIvor et al., *The Operation and Effectiveness of the Scottish Drug Court Pilots*, 56.

64. Ben Leapman, "In Session: London's First Drugs-Only Court," *Evening Standard* (December 23, 2005).

65. Hiller, "Language, Law, Sports and Culture," 443.

66. Peter Berger, "Four Faces of Global Culutre," *National Interest* (Fall 1997): 26–27.

NOTES TO CHAPTER EIGHT:
BUILDING CONFIDENCE, JUSTIFYING JUSTICE

1. Greg Berman and John Feinblatt, *Judges and Problem-Solving Courts*, Center for Court Innovation Think Piece, State Judicial Institute (2002): 19.

2. Greg Berman and John Feinblatt, *Good Courts: The Case for Problem-Solving Justice* (New York: New Press, 2005), 3.

3. Kimon Howland Sargeant, *Seeker Churches: Promoting Traditional Religion in a Nontraditional Way* (New Brunswick, NJ: Rutgers University Press, 2000), 85.

4. David Rottman and Pamela Casey, "Therapeutic Jurisprudence and the Emergence of Problem-Solving Courts," *Journal,* National Institute of Justice (July 1999): 13.

5. "A Decade of Change: The First 10 Years of the Center for Court Innovation," Center for Court Innovation, White Paper, Center for Court Innovation, New York (2006): 2.

6. Berman and Feinblatt, *Good Courts,* 3.

7. After the Supreme Court's final ruling in the contested Bush/Gore elections in 2000, for example, many commentators openly questioned the legitimacy of the Supreme Court. After the Supreme Court made its final ruling, Mortimer B. Zuckerman, editor in chief of *U.S. News and World Report*, wrote that as a consequence of the decision, "the legitimacy of the Supreme Court has been compro-

mised" (December 25, 2000); available at http://www.usnews.com/usnews/
opinion/articles/001225/archive_008259.htm. In stronger terms, Jeffrey Rosen, a
law professor at George Washington University, in a *New Republic* article tendentiously titled "The Supreme Court Commits Suicide," wrote that the *Bush v. Gore*
Supreme Court decision had resulted in "destroying the legitimacy of the Court"
(December 2000). Several years earlier, the editors of *First Things* also expressed
concerns about the legitimacy of the court. Following a federal district court decision on doctor-assisted suicide, editors of *First Things*, in a November 1996 issue,
directly raised the possibility that American courts no longer deserved the consent
of the people. The editors declared that "the Supreme Court has raised the question of the legitimacy of its law" and expressed worries that "we have reached or
are reaching the point where conscientious citizens can no longer give moral assent
to the existing regime." In light of the judiciary's activist orientation, they observe,
"The courts have not, and perhaps cannot, restrain themselves, and it may be
that in the present regime no other effective restraints are available. If so, we are
witnessing the end of democracy." Given this condition, they propose that the
consent of the citizenry may be in jeopardy: "What is happening now is the dis-
placement of a constitutional order by a regime that does not have, will not obtain,
and cannot command the consent of the people." The original editorial was re-
printed in an edited collection: *The End of Democracy?* ed. Mitchell S. Muncy
(Dallas: Spence Publishing, 1997), 3–9.

8. Mike Hough and Julian V. Roberts, *Confidence in Justice: An International
Review* (March 2004): 34.

9. The American National Elections Studies, 1958–2004 Cumulative File. Percentages represent those who said the government in Washington could be trusted
to do what is right "just about always" and "most of the time."

10. American Bar Association, *Perceptions of the U.S. Justice System* (1999):
50–52.

11. Terry Carter, "Red Hook Experiment: How a Neighborhood Court Fights
Crime and Solves Problems," *American Bar Association Journal* (June 2004): 42.

12. Peggy Fulton Hora and Deborah J. Chase, "Judicial Satisfaction When
Judging in a Therapeutic Key," *Contemporary Issues in Law* 7, no. 1 (2003–
2004): 37.

13. CCJ/COSCA, Resolution 22, In Support of Problem-Solving Courts Principles and Methods, Adopted at 56th Annual Meeting on July 29, 2004; see also
2000 resolution in *Judging in a Therapeutic Key*, 113.

14. Eric Lee, *Community Courts: An Evolving Model*, Bureau of Justice
Assistance Monograph, Office of Justice Programs, U.S. Department of Justice
(October 2000): 15–16.

15. "Good Courts: An Interview with Greg Berman," interviewed by Onnesha
Roychoudhuri, *Mother Jones* (June 18, 2005); available at http://www.mother
jones.com/news/qa/2005/06/good_courts.html.

16. Laurie O. Robinson, "Commentary on Candace McCoy Paper," *American
Criminal Law Review* 40, no. 4 (Fall 2003): 1535–36.

17. Robert V. Wolf, "Community Justice Around the Globe: An International
Overview," *Crime and Justice International* 22, no. 93 (July–August 2006): 4.

18. Charlotte Day, "Key Principles for Community Justice Projects," Community Justice National Programme, Department of Constitutional Affairs, London, United Kingdom, Version 2.2 (August 17, 2006): 6.

19. Joyce Plontnikoff and Richard Woolfson, *Review of the Effectiveness of Specialist Courts in Other Jurisdictions*, Department of Constitutional Affairs, London, United Kingdom (May 2005): 54.

20. Ibid., 61.

21. "Problem Solving Justice: The Case for Community Courts in Ireland," National Crime Council, Dublin, Ireland (April 2007): 24.

22. Ibid., 26.

23. Ibid., 31–32.

24. "Beyond the Revolving Door: A New Response to Chronic Offenders," Report of the Street Crime Working Group to the Justice Review Task Force, British Columbia Justice Review Task Force, Vancouver, British Columbia, Canada (March 31, 2005): iii.

25. Ibid., 11.

26. Ibid., 92.

27. Ibid., 37.

28. As Hough and Roberts put it, there is "more cause for optimism than pessimism" (Mike Hough and Julian V. Roberts, *Confidence in Justice: An International Review* [March 2004], 23).

29. Ibid., 19.

30. Julian V. Roberts, "Public Confidence in Criminal Justice in Canada: A Comparative and Contextual Analysis," *Canadian Journal of Criminology and Criminal Justice* 49 (April 2007): 167.

31. Hough and Roberts, *Confidence in Justice*, 23.

32. Ibid., 18.

33. Roberts, "Public Confidence in Criminal Justice in Canada," 173–74.

34. David Healy, for example, writes of the "mass creation of diseases" by pharmaceutical companies. See David Healy, *The Creation of Psychopharmacology* (Cambridge: Harvard University Press, 2002): 371.

35. Given the essential purpose of criminal justice, Julian Roberts questions whether being relevant or building confidence are appropriate goals for the justice system: "The mission of the criminal justice system is not primarily to help crime victims but rather to promote public safety and impose appropriate punishments. It is, therefore, unreasonable to expect confidence levels to be comparable for the justice and health systems, when the well-being of members of the public entering the system is the primary goal of the latter. Nurses, educators, and military personnel receive higher ratings from the public than lawyers, judges, or prosecutors. . . . However, it must be recalled that these professions (health care, education, and the military) all share a mandate to help or protect members of the public. In contrast, judges must discharge multiple mandates, one of which is ensuring that defendants receive a fair trial. Similarly, prosecutors must act in the public interest, which may mean discontinuing a prosecution or declining to launch an appeal against an acquittal or a sentence. Members of the public may well lose sight of these functions, and this may explain why confidence levels are lower for criminal justice" (Roberts, "Public Confidence in Criminal Justice in Canada," 163).

36. Sian Llewellyn-Thomas and Gillian Prior, "North Liverpool Community Justice Centre: Surveys of Local Residents," Ministry of Justice Research Series 13/07, Ministry of Justice (October 2007): 22.

37. Ibid., 25.

38. Andrew Phelan, "Solving Problems or Deciding Cases? Judicial Innovation in New York and Its Relevance to Australia, Part II," *Journal of Judicial Administration* 13 (2004): 164.

39. Arie Freiberg, "Problem Oriented Courts: An Update," *Journal of Judicial Administration* 14 (2005): 205.

40. Ibid., 206.

41. Magistrate Michael King, for example, in his advocacy of therapeutic jurisprudence more generally, argues that one "outcome of therapeutic jurisprudence . . . should be greater litigant and public confidence in the judiciary." However, he also speaks of how litigant satisfaction is determined by a perceived "fairness of the court process." See Michael S. King, "Applying Therapeutic Jurisprudence in Regional Areas: The Western Australian Experience," *ELaw*, Murdoch University Electronic Journal of Law 10, no. 2 (June 2003), available at http://www.murdoch.edu.au/elaw/issues/v10n2/king102.txt.

42. Jelena Popovic, "Court Process and Therapeutic Jurisprudence: Have we Thrown the Baby Out with the Bathwater?" *eLaw Journal,* Special Series 1 (2006): 63, available at https://elaw.murdoch.edu.au/special_series.html.

43. Ibid., 63.

44. David Indermaur, Lynne Roberts, Neil Morgan, and Giulietta Valuri, "Evaluation of the Perth Drug Court Pilot Project, Final Report," prepared by the Crime Research Centre for the Western Australia Department of Justice (May 2003): vi.

45. Ibid., 250.

46. Gill McIvor, Lee Barnsdale, Susan Eley, Margaret Malloch, Rowdy Yates, and Alison Brown, "The Operation and Effectiveness of the Scottish Drug Court Pilots," Scottish Executive Social Research (Edinburgh, 2006): 76.

47. "The Glasgow Drug Court in Action: The First Six Months," 89.

48. Tina Previtera, "Responsibilities of TJ Team Members v. Rights of Offenders," *eLaw Journal,* Special Series 1 (2006): 51, available at https://elaw.murdoch.edu.au/special_series.html.

49. Jerome Bruner, *Making Stories: Law, Literature, Life* (New York: Farrar, Straus, and Giroux, 2002): 44.

50. Ibid., 45–46.

51. David Beetham, *The Legitimation of Power* (Atlantic Highlands, NJ: Humanities Press International): 13.

52. See James L. Nolan Jr., *Reinventing Justice: The American Drug Court Movement* (Princeton, NJ: Princeton University Press, 2001), 51–57.

53. Jeffrey Tauber, for example, told an audience at the COSLA conference in Scotland, "For a long time criminal justice practitioners thought that they could successfully deal with a drug offender on their own, as did, quite frankly, treatment providers. They felt the only way to deal with drug abuse was to do so with the persons who entered drug treatment programs voluntarily, that they [drug abusers] had to be ready for treatment, that coercion was inappropriate. We know

now—after 20 years of data, statistics, and scientific surveys and studies—that coercion is not only as effective, but it is in fact more effective in dealing with the drug-using offender than voluntary entry into a program." Similarly, a Department of Justice document states: "Research indicates that a person coerced to enter treatment by the criminal justice system is likely to do as well as one who volunteers." See "Defining Drug Courts: The Key Components" Drug Courts Program Office, Office of Justice Programs, U.S. Dept. of Justice (January 1997), 9, citing R. Hubbard, M. Marsden, J. Rachal, H. Harwood, E. Cavanaugh, and H. Ginzburg, *Drug Abuse Treatment: A National Study of Effectiveness* (Chapel Hill: University of North Carolina Press, 1989). For a comprehensive discussion of the efficacy of coerced treatment, see Sally Satel, *Drug Treatment: The Case for Coercion* (Washington, DC: AEI Press, 1999).

54. Eric J. Miller, "Embracing Addiction: Drug Courts and the False Promise of Judicial Interventionism," *Ohio State Law Journal* 65 (2004): 1503.

55. David Nelken, "Using the Concept of Legal Culture," *Australian Journal of Legal Philosophy* 29 (2004): 21.

56. Ibid.

57. A. Stevens, D. Berto, W. Heckmann, V. Kerschl, K. Oeuvray, M. van Ooyen, E. Steffan, and A. Uchtenhagen, "Quasi-Compulsory Treatment of Drug Dependant Offenders: An International Literature Review," *Substance Use and Misuse* 40 (2005): 269–83.

58. See Mae Quinn, "An RSVP to Professor Wexler's Warm Invitation to the Criminal Defense Bar: Unable to Join You, Already (Somewhat Similarly) Engaged," *Boston College Law Review* 48 (2007): 539–95; Timothy Casey, "When Good Intentions Are Not Enough: Problem-Solving Courts and the Impending Crisis of Legitimacy," *Southern Methodist University Law Review* 57 (2004): 1459–1519; Eric Miller, "Embracing Addiction: Drug Courts and the False Promise of Judicial Interventionism," *Ohio State Law Journal* 65 (2004): 1479–1576; and Morris B. Hoffman, "Therapeutic Jurisprudence, Neo-Rehabilitationism, and Judicial Collectivism: The Least Dangerous Branch Becomes the Most Dangerous," *Fordham Urban Law Journal* 29 (June, 2002): 2063–98.

59. Casey, "When Good Intentions Are Not Enough," 1495.

60. Ibid., 1500–1501.

61. Ibid., 1503–4.

62. Ibid., 1497.

63. "Community Justice: A US-UK Exchange," a summary report of a meeting convened by the Center for Court Innovation and the Office for Public Management at the latter's London headquarters on October 22, 2004, available at www.opm.co.uk/resources/papers/justice/comm_justice_CCI_OPM.pdf.

64. Ibid.

65. As cited in Dennis E. Curtis and Judith Resnick, "Images of Justice," *Yale Law Journal* 96 (1987): 1728.

66. Judith Resnick, "Managerial Judges," *Harvard Law Review* 96 (1982): 431.

SELECTED REFERENCES

Bakht, Natasha, and Paul Bentley. "Problem Solving Courts as Agents of Change." National Justice Institute, Canada, 2004.

Barber, Benjamin R. *Jihad vs. McWorld: Terrorism's Challenge to Democracy.* London: Random House, 1995.

Barr, Carl, and Freda F. Solomon. "The Role of Courts—The Two Faces of Justice." In *The Improvement of the Administration of Justice.* Edited by Gordon M. Griller and E. Keith Stott Jr., 3–19. Chicago: American Bar Association, 2002.

Bean, Philip. "Drug Courts, the Judge, and the Rehabilitative Ideal." In *Drug Courts: In Theory and in Practice.* Edited by James L. Nolan Jr., 235–54. New York: Aldine de Gruyer, 2002.

Bean, Philip. "Drug Treatment Courts, British Style: The Drug User Treatment Court Movement in Britain." In *Drug Courts: Current Issues and Future Perspectives.* Edited by Lana D. Harrison, Frank R. Scarpitti, Menachem Amir, and Stanley Einstein, 137–52. Houston: Office of International Criminal Justice, 2002.

Beetham, David. *The Legitimation of Power.* Atlantic Highlands, NJ: Humanities Press International, 1991.

Bellah, Robert, Richard Madsen, William M. Sullivan, Ann Swidler, and Steven M. Tipton. *Habits of the Heart: Individualism and Commitment in American Life.* Berkeley: University of California Press, 1985.

Bentley, Paul. "Canada's First Drug Treatment Court." *Criminal Reports* 31, no. 5 (2000): 257–74.

Berger, Peter. "Four Face of Global Culture." *National Interest* (Fall 1997): 23–29.

Berger, Peter, Brigitte Berger, and Hansfried Kellner. *The Homeless Mind: Modernization and Consciousness.* New York: Random House, 1973.

Berger, Peter, and Samuel P. Huntington. *Many Globalizations: Cultural Diversity in the Contemporary World.* Oxford: Oxford University Press, 2002.

Berman, Greg. "The Hardest Sell? Problem-Solving Justice and the Challenges of Statewide Implementation." Center for Court Innovation Think Piece (June 2004).

Berman, Greg. "What Is a Traditional Judge Anyway? Problem Solving in the State Courts." *Judicature* 84, no. 2 (September–October 2000): 78–85.

Berman, Greg, and John Feinblatt. *Good Courts: The Case for Problem-Solving Justice.* New York: New Press, 2005.

Berman, Greg, and John Feinblatt. "Problem-Solving Courts: A Brief Primer." *Law and Policy* 23, no. 2 (April 2001): 125–40.

Berman, Greg, Aubrey Fox, and Robert V. Wolf, editors. *A Problem-Solving Revolution: Making Change Happen in State Courts.* New York: Center for Court Innovation, 2004.

Best, Joel. *Random Violence: How We Talk About New Crimes and New Victims.* Berkeley: University of California Press, 1999.

Boldt, Richard. "Rehabilitative Punishment and the Drug Treatment Court Movement." *Washington University Law Quarterly* 76 (1998): 1205–1306.

Boldt, Richard, and Jana Singer. "Problem-Solving Judges and Therapeutic Jurisprudence in Drug Treatment Courts and Unified Family Courts." *Maryland Law Review* 65 (2002): 82–99.

Braithwaite, John. *Crime, Shame, and Integration.* Cambridge: Cambridge University Press, 1989.

Braithwaite, John. "Restorative Justice and Therapeutic Jurisprudence." *Criminal Law Bulletin* 38, no. 2 (March–April 2002): 244–62.

Braithwaite, John, and Philip Pettit. *Not Just Deserts: A Republican Theory of Criminal Justice.* Oxford: Clarendon Press, 1990.

Burton, Mandy. "Judicial Monitoring of Compliance: Introducing 'Problem Solving' Approaches to Domestic Violence Courts in England and Wales." *International Journal of Law, Policy, and Family* 20, no. 3 (December 1, 2006): 366–78.

Casey, Timothy. "When Good Intentions Are Not Enough: Problem-Solving Courts and the Impending Crisis of Legitimacy." *Southern Methodist University Law Review* 57 (Fall 2004): 1459–1519.

Chase, Oscar G. *Law, Culture, and Ritual: Disputing Systems in Cross-Cultural Context.* New York: New York University Press, 2005.

Clear, Todd R., and Judith Rumgay. "Divided by a Common Language: British and American Probation Cultures." *Federal Probation* (September 1992): 2–11.

Cooper, Caroline S., Shanie R. Bartlett, Michelle A. Shaw, and Kayla K. Yang. "Drug Courts: 1997 Overview of Operational Characteristics and Implementation Issues, Part Six: Drug Court Treatment Services" (1997).

Daicoff, Susan. "The Role of Therapeutic Jurisprudence within the Comprehensive Law Movement." In *Practicing Therapeutic Jurisprudence: Law as Helping Profession.* Edited by Dennis P. Stolle, David B. Wexler, and Bruce J. Winick. Durham, NC: Carolina Academic Press, 2000.

Dalrymple, Theodore. *Our Culture, What's Left of It: The Mandarins and the Masses.* Chicago: Ivan R. Dee, 2005.

Davis, Wendy. "Special Problems for Specialty Courts." *ABA Journal* 89 (February 2003): 32–37.

Dickstein, Morris, editor. *The Revival of Pragmatism: New Essays on Social Thought, Law, and Culture.* Durham, NC: Duke University Press, 1998.

Ehrman, Henry W. *Comparative Legal Cultures.* Englewood Cliffs, NJ: Prentice-Hall, 1976.

Eley, Susan. "Changing Practices: The Specialised Domestic Violence Court Process." *Howard Journal* 44, no. 2 (May 2005): 113–24.

Ewald, William. "Comparative Jurisprudence (II): The Logic of Legal Transplants." *American Journal of Comparative Law* 43, no. 4 (Autumn 1995): 489–510.

Fagan, Jeffrey, and Victoria Malkin. "Theorizing Community Justice Through Community Courts." *Fordham Urban Law Journal* 30 (March 2003): 897–953.

Farber, Daniel Farber. "Reinventing Brandeis: Legal Pragmatism for the Twenty-First Century." *University of Illinois Law Review* (1995): 163–90.

Feinblatt, John, Greg Berman, and Derek Denckla. "Judicial Innovation at the Crossroads: The Future of Problem-Solving Courts." *Court Manager* 15, no. 3 (2000): 28–34.

Ferrarese, Maria Rosaria. "An Entrepreneurial Conception of the Law? The American Model through Italian Eyes," In *Comparing Legal Cultures*. Edited by David Nelken, 157–181. Aldershot: Dartmouth, 1997.

Fox, Aubrey, and Greg Berman. "Going to Scale: A Conversation About the Future of Drug Courts." *Court Review* (Fall 2002): 4–13.

Fox, Aubrey, and Robert V. Wolf. *The Future of Drug Courts: How States Are Mainstreaming the Drug Court Model*. New York: Center for Court Innovation, 2004.

Freedland, Jonathan. *Bring Home the Revolution: The Case for a British Republic*. London: Fourth Estate, 1998.

Freiberg, Arie. "Affective versus Effective Justice." *Punishment and Society* 3, no. 2 (2001) 265–78.

Freiberg, Arie. "Australian Drug Courts." *Criminal Law Journal* 24, no. 4 (August 2000): 213–35.

Freiberg, Arie. "Problem-Oriented Courts: Innovative Solutions to Intractable Problems?" *Journal of Judicial Adminstration* 11, no. 1 (August 2001): 8–27.

Freiberg, Arie. "Problem-Oriented Courts: An Update." *Journal of Judicial Administration* 14 (2005): 196–219.

Freiberg, Arie. "Specialized Courts and Sentencing." Paper presented at the Probation and Community Corrections: Making the Community Safer Conference in Perth, Australia, September 23–24, 2002.

Freiberg, Arie. "Three Strikes and You're Out—It's Not Cricket: Colonization and Resistance in Australian Sentencing." In *Sentencing and Sanctions in Western Countries*. Edited by Michael Tonry and Richard S. Frase. Oxford: Oxford University Press, 2001.

Freiberg, Arie, and Neil Morgan. "Between Bail and Sentence: The Conflation of Dispositional Options." *Journal of the Institute of Criminology* 15, no. 3 (March 2004): 220–36.

Friedman, Lawrence M. "Borders: On the Emerging Sociology of Transnational Law." *Stanford Journal of International Law* 32, no. 65 (Winter 1996): 65–90.

Friedman, Lawrence M. "Some Comments on Cotterrell and Legal Transplants." In *Adapting Legal Cultures*. Edited by David Nelken, 93–98. Oxford: Hart, 2001.

Fritzler, Randal B., and Leonore M. J. Simon. "The Development of a Specialized Domestic Violence Court in Vancouver, Washington Utilizing Innovative Judicial Paradigms." *UMKC Law Review* 69 (2000): 139–77.

Furedi, Frank. *Therapy Culture: Cultivating Vulnerability in an Uncertain Age*. New York: Routledge, 2004.

Garland, David. *Punishment and Modern Society: A Study in Social Theory*. Chicago: University of Chicago Press, 1990.

Geertz, Clifford. *Local Knowledge: Further Essays in Interpretive Anthropology*. New York: Basic Books, 1983.

Glendon, Mary Ann. *Abortion and Divorce in Western Law: American Failures, European Challenges*. Cambridge: Harvard University Press, 1990.

Glendon, Mary Ann. *A Nation Under Lawyers: How the Crisis in the Legal Profession Is Transforming American Society*. New York: Farrar, Straus, and Giroux, 1994.

Glendon, Mary Ann, Michael W. Gordon, and Christopher Osakwe. *Comparative Legal Traditions*. St. Paul: West Publishing, 1982.

Goldberg, Susan. "Judging for the 21st Century: A Problem-Solving Approach." Ottawa, Canada: National Judicial Institute, 2005.

Goldkamp, John, and Cheryl Irons-Guynn. "Emerging Judicial Strategies for the Mentally Ill in the Criminal Caseload: Mental Health Courts in Fort Lauderdale, Seattle, San Bernardino, and Anchorage." Bureau of Justice Assistance, U.S. Department of Justice, April 2000.

Grossfeld, Bernhard. *The Strengths and Weakness of Comparative Law*. Translated by Tony Weir. Oxford: Clarendon Press, 1990.

Hiller, Jack A. "Language, Law, Sports and Culture: The Transferability or Non-Transferability of Words, Lifestyles, and Attitudes Through Law." *Valparaiso University Law Review* 12, no. 3 (1978): 432–65.

Hoffman, Morris B. "Therapeutic Jurisprudence, Neo-Rehabilitationism, and Judicial Collectivism: The Least Dangerous Branch Becomes the Most Dangerous." *Fordham Urban Law Journal* 29 (June 2002): 2063–98.

Hora, Peggy Fulton, and Deborah J. Chase. "Judicial Satisfaction When Judging in a Therapeutic Key." *Contemporary Issues in Law* 7, no. 1 (2003–2004): 8–38.

Hsin-Huang, Michael Hsiao. "Coexistence and Synthesis: Cultural Globalization and Localization in Contemporary Taiwan" In *Many Globalizations*. Edited by Peter L. Berger and Samuel P. Huntington, 68–88. Oxford: Oxford University Press, 2002.

Illouz, Eva. *Saving the Modern Soul: Therapy, Emotions, and the Culture of Self-Help*. Berkeley: University of California Press, 2008.

Imber, Jonathan B., editor. *Therapeutic Culture: Triumph and Defeat*. New Brunswick, NJ: Transaction, 2004.

Indermaur, David, Lynne Roberts, Neil Morgan, and Giulietta Valuri. "Evaluation of the Perth Drug Court Pilot Project, Final Report." Prepared by the Crime Research Centre for the Western Australia Department of Justice (May 2003).

Jacob, Herbert, Erhard Blankenburg, Herbert M. Kritzer, Doris Marie Provine, and Joseph Sanders. *Courts, Law and Politics in Comparative Perspective*. New Haven, NJ: Yale University Press, 1996.

Jacobsohn, Gary Jeffrey. "The Permeability of Constitutional Borders." *Texas Law Review* 82, no. 7 (June 2004): 1763–1818.

Johnstone, Quintin. "The Hartford Community Court: An Experiment That Has Succeeded." *Connecticut Law Review* 34, no. 1 (Fall 2001): 123–56.

Joralemon, Donald. "Organ Wars: The Battle for Body Parts." *Medical Anthropology Quarterly* 9, no. 3 (1995): 335–56.

Kahn-Freund, Otto. "On the Uses and Misuses of Comparative Law." *Modern Law Review* 37, no. 1 (1974): 1–27.

Karsten, Peter. *Between Law and Custom: "High" and "Low" Legal Cultures in the Lands of the British Diaspora—The United States, Canada, Australia, and New Zealand, 1600–1900*. Cambridge: Cambridge University Press, 2002.

Kaye, Judith S. "Delivering Justice Today: A Problem-Solving Approach." *Yale Law and Policy Review* 22 (Winter 2004): 125–51.

Kaye, Judith S. "Lawyering for a New Age." *Fordham Law Review* 67, no. 1 (October 1998): 1–12.

King, Michael S. "Innovation in Court Practice: Using Therapeutic Jurisprudence in a Multi-Jurisdictional Regional Magistrates' Court." *Contemporary Issues in Law* 7, no. 1 (2003–2004): 86–99.

Kumar, Krishan. "Nation and Empire: English and British National Identity in Comparative Perspective." *Theory and Society* 29 (2000): 575–608.

Lane, Eric. "Due Process and Problem-Solving Courts." *Fordham Urban Law Journal* 30 (March 2003): 955–1025.

Legrand, Pierre. "What 'Legal Transplants'?" In *Adapting Legal Cultures*. Edited by David Nelken, 55–70. Oxford: Hart, 2001.

MacIntyre, Alasdair. *After Virtue: A Study in Moral Theory*. Notre Dame, IN: University of Notre Dame Press, 1984.

Malkin, Victoria. "Community Courts and the Process of Accountability: Consensus and Conflict at the Red Hook Community Justice Center." *American Criminal Law Review* 40, no. 4 (Fall 2003): 1573–93.

Mazur, Robyn, and Liberty Aldrich. "What Makes a Domestic Violence Court Work? Lessons from New York." *Judges' Journal* (American Bar Association) 42, no. 2 (Spring 2003): 5–9, 41–42.

McCoy, Candace. "The Politics of Problem-Solving: An Overview of the Origins and Development of Therapeutic Courts." *American Criminal Law Review* 40, no. 4 (Fall 2003): 1513–34.

Miller, Eric J. "Embracing Addiction: Drug Courts and the False Promise of Judicial Interventionism," *Ohio State Law Journal* 65 (2004): 1479–1576.

Mirchandani, Rekha. "What's So Special about Specialized Courts? The State and Social Change in Salt Lake City's Domestic Violence Court." *Law and Society Review* 39 (June 2005): 379–417.

Montesquieu, Baron de, Charles de Secondat. *The Spirit of Law* (1748). Translated by Thomas Nugent in 1752. Kitchener, Ontario: Batoche Books, 2001.

Moore, Dawn. "Translating Justice and Therapy." *British Journal of Criminology* 47 (2007): 42–60.

Murrell, Gay. "Breaking the Cycle: NSW Drug Court." *Reform* 77 (Spring 2000): 20–24, 90.

Nelken, David. "Beyond the Metaphor of Legal Transplants? Consequences of Autopoietic Theory for the Study of Cross-Cultural Legal Adaptation." In *The New Boundaries of Law: The Debate over Legal Autopoiesis*. Edited by Jiri Priban and David Nelken, 265–302. Aldershot: Ashgate, 2001.

Nelken, David, editor. *Comparing Legal Cultures*. Aldershot, England: Dartmouth, 1997.

Nelken, David. "Legal Transplants and Beyond: Of Disciplines and Metaphors." In *Comparative Law in the 21ˢᵗ Century*. Edited by Andrew Harding and Esin Orucu, 19–34. The Hague: Kluwer Law International, 2002.

Nelken, David. "Using the Concept of Legal Culture." *Australian Journal of Legal Philosophy* 29 (2004): 1–26.

Nolan, James L., Jr., editor. *Drug Courts: In Theory and in Practice*. New York: Aldine de Gruyter, 2002.

Nolan, James L., Jr. *Reinventing Justice: The American Drug Court Movement*. Princeton, NJ: Princeton University Press, 2001.

Nolan, James L., Jr. *The Therapeutic State: Justifying Government at Century's End*. New York: New York University Press, 1998.

Petrucci, Carrie J. "Respect as a Component in the Judge-Defendant Interaction in a Specialized Domestic Violence Court That Utilizes Therapeutic Jursiprudence." *Criminal Law Bulletin* 38, no. 2 (March–April 2002): 263–95.

Plotnikoff, Joyce, and Richard Woolfson. "Review of the Effectiveness of Specialist Courts in Other Jurisdictions." Department of Constitutional Affairs, United Kingdom, May 2005.

Posner, Richard A. *Law, Pragmatism, and Democracy*. Cambridge: Harvard University Press, 2003.

Posner, Richard A. "What Has Pragmatism to Offer the Law?" *Southern California Law Review* 63 (1990): 1653–69.

Quinn, Mae. "An RSVP to Professor Wexler's Warm Invitation to the Criminal Defense Bar: Unable to Join You, Already (Somewhat Similarly) Engaged." *Boston College Law Review* 48 (2007): 539–95.

Rheinstein, Max. "Teaching Tools in Comparative Law." *American Journal of Comparative Law* 1 (1952): 95–114.

Rieff, Philip. *The Triumph of the Therapeutic*. Chicago: University of Chicago Press, 1966.

Ritzer, George. *The McDonaldization of Society: Revised New Century Edition*. Thousand Oaks, CA: Pine Forge Press, 2004.

Roberts, Julian V. "Public Confidence in Criminal Justice in Canada: A Comparative and Contextual Analysis." *Canadian Journal of Criminology and Criminal Justice* (April 2007): 153–84.

Robertson, Roland. *Globalization: Social Theory and Global Culture*. London: Sage, 1992.

Robertson, Roland. "Glocalization: Time-Space and Homogeneity-Heterogeneity." In *Global Modernities*. Edited by M. Featherstone, S. Lash, and R. Robertson, 25–44. London: Sage, 1995.

Robinson, Laurie O. "Commentary on Candace McCoy Paper." *American Criminal Law Review* 40, no. 4 (Fall 2003): 1535–39.

Rottman, David. "On Public Trust and Confidence: Does Experience with the Courts Promote or Diminish It?" *Court Review* (Winter 1998): 14–22.

Rottman, David, and Pamela Casey. "Therapeutic Jurisprudence and the Emergence of Problem-Solving Courts." *National Institute of Justice Journal* 12 (July 1999): 13–19.

Salzman, Elena. "The Quincy District Court Domestic Violence Prevention Program: A Model Legal Framework for Domestic Violence Intervention." *Boston University Law Review* 74 (1994): 329–64.

Satel, Sally. "Observational Study of Courtroom Dynamics in Selected Drug Courts." *National Drug Court Institute Review* 1, no. 1 (Summer 1998): 43–72.

Schauer, Frederick. "The Politics and Incentives of Legal Transplantation." In *Governance in a Globalizing World.* Edited by Joseph S. Nye, Jr., and John D. Donahue. Washington, DC: Brookings Institution, 2000.

Schneider, Richard, Hy Bloom, and Mark Heerema. *Mental Health Courts: Decriminalizing the Mentally Ill.* Toronto: Irwin Law, 2007.

Schopp, Robert F. "Therapeutic Jurisprudence Forum: Integrating Restorative Justice and Therapeutic Jurisprudence." *Revista Juridica Universidad de Puerto Rico* 67 (1998): 665–69.

Schur, Edwin M. *The Awareness Trap: Self-Absorption Instead of Social Change.* New York: Quadrangle/New York Times Book, 1976.

Shearer, Robert A. "Coerced Substance Abuse Counseling Revisited." *Journal of Offender Rehabilitation* 34 (2000): 153–71.

Slaughter, Anne-Marie. *A New World Order.* Princeton, NJ: Princeton University Press, 2004.

Stolle, Dennis P., David B. Wexler, and Bruce J. Winick, editors. *Practicing Therapeutic Jurisprudence: Law as Helping Profession.* Durham, NC: Carolina Academic Press, 2000.

Teubner, Gunther. "Legal Irritants: How Unifying Law Ends Up in New Divergences." In *Varieties of Capitalism.* Edited by Peter A. Hall and David Soskice, 417–41. Oxford: Oxford University Press, 2001.

Tonry, Michael, and Richard S. Frase. *Sentencing and Sanctions in Western Countries.* Oxford: Oxford University Press, 2001.

Tsai, Betsy. "The Trend Toward Specialized Domestic Violence Courts: Improvements on an Effective Innovation." *Fordham Law Review* 68 (2000): 1285–1327.

Van de Veen, Sherry L. "Some Canadian Problem Solving Court Processes." *Canadian Bar Review* 83 (2004): 91–158.

Von Hirsch, Andrew, and Andrew Ashworth. "Not Not Just Deserts: A Response to Braithwaite and Pettit." *Oxford Journal of Legal Studies* 12, no. 1 (Spring 1992).

Walsh, Charlotte. "The Trend Towards Specialisation: West Yorkshire Innovations in Drug and Domestic Violence Courts." *Howard Journal* 40, no. 1 (February 2001): 26–38.

Watson, Alan. *Legal Transplants: An Approach to Comparative Law.* 2nd ed. Athens, GA: University of Georgia Press, 1993.

Wilson, James Q., and George L. Kelling. "Broken Windows." *Atlantic Monthly* (March 1982): 29–38.

Winick, Bruce J., and David B. Wexler, editors. *Judging in a Therapeutic Key: Therapeutic Jurisprudence and the Courts.* Durham, NC: Carolina Academic Press, 2003.

Wolf, Robert V. "Community Justice Around the Globe: An International Over-
  view." *Crime and Justice International* 22, no. 93 (July–August 2006): 4–22.
Young, Richard, and Carolyn Hoyle. "Restorative Justice and Punishment." In
  The Use of Punishment. Edited by S. McConville. Collompton: Willian, 2003.
Zedner, Lucia. "Comparative Research in Criminal Justice." In *Contemporary
  Issues in Criminology.* Edited by Michael Levy, Mike Maguire, and Lesley
  Noaks, 8–25. Cardiff: University of Wales Press, 1995.
Zimmerman, Michael D. "A New Approach to Court Reform." *Judicature* 82,
  no. 3 (November–December 1998): 108–11.

INDEX

Aboriginal Community Code of Conduct, 108
Aitken, Bill, 147
Alberta Health Innovation Fund, 79
Alcoholics Anonymous (AA), 11, 12, 15, 133
American Bar Association (ABA), 7
Americanization, 171–72, 196; viewed as a negative development, 157–58
anti-Americanism, 166; ambivalence of, 157–59, 169, 170, 178, 226n9; and legal borrowing, 177–78
Arkfeld, Louraine, 17
Armytage, Penny, 85
Ashworth, Andrew, 33
Atkins v. Virginia (2002), 161
Australia, 35, 41; influence of American culture on, 170–71; needle and syringe exchange program of, 103; therapeutic jurisprudence in, 86–88. *See also* Australia, aboriginal courts in; Australia, problem-solving courts in
Australia, aboriginal courts in, 77–78, 86, 106–7, 136, 154; Koori Court , 86, 107–8; Murri courts, 86, therapeutic jurisprudence as a common feature of, 86; Yandeyarra Court, 86
Australia, problem-solving courts in, 76–78, 83–86, 154–55, 227n27; concern over statutory (legislative) basis of, 98, 188; criticism of therapeutic jurisprudence in problem-solving courts, 92–93; differences of from English courts, 104–5; domestic violence courts, 84, 216–17n24; drug courts, 83, 91, 96–97, 152, 154, 215n3; embrace of therapeutic jurisprudence by, 77; harm reduction policy of, 102–4; influence of British and American courts on, 76–77; mental health courts, 83–84; methadone maintenance program of drug courts, 103–4; monitoring of defendants in, 84; in New South Wales, 83; and the preservation of the open justice system, 187–88; problem of with the efficacy of U.S. drug courts, 161, 226n11; prostitution courts, 148; and public confidence in the justice system, 188–89; role of the legislature in formation of, 96–99
Auty, Kate, 86

Bail Act (1982 [Australia]), 97
Bakht, Natasha, 89, 95
Barber, Benjamin, 25
Barker, Val, 45, 55
Bean, Philip, 41, 50, 109, 127, 209n3; on selective borrowing of American court procedures, 167–68, 169, 170, 171
Beckett, Brenden, 68–69
Beetham, David, 189, 192
Bellah, Robert, 54, 190–91, 210–11n24
Bentley, Paul, 78–79, 89, 94, 95, 101, 114, 153; opinion of Proposition 36 (California), 146; promotion of problem-solving courts in Canada, 159–60
Berger, Peter, 7, 24, 25, 172, 177
Berman, Greg, 9, 10, 11, 22, 36, 137, 144, 180, 183, 199n16; on pragmatism, 225n37
Best, Joel, 59
Bishop, Des, 135
Blair, Tony, 119
Bloomberg, Michael, 65, 177
Blunkett, David, 3, 64
Boruchowitz, Robert, 22
Bragg, Melvyn, 169
Braithwaite, John, 32–33, 33–34, 103, 206n39; on "reintegrative shaming," 34, 206n48
British Columbia Justice Review Taskforce, 184
British Crown Courts, 47, 51, 67–68
"broken windows" theory, 12
Bruner, Jerome, 189
Burton, Mandy, 62
Bush, George W., 145

Calabrese, Alex, 1–2, 14, 64; on the role of a judge in the Red Hook (Brooklyn) community, 142